I0157742

THE DYKE DYKIGNOSTIC MANUAL (DDM-IV)

Mickey Eliason, PhDyk
Rotating Co-Coordinator of Dycological Research
DDM DycologyAcademy Collective,
[Address withheld for security purposes]
Lesbianville, U.S.A.
DDMAcademy@gmail.com

All rights reserved for dykes everywhere

TABLE OF CONTENTS

ACKNOWLEDGMENTS

This book is dedicated to all the lesbians in my life, past, present, and future, who have variously loved me, supported me, befriended me, dumped me, made me miserable, irritated me, puzzled me, or made me smile. For fear of missing someone, I will not even attempt to list the many dykes who listened to me and helped me work out the DDM categories. One colleague in particular, who wished to remain anonymous because of her notoriety in the local community, helped me get the project completed through her encouragement, astute observations of dyke cultures and behaviors, and editorial comments. I could not have survived without the LGBTQ social, political, recreational, and academic communities in which I have lived and worked. I have special appreciation for the San Francisco Walking Dykes who have nourished my soul with friendships and long walks in beautiful places. Finally, much gratitude to my partner Julie, who after the publication of the DDM-III-R, declared it to be the "best book she ever read" and won my heart.

PREFACE

Lesbian communities across the United States are threatened by a growing epidemic of dyke drama. Although often discussed in the lesbian press and in informal gatherings of lesbians, the full impact of dyke drama has not been thoroughly studied until recently. This contemporary research has revealed the underlying etiology of the complex and multi-faceted phenomenon. Dyke drama is caused primarily by the presence and interaction of dykignoses, potentially pathological conditions unique to lesbian individuals and communities. This is the first book dedicated to exploring these dyke conditions and ultimately eradicating them, thus reducing the harmful effects of dyke drama, which have been declared a public health epidemic in lesbian communities through-out the United States. Dyke drama is responsible for thousands of hours of lost productivity, takes an enormous toll on relationship stability, and is the underlying cause of poor lesbian dental health.

This book answers important questions that most lesbians have pondered in their lives. For example, have you ever experienced a relationship with a woman that was so unusual that you were unable to explain it to yourself or others later? Have you had encounters with dykes who seemed odd in ways that your heterosexual women friends and acquaintances never exhibited? Do you know lesbian couples that seem to be totally ill suited for each other, but somehow their relationship works? Have you ever acted in ways that led a lover or ex-lover-now-best-friend to declare that you were "deranged?" This manual addresses these previously taboo topics and openly discusses lesbian bad behaviors. It will provide the insights you need to label other dyke's inexplicable behaviors, or understand your own irrational thoughts, actions, and relationship dynamics. Perhaps this book might even serve as a new activity for lesbian game nights, whereby teams compete to "name that dykignosis" of all of the lesbians in the community who are not present at the event. This game may ultimately prove to be second in popularity only to the current favorite, "name that ex." Finally, the manual may be useful to women who are newly out lesbians and who are perplexed and overwhelmed by the puzzling dynamics in their new communities and relationships.

Think of this book as a lesbian tool belt. This particular tool belt is not the same one as the literal tool belt that so many lesbians strap on to hold screwdrivers, pliers, or sex toys of any variety. This manual contains a set of psychological tools for leading a healthy lesbian life.

Actually, the tool belt may not be the best analogy; dykes need a much bigger container for all the items needed to safely navigate the world. They need the psychological version of jackhammers, wrenches, and sanders to survive in a homophobic, racist, classist, and sexist society and cope with dysfunctional families of origin. They need tools to deal with the beginnings and endings of intimate relationships and to learn the appropriate etiquette for behaving at lesbian potlucks. Dykes have to learn how to survive the dynamics of lesbian collectives, know the best way to gracefully extricate oneself from a lesbian priestess who tries to convert you to goddess worship at a dyke dance, and successfully navigate traffic snarls and parking stresses on the way to lesbian events. Perhaps a toolbox is a better metaphor: a really big toolbox, like the one found in the back of a butch lesbian's pickup truck. Lesbians have so much adversity to deal with that virtually all dykes suffer from some dysfunctions. In fact, the expert panel for this manual has not been able to find a single lesbian who does not have at least one of the disorders described in this manual. Perhaps a dyke raised by wolves in the wilderness would be free of dyke dysfunction, but the rest of the population needs some assistance. In fact, no doubt wolves have their own brand of pathologies.

The Need for the Dyke Dykignostic Manual

One of the most important implements in the lesbian toolbox is the Dyke Dykignostic Manual (or DDM), the lesbian equivalent of the Diagnostic and Statistical Manual (DSM). The DSM is the reference book that psychiatrists and psychologists use to diagnose adjustment problems and psychopathology in straight people. Of course, sometimes the DSM categories apply to lesbians, and the author of this manual does not recommend replacing it with the DDM. Instead, the DDM is intended to be a supplement to the DSM because experts have observed some unusual behaviors among many members of the Lesbian Nation that are simply not addressed in the DSM. These are not medical diagnoses, as in the DSM, but rather are "dykignoses" signaling a unique lesbian pattern of behavior that can sometimes cause problems in the person's life, relationships, and communities. The DSM refers to disorders, but in the DDM, we prefer to refer to these sets of symptoms as "dyke drama generators."

Irrational behaviors sometimes emerge in unique fashion among lesbians. There are many potential reasons for this, but one critical factor is the lack of a lesbian rulebook. When dykes were children, they were socialized to be good little heterosexual girls, or boys in the case of trans and gender queer sisters, according to the cisgender heterosexual rulebook. Some lesbians already started to resist those heterosexist rules in childhood or adolescence, so gender and sexuality socialization often went awry in early developing lesbians who failed to see the relevance of the messages they got. They had to accommodate or tweak the bad advice received from parents, religion, peers, school, the media, on the playground, and from all the other sources of (mis) information. Some young lesbians hung on to tomboy ways for as long as possible and learned to keep quiet when friends talked incessantly about some boy. Other lesbians did not recognize their dyke-essence until they were late teens, young adults, or even older women, and they had even more years of heterosexual conditioning to overcome.

Many budding lesbians watched the straight romance movies and TV shows, but fell for the beautiful actress or the spunky "sidekick" (an early code word for dyke) rather than the handsome male lead, and created new endings for these stories in their heads. But all lesbians soaked up heterosexist culture like a sponge, even as they tried to resist it, so when they came out, they had years of errant and irrelevant socialization to overcome. Lesbians often had to enroll in crash courses on lesbian culture at the lesbian community center. In most locales, this is a local gay bar but sometimes it is a coffee house, bookstore, women's center, or internet site. In spite of having new lesbian friends and communities as guides, for most lesbians, first dyke relationships were trial and error learning experiences. Unfortunately, those courses in lesbian culture were fraught with idiosyncrasies and were full of contradictory information, because the unofficial lesbian rulebook is mostly based on stereotypes. So is the heterosexual rulebook, another reason why even heterosexual relationships are often flawed, but the schizophrenic nature of learning one set of arbitrary rules and then having to abandon them for another set of confusing and arbitrary rules is one factor in lesbian coming out emotional breakdowns and relationship trials and tribulations. It is not easy being a lesbian. At present, dyke communities lack the necessary aptitude tests to determine who is ready for relationships and who needs more training before they take leadership roles in the community or are ready for long-term relationships. The lesbian socialization course has not yet been standardized, and is not complete. To be a really healthy dyke, instead of a crash course, a whole degree program with a few years of graduate study as well is needed to debunk the myths and stereotypes and find new and healthier ways to live in the world.

Many lesbians never felt like they fit into the mysterious heterosexual society of girlhood, but did not have anyone to talk to about these things, and no role models for anything other than the heterosexual female life. The result of this alienation and this secretive re-adjusting of the messages dykes-to-be received in their youth, is that they made up their own rules, usually in relative isolation. When people are operating from very different sets of rules, the result is communities populated by rather odd or eccentric members. This makes for some entertaining communities and friendships, but when it comes to intimate relationships, most lesbians want to find a woman with some semblance of "stable." In this DDM, "stable" is defined as having a low dyke drama co-efficient, a factor that consists of four components: 1) the ability to initiate and sustain relationships with other women, both as friends and lovers without making them crazy; 2) the ability to navigate the world successfully more than 80% of the time (everyone deserves a vacation from reality and sanity once in a while); 3) not causing unnecessary pathos and drama in relationships, friendships, lesbian collectives, softball teams, or communities; and 4) a sense of humor about the oddities and dysfunctions in lesbian communities. In fact, this manual proposes that lesbian communities reclaim the original definition of gay as carefree and happy and strive to be gay dykes.

The Development of the Manual

Over the years, the author been a participant observer of lesbian culture in two very different locations in the United States; one a rural Midwestern college town and the other a multicultural urban environment; a "gay mecca." Although there are some differences by geography, she has been surprised to find many similarities in the types of dysfunctions that dykes displayed in both locations, and across many other differences such as age, race, ethnicity, national origin, education, income level and so on. These similarities suggest that many of these disorders appear to represent universal (or at least U.S.) dyke pathologies. The author used a highly scientific multi-method approach to gathering data for this manual. For example, she has over 30 years of copious field notes with details about the unique behaviors of lesbians collected in such diverse locations as lesbian brunches, a widespread lesbian social practice for building community, and dog parks, a sub-cultural phenomenon representing lesbian bonding with their canine friends. Some of the most vital information was gained from hiding behind the sofa in the local women's center and overheard conversations at lesbian film festivals.

Like the DSM, this classification system was built via careful review of the dyke scholarly literature, conducting original ethnographic research, designing and carrying out experimental studies, running focus groups, and assembling expert panels. Funding for these studies came from the Dycology Academy Collective through years of vegan bake sales and begging for donations at lesbian music festivals. Colleagues and readers of the first version of the DDM, published in the *Journal of Lesbian Studies* in 2010, suggested new categories and/or helped to hone the existing dykignoses. The Dycology Academy Collective hopes that future readers will continue to add to these diagnostic categories for the benefit of lesbians everywhere who only want stable and drama-free relationships. Learning to identify these syndromes early on may help lesbians to avoid some of the relationship problems that stem from getting involved with an afflicted dyke or inflicting one's own pathologies on an unsuspecting girlfriend. Those affected lesbians may recognize themselves in these categories and seek help before initiating another disastrous relationship. Lesbians, as a whole, tend to be receptive to therapy (for one exception, see DDM 18b), so there is no stigma associated with seeking the help of a professional or quasi-professional who is familiar with these uniquely lesbian conditions. On the other hand, counseling from a heterosexual professional who is not versed in these conditions may result in misdiagnoses with potentially disastrous consequences. For example, heterosexual male psychologists are ill prepared to deal with lesbian couples that come to therapy for the purpose of improving their relationships with their respective exes. Heterosexual therapists are generally uneducated about dyke dynamics, although metrosexual counselors are a somewhat more knowledgeable. The metrosexual and the professional counselor who watches at least one hour of television per day may know about some of these conditions, such as the U-Haul Syndrome (see DDM 7), but will be totally unaware of more subtle lesbian disorders. Consumers need to be warned to look for the lesbian seal of approval when they seek a therapist. Better yet, they should look for a copy of this book on the therapist's shelf.

This manual has several parts, mirroring in structure the DSM. The next section outlines the foundational information needed to understand lesbian culture, including a history of dycology, a newly emerging academic discipline dedicated to the study of lesbian psychology. This introduction is followed by an exploration of Axis I and II dykignoses as well as information about biological and social determinants of health and assessment tools to measure the presence of some of these conditions. There are many cultural differences in how women are raised and are taught to think of themselves, so this book focuses on the U.S. experience and may not generalize to dykes from other parts of the world. All classification systems are imperfect and are often based on generalizations. In reality, every dyke is different and unique. The author, for example, is biased by her own socialization in youth as a white, working class, rural, stoic Scandinavian from a country-music playing, gun rack on the pickup truck, passive-aggressive, don't ask, don't tell culture. As an adult, she lived in a slightly more diverse, liberal community with a strong lesbian feminist leaning subculture, and over the years, became a highly educated academic, softball-playing, theory-spouting, multiple-serial-monogamist soft butch dyke. She is now middle-aged, if she lives to be 128 as she intends. This manual is the product of her elder-dyke wisdom years, but she has not yet observed all subsets of the lesbian community or witnessed every nuance of dyke drama. Keep this disclaimer in mind as you read the manual. There are likely to be many as yet unlabeled dykignostic categories. Please report them to the DDM Academy as you discover them and contribute to the science of dycology.

The DDM has been designed to be helpful to many different audiences, including lesbian therapists, lay advisers, ordinary lesbians, and new immigrants to dyke communities. Hopefully, this manual can serve as a useful introduction to U.S. lesbian behavior for newcomers to the states who need advice for overcoming the tremendous culture shock of immigrating to a U.S. dyke community. Think of it as the traveler's guide to U.S. dyke culture, including common language, customs, rituals, and food preferences. It contains maps of the lesbian emotional terrain, notes hazardous areas to avoid when visiting, and suggests the off-the-beaten path must-see locations. For example, everyone should witness a lesbian music, cultural festival, or golf tournament at least once in the lifetime to be a well-rounded human being. Similarly, no one can truly understand dyke culture without viewing at least three really bad lesbian-made romance films. To protect the author's safety, these films will not be named. For readers not born in the U.S., or new to the lesbian community, a glossary of terms has been provided at the back of the manual, as the idiom of dyke communities can be quite perplexing to a newcomer.

Cautionary Note

There is one important similarity between the DSM and the DDM. DSM diagnostic categories are based on the premise that if the behavior does not cause significant distress to the individual or her relationships, or affect her ability to work and live independently, the behavior does not represent pathology. The same concept applies here. Do not send the author a threatening note about how "normal" your behavior is, if you find yourself reflected in one of these conditions. Also, remember not to shoot the messenger if you see a disturbing truth about yourself in this manual. This manual is not intended to judge, merely to educate, and perhaps, to entertain.

NOTES ABOUT THE FOURTH EDITION

The DDM is a classification system, and like all such systems, is a useful way of labeling behaviors that are on a continuum from extremely harmful to merely annoying. It is important to make these taken-for-granted lesbian behaviors visible and, therefore, more amenable to change. This manual is a first attempt to classify common lesbian pathologies. Lesbians, however, are notoriously resistant to labels, but only if those labels are imposed on them from the outside. In reality, dykes use more terms for themselves and others than any other segment of the population. For the evidence of this, refer to lesbian online dating sites, where identity labels abound, such as "lesbian-identified bisexual femme bottom crone," "bi-curious bi-racial curvaceous androgyne," and "boidyke with daddy tendencies and a BDSM soul seeks pervy-lipstick lesbian." Lesbians appear to be drawn to experimentation with identity labels for themselves, but stubbornly resist having their pathological behaviors named. There are times when diagnostic systems and labels serve a useful purpose aside from attracting potential girlfriends on dating profiles. There could be no dyke community without labels that lesbians use very productively to form political, social, sexual, theoretical, or recreational communities. Similarly, when any group of people shows consistent patterns of behavior that result in problems for individuals or communities, it is useful to name the behaviors to make them visible, and therefore, changeable, or, at least, to make fun of them.

This manual represents one of the first scientific attempts to label unique lesbian behavior patterns, although lesbian comics have been doing this informally for years. Diagnostic systems are constantly evolving entities, as ongoing research provides more precise classifications, insights into causative factors, and improved treatment options. As with the corresponding Diagnostic and Statistical Manual of Mental Disorders (DSM), used to identify mental aberrations and dysfunctions in the general population, this classification system of lesbian quirk-ologies has undergone serious revision and expansion since its first appearance in print in early 2010. The first published edition of the DDM had only 13 diagnostic categories and only cursory descriptions of the symptoms of each disorder. Since that first rudimentary attempt to classify lesbian pathologies, countless concerned dykes have written to the author to submit new disorders or expand on the symptoms of the existing ones. They have demanded that the manual be expanded to include prevalence, etiology and treatment considerations. A second unpublished edition was circulated among a small group of experts on dyke culture for validity checks and feedback, and still was found to be lacking, so more research was conducted.

The DDM-III-R, published in 2012, was an initial attempt to comprehensively catalog the unique pathologies of lesbians in the western world, although the focus of this early version is on the mostly White dyke communities of the United States. Other groups are less vocal about their dysfunctions in public, so we know the most about middle class white dykes who have a tendency to flaunt their pathologies (think of Alice's Chart on *The L Word*). Dyke dykignostic categories are highly culture-bound conditions, thus not all of the categories in this manual may generalize to all subsets of lesbians in the world, or even to other unique subcultures of lesbians in the U.S. However, some of these conditions appear to cut across social identities and geographic boundaries and are found in dykes everywhere. For example, the phenomenon of falling in love too fast tends to manifest as U-Haul Syndrome in the U.S (see DDM 7), but as a more generalized love addiction in some other countries that are deprived of the U-Haul branding of the U.S., and where living together is not feasible. This penchant for falling in love in the blink of an eye appears to be a universal trait of lesbians, but manifests differently depending on local and national popular culture and commercial influences. Further research is needed to sort out other nature/nurture influences on lesbian behaviors.

The third edition of the manual has now been revised and expanded into this version, the DDM IV. It is offered in the spirit of service to lesbian communities, in hopes of improving the quality of lesbian lives and loves by reducing the harmful effects of dyke drama. It must be read as a work in progress, though, as the issues affecting lesbians in the U.S. and in the world are constantly shifting and evolving along with societal attitudes, politics, and the latest lesbian celebrities. No doubt, new forms of dyke drama are originating even as readers finish this sentence, and the DDM V is already underway.

BRIEF HISTORY OF DYCOLOGY

Introduction to Dycology

Dycology, the study of lesbian psychological development and adjustment, is a relatively new field. In fact, the author of this manual is the first in the world to claim a doctoral degree in dycology after 30 years of rigorous training. She completed years of intensive field study of lesbian behavior, including being a participant observer at dyke events, and surreptitiously observing lesbian behavior from behind softball bleachers and in the bushes of lesbian music festivals. In 2005, she completed a post-dyke fellowship on lesbian relationships, and for her dykertation, conducted meticulous analysis of lesbian online dating sites and blogs. She will soon be launching the first entire university dedicated to this discipline, because dyke behaviors in individuals and communities cannot fully be understood through the methods and theories of only one or a few academic disciplines. Only an interdisciplinary approach, drawing from all existing academic endeavors could ever address such a complex phenomenon. For example, understanding how and why there is a disproportionate number of lesbian gym teachers requires experts in psychology, biology, musicology, physical education, and sociology, at a minimum, to sort out potential causative factors. Another complicated social entity is the lesbian republican. There is no existing academic methodology to explain this puzzling phenomenon. These are only a few of the paradoxes found in lesbian communities.

The field of dycology emerged in the 1970s, when lesbians began to challenge their marginalization in both the gay liberation and women's liberation movements and started to create specific and uniquely dyke political and social structures. The lack of acknowledgement or recognition of dyke pathologies until the beginning of the twenty-first century is mostly related to early lesbian feminist ideas of the superiority of lesbians, rendering the pathologies invisible or deliberately hidden to preserve a mythological image of the perfect lesbian. On retrospect, some of those early feminist lesbians who made the dyke superiority speeches suffered from many of the conditions described in this manual. For example, Rita Mae Brown clearly exhibits most of the symptoms of DDM 1a, the femi-feline cat fetish, a serious disorder that involves blurring the boundary between cat and dyke. A few other early separatist lesbians, who are unnamed to avoid sullying their reputations, were afflicted with the Lesbian Mother Superior Syndrome (see DDM 6), an irrational need to be seen as leaders of a lesbian community and to control her members. In recent years, dyke drama has escalated unabated, because of the influence of media such as *The L Word* and antics of out lesbians behaving badly, like Lindsay Lohan and Miley Cyrus. Lesbian community leaders are finally acknowledging the need to openly address dyke pathological behaviors. This book is a first start in that direction.

Notes on Terminology

Any new field of study must begin with the definition of terms, and a tracing of its history, so these are the topics of this section of the manual. Dycology has been slow to progress as an academic discipline because of the lack of widely accepted terms, and lesbian communities everywhere have experienced considerable drama and conflict from the debates about language. Many U.S. dykes speak a peculiar dialect of the English language called "lesbianese." To the casual listener, the language may sound like Standard English, but on closer inspection, words and phrases have taken on whole new meanings than when the same words are used by heterosexual English speakers. For example, words such as "breeder," "closet," "U-Haul," "brunch," "turkey baster," "toaster oven," and "girlfriend" take on unique meanings. Other words are specific to the lesbian or the wider LGBT or queer communities, and are not widely understood by heterosexuals, such as "gaydar." This manual will explore some of the commonly used lesbianese words and phrases, but others are closely guarded secret codes in the lesbian underworld, and the author cannot reveal them without risk of grave consequences. Next, public domain terminology related to sexual identity, gender, and personal naming is discussed in regards to lesbian individuals and communities.

Sexual Identity Labels

This manual uses the emphatic term, Dyke, as an umbrella term for women who have relationships with other women, or who claim this identity. A subcommittee of the DDM Academy, the San Francisco Dyke March Committee, has this definition, which we adopt:

> "It's a political identity. It stands for community. It stands for solidarity. It stands for radical fight. It stands for trans*, black, brown, queer, bisexual, lesbian, disabled, chronically ill, fat, femme, butch, indigenous, gender expansive love. It does not stand by erasure. By displacement. By appropriation."

According to the definition used in this manual, if a woman says she is a dyke, then she is a dyke. Dyke is not a label that anyone can impose on another person; it must be self-proclaimed. There is considerable controversy among community members who vociferously debate which term is the most correct: dyke, dike, lesbian, womyn-loving womyn, homosexual, sapphite, two-spirit, political lesbian, bull dagger, chapstick lesbian, gay gal, queer, lesbian identified bisexual, friend of Dorothy, same-gender loving woman, wimmin-loving-wimmin, gay women, gold star lesbian, one of the tribe, vagitarian, lone star lesbian, aggressive, baby dyke, grrl, granola lesbian (also called a crunchy lesbian), bisexual-identified lesbian, member of the choir, ambisexual, pansexual, omnisexual, family, stud, bi-dykes (or Bykes), or a host of other terms. There are also terms for women who are no longer lesbians, such as hasbians and ex-lesbians, and some derogatory terms for women who emulate some lesbian behaviors, but for the enjoyment of or to attract men (barsexuals, lesbian pretenders, phony lesbians, fake lesbians, bi-curious) or those thought to be posing as lesbians as a fad such as LUGs (lesbians until graduation) or LUTs (lesbians until thirty). For those not familiar with some of these terms, they are defined in the glossary of this manual.

The debates about terminology become louder and more heated when it comes to deciding upon a name for a lesbian group or organization, and some groups fold prematurely solely because of lack of agreement on the name. Some women argue that labels are for clothes, not people, and refuse to use a label at all. This refusal of labels creates considerable problems for organizations or groups that need to be identified by some words. The "No Labels" Center and the "We Can't Agree on a Name Political Action Group" are not effective or powerful names and do not generate satisfactory t-shirt or bumper sticker slogans. Sometimes names are chosen that have some level of recognition within dyke communities, but outsiders may often have no idea what the group is about, for example, Lavender Americans, Rainbow Political Action Group, or the Human Rights Campaign.

In dating situations, the refusal of labels can create some difficulties in finding partners, as this actual verbatim selection from an online dating profile suggests:

"I am femme identified...and I don't think it's a label so let's not have that discussion...lol. If you are butch that rocks...if you are

butch and don't like the 'label' say hi anyway I don't necessarily expect everyone to id even when they know they are...lol."

If subjected to a close dyco-analytic reading, this online dating profile post indicates the existence of an ambivalent-avoidant lesbian-labeling syndrome. This woman denies a label at the same time she labels herself (and the purported butch she seeks), but refuses to have an open discussion about it. Unfortunately, this is a typical dyke communication pattern; one that often leads to misunderstandings and dyke drama. The years of hiding one's sexuality and using secretive, coded language are hard to overcome, so many dykes continue indirect communication patterns for years after coming out, often to the detriment of their relationships.

Even dykes who refuse labels for themselves, when out in groups in mainstream society, often rate other women for their lesbian potential (LP) and/or assign a butch-femme number (see the section below on lesbian gender) without ever asking that woman about her self-identifications. Everyone has a right to use (or refuse) a label in her own personal life and self-concept, but for the purposes of communication and getting tasks accomplished, some term must be adopted, or even embraced. And in fact, to refuse a label is to label oneself as a label refuser, so we cannot ever get past the labeling issue as long as we are a verbal culture.

In this manual, the term dyke is preferred because of its monosyllabic simplicity, for the sheer pleasure of saying the word, and for the power that it gives the one who pronounces the word out loud in mixed company. Many lesbians get deep satisfaction from witnessing grown macho men cringe or shiver in fear when the word is uttered in public. There is some debate as to the origins of the word, but an ancient crone who frequented one of the first dyke bars in the U.S. told the author with great authority and only a little inebriety that the term came from a Dutch working class woman in the 1700s who was known for visiting housewives when their husbands were away. She was named Dyke after the famous story of the resourceful child who saved her village from destruction by plugging the hole in the dam with her finger. Those who are offended by the term or use other terms are welcome to create their own manuals. This edition uses dyke and lesbian more or less interchangeably.

The origins of the word lesbian are also hazy. Whereas some suggest that it derives from the island of Lesbos, where the woman-loving poet Sappho lived, other historians report that in the 18th century, women throughout the world who were marriage resisters were said to have a secret society. These early dykes used the code phrase of "Let's be in love," to identify other members, reflecting that universal lesbian tendency to fall in love in the blink of an eye. This was shortened over time to "lez-be-in-love," and finally to "lesbian" by the early 20th century.

Lesbian Gender Labels

The next topic to address is the complicated and nuanced language about gender expression and presentation. Gender is on a continuum, but there is no consensus as to how to label various points along the scale. On rare occasions, dykes use simple terms like butch or femme to describe themselves, but typically the terms are much more nuanced than a simple butch-femme dichotomy. Gendered terms for those on the more masculine (that term is also hotly contested in some circles) side of the gender continuum include transmasculine, stone butch, stud, bull dagger, boidyke, bulldyke, diesel dyke, glamour butch, Saturday night butch, tomboy, tomboi, soft butch, academic butch, metrosexual butch, and mild butch (one who presents as a butch in public, but has femme behaviors and personality traits in private). Butch queens are generally girly, sassy, gay men, and no self-respecting dyke would pair butch and queen together in the same phrase to describe a woman.

Terms that describe the "feminine" side of the continuum include high femme, stone femme, plumber femme (one who will get her hands dirty), versatile femme, lipstick lesbian, and blue jean femme. Those who are somewhere around the midpoint of the gender continuum may use kiki, stem (halfway between stud and femme), gay gal, queer, androgynous, butchy-femme, femme-y butch, or chapstick lesbian. Others avoid gendered terms entirely and call themselves sports dykes or jocks or some other term of their own creation. Those who move around the gender continuum at will might call themselves (or be called) switch lesbians or "tweens" (between butch and femme). Some merely refer to a number from 1 to 10 (or 0 to 10) on the butch-femme (BF) scale. Usually a ten refers to an extremely femme woman, although the field of dycology still lacks any standardized scale of lesbian gender, so it behooves the individual lesbian to inquire about the meaning of the numbers before replying to a dating profile without a picture, if one cares about the position on the BF continuum. Even with the confusion about the specific meaning of the numbers, more lesbians know their BF number than their credit rating score.

Personal Names

In addition to controversies about the terms to use about the sexuality or gender of communities or individuals, dykes are notorious for changing their birth names, with some lesbians changing names as often as changing partners. Reasons for the name changes are varied, but may include feminist motivations to name themselves along a matriarchal line, rather than take on the father's name. This convention may often lead to names such as Sheri Donnasgreatgranddaughter or Ellen Cronewoman. Other motives are related to the high prevalence of earth mother, wiccan, pagan, and goddess orientations that lead to changing one's name to some form of nature, such as Willow, Moon, Dolphin, Tree, or Dirt. In addition, some women reject gendered names and choose neutral or non-gendered names. Hence, Tiffany becomes Pat, Belinda becomes Blue, and Jessica becomes J. When lesbians become coupled, they sometimes decide to change their last names as well. These decisions are always difficult as the couple negotiate whether to hyphenate their birth names or create something new. Sometimes they choose to blend their names in new creations, so that Suzie Lin and Dori Jain become "the JaLins." When they break up and eventually find other partners, names must be re-negotiated, and even if relationships end, sometimes names of exes (along with tattoos of her name) might be carried on through subsequent relationships to "honor the deep connection" the dyke had with her ex. For example, when Suzie JaLin breaks up with Dori, and moves in with Jane Doe, they may change their name to the JaLinDoes. Others may take their pet's name as their new surname, as in Gayle and Pat Fido or Minna and Lou Kitty-Poo. This creates potential jealousy situations if the couple adopts any new pets after the naming.

Proper lesbian etiquette requires that upon meeting a new dyke, at least three topics must be covered; 1) the coming out story (this may require a minimum of three hours); 2) the term she prefers to use to label her sexuality and gender (or lack of term thereof as well as the political reasons for not using any label); and 3) the various iterations of her name. Second meetings typically add discussions about the relationship history (the ritualistic naming of the exes, another conversation that can take hours), pets (past and present), and children, in that order.

LESBIAN COMMUNITY FORMATIONS

Community is typically defined as a group of people living in the same locale, having the same government, having common interests, or constituting a distinct subset of a larger group based on a shared identity. Lesbian communities may loosely adopt some of these definitions, but are sometimes organized in subtly different configurations, and constantly shift and evolve. Dykes often have informal internal community governing boards that are comprised of lesbian potluck hostesses, political activists, owners of the lesbian bar, moderators of lesbian listservs, and softball coaches. One of these governing board members may assume the role of mayor of dykeville in some communities.

Members of lesbian communities include individuals, couples, communes, collectives, pets, ex-pets, step-pets, ex-lover networks, activist groups, competing sports teams, recovery groups (e.g., Co-Dyke-Dependents Anonymous), and differing subgroups based on interests (e.g., lesbian Appalachian clog dancers) and political orientations (e.g., the Lavender Green League). Lesbian social institutions may include dog parks, feminist bookstores, lesbian coffee shops, women's centers, softball diamonds, online dating sites and blogs, dance clubs, covens, and animal shelters. For the purposes of this manual, a lesbian community is defined as any network of lesbians who know each other and interact on a regular basis, whether in person or via communication technologies including Facebook friends, online dating dabblers, Skype daters, email pen pals, listserv members, meet-up groups, and so on.

One of the most powerful but mysterious organizing factor in any lesbian community is socioeconomic class. Unfortunately, there is little scientific study of the influence of social and economic class in lesbian communities, because the dykes who are typically in charge of organizing lesbian events and running lesbian social and political groups often flatly refuse to discuss these issues. Some speculate that deep, dark secrets revolve around the class distinctions that lesbian leaders fear to reveal to the general public. Others propose that the lesbians who emerge as leaders in many communities are those who are "downwardly mobile." These are lesbians who are highly educated but choose or are forced into low-paying careers such as human and social services or non-profit community work. To deal with the cognitive dissonance of high education and low income, they may subconsciously glorify their lower economic status and thus be blind to the larger effects of socioeconomic class status in the dyke community and squelch any open discussion of class. Lesbian festivals and fairs will typically feature ten workshops on various sexual practices, five on embracing one's genitals and menstruation, four naked drumming circles, and eight sessions on alternative spiritualities, but none on the caste system in lesbian communities created by social class and income. Apparently class issues are the dyke version of Pandora's box.

Similarly, discussions of race and ethnicity are often framed in terms of a philosophy of dyke inclusivity, but without serious social action that might actually reduce racism in lesbian communities. Some individual White lesbians suffer from a delusion that the mere fact of being a lesbian themselves makes them more highly evolved and inclusive, and that all people who are different from them should recognize that fact. In reality, lesbian communities are almost as segregated and fragmented as any other social grouping, but lesbian-correctness (LC) disallows any open discussion of the segregation. Any geographical region will have multiple, evolving, overlapping, complicated, lesbian sub-communities based on class and race. The community is further sub-divided by other factors such as cultural and religious identities, feminist ideologies, hairstyles, and cat versus dog affinities. In fact, animosity between cat dykes and dog dykes may be strong enough to outweigh class differences. Cat lovers often band together even across racial, ethnic, and religious lines to defend their turf from encroachment by dog dykes. Some communities even have cat supremacist groups.

Family values coalitions that have declared the lesbian community a threat to society have obviously not studied all the nuances of lesbian social organization and the fragmentation of dyke unity caused by the wide diversity found in lesbians. Clearly fundamentalists have much to fear from some sub-groups of the lesbian community, but unfortunately, there is no one unified lesbian community from which a lesbian agenda might emanate in the near future, so the world is free from the threat of a lesbian revolution for the time being. If, however, the dykignoses addressed in this manual were adequately treated or prevented, lesbians would be a force to be reckoned with.

In the past twenty years, dyke cyber communities have been created, negating the need for physical or geographic proximity. These have not yet been studied sufficiently to truly understand their impact on individual lesbian and community wellbeing, but there is increasing anecdotal evidence that dyke drama can often occur on these sites. For example, a large and well-respected lesbian listserv in one major metropolis underwent a meltdown when a lesbian mother superior (see DDM 6) tried to impose and enforce rules that upset many of the members. Her efforts to ensure that only "pure lesbians" could be members of the list created discord among the non-hierarchical leadership team of the listserv. The drama that followed included threats of lawsuits, hysterical mediation meetings, and caused two break-ups. Ultimately, half of the members left and started their own competing listserv. Ten years later, mere mention of the incident can set off a riot at a lesbian brunch.

Although there are a few known cases of lesbian hermits, living on mountaintops or deep in forest glens, most dykes exist within well-established communities. Lesbian communities are ultimately organized via relationship status into dyads, triads, small closely-knit ex-lover enclaves, as well as larger social groups, as described in the next section.

Lesbian Social Organization: Dyads, Triads, and Laggles

Only on rare occasions do lesbians operate as single individuals. Rather, three social formations dominate the lesbian community landscape. The dyad, or lesbian couple, bears some superficial resemblance to the heterosexual couple relationship, with a tendency to nest and create a nuclear family with children or pets. In some cases, lesbian couples become unusually close (see DDM 3, Lesbian Fusion Disorders for more about this). Lesbian triads are also common. These triads can take many forms, but there are two particularly common dyke triad formations. The first involves a lesbian couple plus a still emotionally enmeshed ex-lover of one of the pair. Triads of this nature are rarely found in heterosexual communities, and create tremendous amounts of dyke drama in lesbian communities. They are also one of the major causes of relationship breakup, and affect the climate at lesbian social institutions such as brunches and potlucks. In the world as a whole, it is said that there are six degrees of separation between any two people, but lesbian communities are much smaller and more inbred, thus there are only three degrees of separation between any two lesbians. Every triad of lesbians consists of overlap with other triads, dyads, and laggles, making them infinitely complex.

The other common form of triad is the lesbian couple plus a cat or dog companion of one of the pair from a previous relationship. These triads are typically characterized by a great deal of animosity and jealousy in the first six months of a new relationship, and many couples

24

cannot survive because of rejection by the feline or canine member of the threesome. It is not uncommon for the new partner in the relationship to come home from work to find all of her shoes gnawed to pieces by a jealous dog, or her priceless jade plant used as a cat litter box.

When lesbians band together in social, political, or recreational groups, they create another social formation with unique characteristics. Most groups of social beings are labeled with a specific term, such as herds of cattle, flocks of sparrows, a pride of lions, a pod of dolphins, a murder of crows, and a school of fish. Thus far, there is not a universally accepted term for a group of lesbians. "Herd" is obviously not a satisfactory term, as lesbian community organizers will attest—herding lesbians is much like herding cats. "Pride" works well for one month out of the year, but is not the best term for the remaining 11 months, and lacks dyke specificity, as the term is shared with gay, bisexual, and transgender people. The DDM Academy Advisory Group proposes that lesbians most closely resemble geese in their social organization, thus "gaggle" is the best term. Geese fly in a characteristic V formation, which is the closest that one can get to a circle when moving forward. They take turns flying the point position, much like lesbian collectives who eschew hierarchical structures and share leadership. Geese honk loudly when an intruder violates their sacred territory, and fiercely defend "goose-only" safe spaces. Geese, on the surface, appear to be non-competitive, but when dyads and triads of geese come into conflict, considerable goose drama ensues and feathers fly. When a goose falls out of the formation, she soon feels the stress of flying alone and quickly rejoins the gaggle to take advantage of group power. When a goose gets sick or injured and leaves the formation, two other geese drop out of formation to protect it, forming a triad, until the impaired goose dies or is able to fly again, and then they rejoin the formation. Finally, when they have a strong purpose to unite them, like migration, geese form strong bonds and support one another, despite class, species, or gender differences, much like lesbians on a mission for same-sex marriage or family discounts at the local gym. Because of all of these similarities between lesbians and geese, the term used for groups of dykes will be a gaggle of lesbians, or laggle, for short.

Causes of Realignments of Lesbian Communities

Within each gaggle of lesbians, every time a couple breaks up, that laggle shifts slightly or greatly, depending on the relative influence of this couple. These seismic shifts create instabilities in both communities and individuals. Break-ups of couples where both members are leaders in the community can completely re-configure the lesbian landscape. For example, in one liberal college town, the director of the women's center and the chair of the women's studies department became a couple, temporarily healing a deep rift in the community between the activist dykes and the intellectual theorists. For the two years that the relationship was harmonious, women's activism in the community was guided by theory, and the academic dykes actually got involved in political actions. However, when the relationship began to sour, the factions split again, after two ugly events rocked the community. The women's center director engaged in hysterical name-calling from the stage at a gay pride event, calling her ex an "elitist theory-spouter out of touch with the everyday dyke struggle." The women's studies chairperson publicly humiliated her ex from the podium of a feminist theory conference, calling her by the most derogatory name in academics, an "essentialist." Eventually, the university was forced to physically relocate the women's studies department from the building where the women's center was housed because of the depth of the hostilities.

The shifts in lesbian community are created by the constant changes in the sexual and relational landscapes that result from dyke drama. Research on lesbian communities in the past ten years shows these facts in the U.S.:

- a lesbian dyad breaks up every six minutes,
- a dyke falls in love every three-and-one-half minutes,
- a new triad forms every five minutes,
- new lesbian collectives or organizations emerge every ten minutes and implode every twenty minutes, and
- conflicts and hostilities erupt during or following every seventh lesbian brunch or walking group.

The diversity and instability of the social entities that make up the larger lesbian community contribute to some of the pathological conditions outlined in this manual, because of the confusion created by shifting alliances, multiple allegiances, and the sometimes, competing demands of sub-communities. For one simplified example of the complexity of lesbian community allegiances, see the discussion of THE CHART in *The L Word*. This document was a literary device used to attempt to record who slept with whom, but the chart ignored the greater

26

intricacies of lesbian relationships. For example, it failed to address such complex arrangements of dyke communities as ex-lover relationships and co-parenting of pets. In addition to who sleeps with whom, one must record who stayed emotionally enmeshed with each other, who hated each other, who became lesbian stalkers, who got custody of the cats, and so forth. Clearly, much more research is needed to study all these nuances of lesbian community. A forward thinking technologically-oriented dyke has recently developed a smart phone app that records all current and past relationships in a social network of dykes, as well as whether the exes are cordial or homicidal, helping lesbians avoid embarrassing scenes at dyke events. This application, called SaveFacebook, will soon be widely available.

THE LESBIAN THERAPIST AND THERAPIES

Another critically important member of dyke communities is the lesbian therapist, counselor, or advice-giver. Actual professional therapists are most prevalent in White communities with one therapist per every 100 lesbians, because middle class white socialization encourages sharing highly personal information freely with strangers. In fact, for a subset of White lesbians, identification with their mental health disorders is common. This dyke will greet strangers at a brunch with, "Hi, I'm Jesse and I am [fill-in-the-blank: bipolar, co-dependent, alcoholic in recovery, etc]." Those in couple relationships may say, "We're the Smith-Joneses and we take Prosac." Conversations of these women are sprinkled with therapy jargon.

There is evidence, however, that most subsets of lesbians regardless of race and class seek out a wise person with whom they can endlessly process their relationships and crushes. Because there is no lesbian rule book, most dykes on occasion feel lost and in need of guidance when their girlfriends engage in some puzzling behavior. It is perceived as safer to consult another person than to question one's girlfriend's motives directly, particularly in more passive aggressive, conflict avoidant dyke cultures, such as in the Midwest regions of the United States. There are three levels of "wise dykes" in any community: (1) the actual trained therapist who has some degree of formal education in counseling techniques, (2) the "shrinkling" who is a student therapist in training, thus available at a much cheaper rate, and (3) the lay advisor. In some communities, particularly of middle class White dykes, actual counselors or their bargain counterpart, the shrinkling, are preferred because of the acceptability of telling one's secrets to a stranger.

Unfortunately, most professional counselors or counselors in training have been educated only in the ways of heterosexual people and couples, and have not read this manual. They may be puzzled by many forms of lesbian disorder and attempt to apply relationship or couple counseling techniques based on research with only heterosexuals with highly inconsistent results. Some professional therapists, however, are self-trained in the ways of dykes and are skilled at the most effective therapy approach for dykes, lesbianalysis. This form of therapy is a combination of feminist and queer interventions uniquely formulated to help dykes identify their DDM number(s), and it applies a wide variety of activities drawn from this manual. In 2016, a national survey showed that only 46.3% of lesbian therapists had been trained in the ways of dykes and only 32.4% were skilled at lesbianalysis. In comparison, only 12.2% of heterosexual counselors knew anything about dycology, and only 1% were skilled in lesbianalysis.

Other communities of lesbians who are not White or middle class are more suspicious of counselors trained by the bureaucratic, heteronormative, racist, classist, sexist educational institutions of North America, the maintainers of the status quo. In these communities, a lesbian lay counselor may emerge from the ranks of hairdressers, chiropractors, bartenders, softball coaches, homeopaths, potluck hostesses, veterinarians, wiccan priestesses, long-term established lesbian couples, stand-up comics, elders, or survivors of multiple lesbian relationships. For a desperate dyke, sometimes the only necessary qualification for a lay counselor is a willingness to listen.

In general, though, anyone who is considered wise in the ways of the lesbian may take the functional role of lesbian lay counselor for a community. For example, lesbians who live on land communes are thought to be unnaturally wise as a result of their purported unmitigated connection with mother earth spirits, and bartenders are considered experts in lesbian relationships because of their years of observation of lesbian mating rituals. In some communities, dyke hairdressers are sought out for their wisdom as much as their dyke-aesthetic hairstyling abilities. Their abilities to create appealing lesbian hairdos are linked to their intuitive understandings of dycology. The danger of lay counselors is that they may sound wise, but act in ways indicative of pathologies such as those outlined in this manual, and may actually cause more damage to those they counsel than good. Trained therapists may not be much better, if they are only schooled in the DSM and heterosexual relationships. The dearth of culturally appropriate counseling for a desperate dyke in a remote community can create dire circumstances, indeed.

The life of an actual therapist who is educationally prepared to do counseling in a dyke community is a lonely life of social exile. The counselors' professional code of ethics prohibits sexual relationships or close friendships among therapists and their clients or ex-clients. As a result, the lesbian therapist cannot participate in many of the social institutions of a lesbian community, such as regular potluck groups, brunches, or political action groups if any of the members were or might become clients. In predominantly White communities where 87.4% of lesbians seek therapy, the therapist has an extremely limited dating pool. In such communities, the therapist may be compared to the catholic priest or nun who takes a vow of chastity, sacrifice, and service to the community. Lay counselors may have no such ethical restrictions on dating or socializing with those whom they advise, and may be highly sought out as partners. Some dyke hairdressers have very high ethical standards and avoid fraternizing with clients. They are often skilled at identifying risk behaviors of the disorders described in this manual after listening to the woman for the 30-40 minute appointment, and thus, know who to avoid when dating. They are also considered to be great dyke matchmakers, because they know all the lesbian community gossip and the stories/rumors about single dykes. This information tends to be much more accurate than online dating profiles.

For those who are already trained therapists or who have aspirations to become professional or lay counselors, this manual offers a blueprint for conducting therapy or advising dykes with common diagnostic dilemmas. The DDM might soon be considered the "Big Book" for lesbians, or affectionately called, the "big ole dyke book."

Lesbianalysis: Effective Forms of Therapy for Dykes

Most professional counselors have not been trained in the idiosyncratic ways of lesbians or learned how to tailor treatment to their clients' stage in the dykecycle, the four major stages of lesbian life transitions. Lesbianalysis is the form of therapy that is based on the dykecycle and takes into account unique lesbian disorders such as the ones outlined in this manual. There are four universal stages in the dykecycle: predyke, baby dyke, adult dyke, and elder dyke.

Pre-Dyke

Phase 1 of the dykecycle is called the "pre-dyke" stage, and includes the years prior to coming out. Dykes can come out anytime between the ages of 3 and 103, so the predyke stage can encompass much of the chronological lifespan. Therapists working with lesbians at this stage of life must have patience and not push the budding same-sex feelings into the open until the client is ready. Premature outings can have dire consequences and delay coming out by a year or more. Many therapists report feeling extreme frustration with week after week sessions with a woman who obsesses over trivial issues with her best friend and agonizes over why they are affecting her so much. The therapist often reports wanting to shout, "Duh, you're a lesbian and you are in love with your best friend, that's why!" Counselor ethical codes typically prohibit such directive guidance. However, therapists can encourage the coming out by having many lesbian books, magazines, and newsletters in their waiting room, and strategically delaying the start of the session to provide the woman with more time to be exposed to these materials. In some cases, 15 minutes of flipping through Curve Magazine may be sufficient to launch the woman into Phase 2.

Baby Dyke

The second phase of the dykecycle is coming out, or the baby dyke phase. A baby dyke is a newly out lesbian regardless of her chronological age. This phase lasts approximately one year, dating from the "eureka" moment of coming out. When the woman finally admits her same-sex attractions, the therapist can celebrate with her. Families and friends are rarely celebratory with a newly out lesbian in their midst, and to the contrary, are sometimes downright downers about the coming out, so it is imperative for therapists to point out all the good things about adopting a lesbian identity. It may be useful to maintain a library of filmed coming out episodes, such as the *Ellen* show (the sit com, not the talk show), Jenny's coming out in *The L Word,* Wanda Sykes coming out performance, Ellen Page's public coming out address, and others to demonstrate the different experiences and potential hazards of coming out. After the initial disclosure, a time when therapists can mostly provide resources and information, the newly out woman is likely to begin coming out to family members and friends. Therapists can role-play with the client, taking on common personas such as the sexist boss, the guilt-tripping mother, the fundamentalist Christian sister, the macho dad, and the clueless grandmother. Many must also learn to deal with the closeted sibling, cousin, or other relative who may be threatened by the more public coming out of the client.

Once the coming out to others issues are addressed, the next important therapy concerns are crushes and dating. This is the most critical time in the dykecycle for establishing potentially damaging patterns that may affect the rest of her lesbian life, such as emergence of U-Haul tendencies (see DDM 7). The babydyke phase is characterized by intense and painful dyke crushes. Although heterosexual people also experience crushes with quite similar signs and symptoms, the dyke crush has an accelerated onset, greater intensity, and longer duration than the heterosexual crush. Crushes seriously impair judgment and can lead to premature couplings if the crush is reciprocated. The lesbianalysis approach advises therapists to use relationship delay tactics with the baby dyke to avoid painful rushing into bad relationships. Therapists must

31

maintain a strong ego, however, because baby dykes rarely take their advice about going slow in relationships. When a client lapses and U-Hauls her way into premature co-habitation, the therapist must be there to guide her through the inevitable Re-Haul phase (see DDM 7 for details). This period of a lesbian's life is the most vulnerable for lesbian dental health problems.

Most of the research on dyke drama in the literature thus far has focused on the emotional and psychological consequences, that is, mental health, and has ignored the physical aspects. In lesbian communities, however, it is common knowledge that excessive dyke drama causes tooth grinding and gnashing, TMJ symptoms, and even lock-jaw in lesbians who are exposed to chronically high levels of drama. Dyke drama has a visceral, almost immediate physical effect on the body, and causes one's jaw muscles to tighten, the teeth to clench, and the brow to furrow. This chronic stress response can result in excessively high dental bills, pain, and inability to carry on a normal conversation. Lesbians appear to have approximately three times the number of annual dentist visits as straight women, even when controlling for factors such as cute dyke dentists and extreme attention to oral hygiene. Higher rates of poverty among lesbians may be in part related to these excessive dental bills and the high levels of stress in dyke communities, and partly from the debilitating nature of some of the dykignoses described in this book, that take time and energy away from earning a livable wage. Lesbian brain drain has been reported in some communities, when talented lesbians fled the drama in their home communities, seeking out urban areas with larger and more varied dyke networks to diffuse the drama quotient, and with more dentists per capita.

There are a wide variety of causes of dyke drama that can be described according to the ecological model. This theory sees any human problem as a result of interactions between the individual person, their interpersonal relationships, their communities, and the broader society. At the individual level, dyke drama can result from chronic mis-identifications (for example, having to constantly prove that one is a lesbian or justify one's gender expression--the author of this book has to constantly prove herself as a butch lesbian when well-intentioned members of the community feel a need to point out the ways that she does not meet their expectations of butch). There are a variety of addictions that are common to lesbians, including excessive attachments to cats, dogs, and lesbian potlucks. If not addicted, some lesbians experience co-pet-dependent disorders, where they allow their furry friends to dominate them.

At the interpersonal level, several factors may contribute to dyke drama, including living in close proximity to ex-girlfriends. If the former pair were fused or merged lesbians, their breakup may remain as enmeshed and messy as their relationship and spill over into the next relationship. Other relationship stresses that affect dyke drama include the menopausal status of the couple. Although it is challenging when one is menopausal and the other is not, mutual menopausal hot flashing can cause serious fire risk, and the mood swings may lead to considerable conflict. For single lesbians, online dating carries much stress, from trying to decipher the profiles of potential mates for signs of dyke pathologies to knowing whether to message a potential date or wait for her to notice you.

At the community level, there may be a lack of needed community resources, like lesbian-friendly dog parks and vets that provide culturally sensitive care for lesbian cat companions. There may be warring political factions in the community, such as those who experience rifts between academic theory dykes and activist types. A serious factor in high levels of dyke drama may also be related to lack of lesbian-specific therapy options. Communities with fewer lesbian therapists suffer nearly ten times the amount of dyke drama as those communities with good choices. Although heterosexual therapists may be well-intentioned and welcoming of lesbian clients, they may be baffled by the idiosyncrasies of our communities.

Some experts think that poor lesbian dental health is an equivalent to erectile dysfunction in men, because of the multiple effects it has on relationships. First, the tightened jaw has an adverse effect on sexual performance. The rigidity of the tightened jaw muscles has an inhibitory effect on lip and tongue motility and may increase involuntary biting. In addition, the contorted face that accompanies the clenched jaw may contribute to migraine headaches. The extremely furrowed brow may be a turn-off for the partner, who is not attracted to that pinched, constipated facial expression. But the major problem is that a tightened jaw inhibits lesbian relationship processing. Some researchers note that the largest difference between same-sex female couples and other forms of relationship lies in the degree to which relationship processing occurs. In lesbian couples, there is a delicate balancing act between too little and too much processing. One consequence of poor lesbian dental health is too little processing, and indeed, too little communicating of any sort.

In conclusion, it is clear that lesbian dental health is a critical factor in healthy relationships and communities, and must be addressed as a public health crisis. The DDM Collective urges you all to seek out a therapist with a dyke seal of approval to get screened for dyke drama, and if your levels are elevated, start therapy to reduce the dyke drama in your life immediately.

Adult Dyke

Once the painful, but also joyous first year of living as a dyke are over, the now adult lesbian begins to settle into her new lesbian community and starts to nest. This is the time for serious relationships, having children, and adopting pets (or having pets and adopting children). The therapist can help the client work through the potential challenges of choosing the right softball team or potluck group, dealing with ex-lovers acquired during the baby dyke phase, and negotiating new names for the couple or their pets. If they decide to have children, they must consider all the options, such as artificial insemination and whether to use a sperm bank or a known donor, and if a known donor, a friend or relative? They must decide whether to use a medical facility for insemination or the infamous turkey baster (the choice of many impoverished or frugal dykes). They have to make decisions about who gets pregnant, who will oversee their prenatal care, who will be the child's goddess parents, and have a multitude of other choices to make.

Many adult dykes must also make decisions about home-ownership, and what to do with highly divergent incomes in terms of investing in the house. This drama can easily cause a breakup. Career issues are also sources of stress and conflict. Often one member of a couple has a higher status or higher paying job, but in an attempt to achieve equality in the relationship, there is little or no open discussion of what the career disparities mean to their relationship. Because this is a taboo topic in many feminist homes, the therapist may not be consulted about this, but it is an underlying tension that erupts into petty disagreements. Because of ex-lover and other lesbian community ties, when one member of a couple is offered a job in another location, this causes considerable drama, and may result in the commuter or long-distance relationship.

Unfortunately, most of a therapist's time with adult dykes is spent in processing the beginnings and endings of relationships. The typical course of a breakup of a lesbian relationship is prolonged compared to that of heterosexuals. Conflict avoidant dykes typically process whether they should break up or not for one year, and then after making the decision to break up, delay actually telling her partner for another three months. This is followed by three to six months of couples counseling that only rarely saves the relationship. The final mutual decision to break up is followed by one to five years of post-relationship grief processing and letting go exercises for both partners. Some lesbians will continue in therapy for another five years to work on their ex-lover relationship, and integrate new partners into the ex-lover extended family. Conflict avoidant dykes are a goldmine for therapists, and may keep one gainfully employed for years. Lesbian ex-lover relationships can take several different forms, and many of them are pathological. Lesbian ex-lover fusion disorder is described in this manual (see DDM 3) and all therapists need to be trained to deal with this complex condition. Two other common forms of ex-lover are the stalker and the vengeful ex. These forms appear to create havoc in dyke communities, but have not yet been studied extensively, thus therapists do not have effective preventive strategies at their disposal.

Elder Dyke

The last phase of the dykecycle is the elder dyke stage, when the client has reached her mature years and is ready to become a community leader, sage, high priestess, or supreme potluck hostess. Elder dykes may become lay therapists at this time. If they continue with therapy, issues might involve dealing with shared menopause in a relationship (see DDM 15), and selecting the appropriate lesbian land commune in which to retire. Therapists can also help aging dykes keep their brains sharp via lesbian versions of memory games, such as crossword puzzles of all the ex-relationships in one's community, or reciting lyrics from 1970s lesbian musician's songs. These word games appear to be much more effective in maintaining lesbian memory cells than Sudoku or other games aimed at heterosexuals.

Unfortunately, merely reaching the elder dyke phase via the passage of time is no guarantee that all lesbians will become mature or wise, and the majority will continue to demonstrate one or more DDM diagnoses. Some will manifest new ones in their elder years as they navigate the contradictions of mainstream media loathing of older women versus some dyke community's glorification of crone status. Although there is a tendency for dyke drama quotients to decline with advancing age, some elder dykes can retain their high maintenance ways well into their 80s. This fact must be kept in mind in the design of dyke elder supportive housing ventures. The architecture of the old dyke home must be conducive to lowering drama levels as well as being ADA compliant.

Regardless of stage of the dykecycle, therapists must also be aware of some basic facts about lesbians. The first, and most important, is that dykes tend to be rebellious. Therapists must introduce new ways of thinking and behaving in gradual and unobtrusive ways so that the client thinks she reached this conclusion on her own. Therapists rarely have success with being too directive with dykes, unless the client has a crush on her and wants to please the therapist. Second, many dykes spend too much time processing issues in their lives, and some suffer from an actual Lesbian Excessive Emotional Processing (LEEP) disorder (see DDM 30). For these process-oriented lesbians, therapists must early on in therapy establish the upper hand, or this client will talk non-stop for the entire 50-minute session without letting the therapist speak until the last 30 seconds. At this point, the client pleads, "What should I do?" in a ploy to lengthen the therapy session. This client may discuss the same issue endlessly for months, even years. Sometimes lesbianalysis of excessive processers involves banning them from talk therapies entirely. In these cases, all professional and non-professional therapists within a 100-mile radius must be alerted to the ban on therapy so that the client does not merely replace her current therapist with another willing ear.

Some lesbians become fixated at a particular stage of the dykecycle because of life stressors or traumas. Some women never leave the predyke phase and live a life in the closet. Hopefully, she has adequate means so that her closet is well furnished. Others become stuck in the baby dyke phase, putting them at risk for conditions such as the Party Dyke (DDM 9), or get into a pattern of serial monogamy with multiple fusion disorder (DDM 3).

Other therapy considerations

Another important factor to consider is the assignment of dykes to individual versus group counseling sessions. Group counseling is contra-indicated in small lesbian communities because of the high likelihood of having exes, current partners or exes of exes, or women with crushes on another group member in any potential grouping of six or more lesbians. Even in larger urban settings, where it might be possible to find six to eight lesbians who do not know each other or any of each other's exes, there is the strong likelihood of two or more of the group members developing feelings for each other. Crushes on one's therapist are also very common, and counselors must maintain strict boundaries with their clients. Reputations can be tainted by the behavior of a few unethical therapists, such as the counselor in one rural community who encouraged her clients to sit in her lap so she could stroke their hair and backs as a soothing technique. When she admitted to having a sex addiction herself, the community felt betrayed and suspicious of therapists for many years thereafter.

One highly lucrative subspecialty of therapy in lesbian communities is the dyke pet counselor. Whereas in heterosexual communities, pet therapists may help with dog obedience training or kitty litter box avoidance syndromes, dykes with pet fetishes (see DDM 1) need assistance in breaking unhealthy bonds with their pets. Some lesbians lose all sense of boundary between pet and dyke, and sometimes the pet abuses her human companion (see DDM 29, Co(pet)dependent disorder). In these cases, pet batterer education sessions are needed to save the relationship. In addition, any dyke with pets who is considering a new relationship must discuss the compatibility of her pet and her new girlfriend. When new pets or children are introduced into existing pet-dyke relationships, sibling rivalries may create dyke drama. Dykes who are breaking up need guidance about pet custody issues, and when pets die, pet dyke counselors are needed to foster healthy grieving in extended ex-lover communities who have been touched by the pet. Issues related to pets are the second most common reason for lesbians to seek therapy; intimate relationships with humans are the first.

Now that issues of terminology, make-up of lesbian communities, and lesbian psychology have been covered, it is important to address the history of lesbian identities and communities in order to understand how and why dyke drama has developed and escalated in recent years.

HERSTORICAL EVIDENCE OF DYKE CULTURES

Dykes have lived in every culture in every era that has ever been studied. Male anthropologists and missionaries, however, who were among the first to study the native cultures that their governments colonized, often did not recognize them, just as the average heterosexual man today often fails to see dykes when looking right at them. Ancient sacred texts often gloss over the significance of female love because of their patriarchal bent or because of translation errors that changed the gender of protagonists of common stories. Lesbians have always tended to be an oral culture, so traces of their existence are harder to find. If one looks closely at the historical evidence, however, dykes are found everywhere. Well-preserved skeletal remains of two women were found buried together in the heart of Africa. They were clutching each other and wearing exactly the same ornaments. Prehistoric stone carvings in caves in France show two women's figures so merged together as to clearly exhibit lesbian fusion disorder (see DDM 3). Classical paintings celebrate the female form and show women gazing lustily at each other. The writings of classical Greece focused much on men's sexual practices, but this scrutiny of men left women more free to express themselves without scrutiny, out of view of the men who were busy writing about the glories of man-boy love. While the men wrote about sex, women were experimenting with each other, creating the early foundations for lesbian community as we know it today. Only recently have lesbians committed their stories to paper. But their oral traditions are present, if one is willing to dig into the origins of the fairy tale.

Fairy tales have universal appeal—they tell interesting stories with morals that help us deal with life's challenges. Young dykes, like all other children, are exposed to fairy tales, but most are not aware that these stories have been altered over the years to appeal to heterosexuals. The original stories were queer tales (hello---fairy tale!). In the past year, the author of this book spent hours in the fairy tale archives on the Island of Lesbos, the underground tunnels of Mount Holyoke, and the secret caves under Bernal Hill to unearth the original stories. She found that some of the stories were dramatically altered for heterosexual consumption, but others needed only slight modifications to make them hetero-acceptable. For example, to make *Goldilocks and the Three Bears* a heterosexual tale, one only needed to change the hairy gay men into actual bears. The storyline is more or less intact, with a moral related to the challenges of having gay men as roommates. *Hansel and Gretel* came from a story that was originally about two young women, Hannah and Gretel, teen lovers who fled their homophobic parents to live in a witch's coven in the woods. Of course, the Christian right turned coven into "oven" and implied the witches were evil. They changed their names to Madrone and Ash, became Wiccan priestesses, and lived happily ever after with their three cats. The original *Jack and Jill* rhyme began like this: "Pat and Jill went up the hill to fetch a bowl of hummus. Pat went down and broke Jill's frown and Jill came loudly after." *Puss in Boots*, well, the title says it all. *Rapunzel* did not let down a cascade of golden hair, but rather, a very practical long braided tail. *Beauty and the Butch* was a cautionary tale about setting one's expectations too high. Beauty, a femme lesbian, wanted a butch sugar daddy who would also love long, intimate conversations about feelings. She was destined to have her heart broken over and over again by destitute butches of few words. *Little Red Riding Crop* was an S&M story. Red was a lesbian top with auburn hair and a lusty girlfriend who went by "Wolf." They liked to have kinky sex behind Grandma's back during family holidays in the cabin in the woods.

Sleeping Beauty was awakened, not by a handsome prince, but by a majestic queen. There was no poisoned apple, but instead a veggie burger tainted with a sleeping potion by a jealous ex-lover who wanted her out of commission for a while so she could turn the dogs against her for revenge. *Snow White and the Seven Sapphists* told the story of a separatist commune. Born Sally White in rural Ohio, when she moved to Eugene, Oregon and came out, she changed her name to Snow and wore long flowing white robes while she cleaned the house. Her housemates at the radical lesbian commune were Sapphy, Bitchy, Tomboy, Dyky, Femmy, Willowy, and Lesbiana. *Cinderella* was a femme lesbian living in a sorority. She fit in well with her sisters on the step team because they shared an interest in shopping and make-up tips, but Ella stayed home to clean up after her slovenly roommates while they went to frat parties. She grew organic pumpkins in the backyard. The glass slipper was actually a well-worn pair of birkenstocks.

Some scholars speculate that Shakespeare was actually a dyke. There is considerable evidence that an early draft of the manuscript of Romeo and Juliet had a different title: Roma and Juliet. This fact explains the family animosities, the falling in love far too quickly, and the extreme drama that this romance created. The give-away that the story was originally about two women's love affair is the telling dialogue in the famous balcony scene. Juliet says, "Deny thy father and refuse thy name," referring to the lesbian penchant for resisting the patriarchy and changing their names. She also pleaded, "O swear not by the moon, the inconstant moon that monthly changes in her circled orb, lest that thy love prove likewise variable," obviously referring to PMS mood swings. If U-Haul had been available in fair Verona, much drama could have been averted in the short run, although no doubt considerable drama might have still manifested in the long run. Many other Shakespearian plays can be read for lesbian subplots related to women cavorting naked in the woods, capricious attempts to manipulate others through intrigue and indirect communications, love addictions, manipulative fairies, mistaken identities, and gender confusions.

Another example of the manipulation of Shakespeare for heterosexual audiences can be found in the original manuscript of Hamlet. In the first draft, Shakespeare's most famous speech was about the anguish of lesbian break-ups, and in particular, a philosophical treatise on who initiates the break-up. The original soliloquy went like this:

> To dump or be dumped, that is the question;
> Whether tis nobler for a dyke to suffer the slings and arrows of a
> no longer cherished lover or take arms against a sea of
> processing hell, and by opposing dump them;
>
> To dump, to be dumped, No more, and by being dumped, to say
> we end the heart-ache and the thousand natural shocks that
> lesbian flesh is heir to?
>
> Tis a consummation devoutly to be wished.
>
> To dump, to be dumped; to be dumped, perchance to feel
> rejected; aye there's the rub. For in that being dumped, what
> horrors may come when we have shuffled off the lesbian
> relationship coil, must give us pause.

Civil war historians have found countless examples of women cross-dressed as men so that they could wear uniforms and fight in the war. Many of them had female partners. Folktales from the old west of the United States are full of stories of women settlers traveling together in covered wagons to start new lives on the frontiers, some toting six guns, wearing cowboy boots, and exhibiting a fetish for leather holsters. Sometimes these journeys were described as impulsive escapes from family and society, perhaps reflecting the early pioneer form of the U-Haul syndrome (see DDM 7).

Most lesbians know about Radcliffe Hall's controversial book, *The Well of Loneliness*. Published in 1928, the book is about the angst and despair associated with being a lesbian. There is evidence, however, that the first version of the manuscript was called *The Well of Wanton Women*, and was about her mind-blowing, ecstatic sexual relationship with two Parisian chorus girls. Hall's publisher convinced her that the world was not ready to accept happy lesbians, so she re-wrote the book to conform to prevailing societal attitudes about lonely and desperate dykes. The success of *Well of Loneliness* led to a plethora of books and movies about seriously depraved or depressed lesbians, creating the stereotype that lesbians are deadly serious and have no sense of humor. There is also evidence that Louisa May Alcott's best seller, *Little Women*, was altered in the minutes prior to the first printing, and the character Laurie, was changed to a boy at the last minute to satisfy censors. The story makes so much more sense with Laurie as a girl. Jo's marriage to a chubby man with a beard was one of the first examples in literary history of a lesbian and a gay man marrying each other to avoid discovery. Finally, the term "purple prose" that today means overblown writing, originally referred to lesbian writers' penchant for flowery euphemistic phrases about female body parts.

In addition to the literary evidence, there is long-standing historical research about the presence of woman-loving women in all girls' schools, convents, and other sex-segregated settings in many different time periods and geographical locations. Saint Joan had a penchant for short hair and men's garb, as did Queen Christina of Sweden, who abdicated the throne rather than marry a man and give up cigars. No doubt, the first female martyr was a lesbian.

RECENT SCIENTIFIC STUDIES IN DYCOLOGY

Since the 1970s, there has been a growing research literature on psychological factors related to lesbian life and relationships. Dykes in general have been suspicious of academic research, unless they happen to be academics themselves, and then only believe their own research, so the scholarly literature has been largely ignored or dismissed until recently. Current dykes are obsessed with studying themselves. Another rich source of information about lesbian behavior can be discerned from lesbian cultural productions, including fiction, erotica, plays, TV shows, films, dyke marches, lesbian comics and comedians, blog sites, online dating sites, newsletters, flyers, observation of signs at dyke marches, and political writing. Important insights about lesbian life for this manual were also gleaned from the theoretical philosophies of *Lizzy the Lezzy* (by Ruth Selwyn), *Paisan Hothead, Homicidal Lesbian* (by Diana DiMassa), *Dykes to Watch Out For* (by Alison Bechdel) and *Dyke Drama* (by Leslie Lange). While generally helpful tools to understanding dyke behavior, some lesbian cultural productions, such as the fiction genre, must be viewed with some suspicion, as there appears to be an overrepresentation of lesbian vampires and dyke detectives in the lesbian literature. If the lesbian mystery genre were a true representation of lesbians, every seventh lesbian would be a detective.

In the past, scientists had to rely on animal studies to explore same-sex behaviors, because dykes were hidden and knew better than to volunteer for research. The earliest studies used fruit flies to model sexual orientation-related community structures and pair-mating behaviors. The researchers found that most of the flies paired off in girl-boy manner during mating season, however, a subset of male fruit flies congregated around dark corners of the forest, where fermented apples rotted. They feasted on the fruit and frolicked gaily as a group. A few female flies joined them in the merriment. A larger subset of female fruit flies formed inseparable pair bonds with each other that lasted one mating season, although many of these pairings ended with group disharmony and chaos, before new pairings were formed for the next mating season. There have also been reports of lesbian seagulls, flocking to certain neighborhoods of the coastal cities of the U.S. to nest, and certain varieties of female hoot owl dyads drawn to lesbian land communes.

One important human experimental study that began in the mid 1950s addressed the question of nature versus nurture in the development of lesbian sexual identities and behaviors. Senator Joseph McCarthy secretly secured funding from the FBI for the project. Senator McCarthy was best known for his attempts to purge homosexuals and communists, who he thought were one and the same, from government service, but recent documents have been found that show his involvement in classified government research. This study was an attempt to identify ways to prevent women from becoming lesbians and complicating his heterosexual world. The government-funded study was kept secret for years, but recently came to light when a dyke graduate student found the records buried in the dark recesses of the basement of the Library of Congress. The principal investigator, a young Dr. Laura Schlessinger, conducted genetic tests of female twin pairs to identify potential lesbians, and then separated them at birth. One twin was assigned to live in a militia compound in Idaho with no TV, internet, or dyke literature and very strict gender socialization, and the other twin was raised in a typical U.S. middle class suburban home. When evaluated at the age of 30, the same number in each group reported same-sex attractions (100%), but the militia-raised groups without the benefit of lesbian romance novels were much less likely to call themselves lesbians or dykes, and were significantly less likely to have ever met a partner at a women's music festival. There were no differences in the prevalence of cat or dog fetishes, but virtually no lesbian potluck hostesses were found among the militia-reared group. LOLs (see DDM 25. Late-Onset Lesbians) were much more common among the militia-reared group. The role of socialization effects on lesbian personality and behavior needs to be studied more extensively, but the study points to the possibility that some lesbian behavioral patterns are innate, whereas others derive from forces in the environment. This idea is supported by the fact that lesbians born in other parts of the world often have difficulty understanding or relating to U.S. dyke behaviors.

There is a small but growing body of research on lesbian inbreeding. Small rural communities, or highly exclusive urban enclaves of dykes may be very small, and because of lesbian multiple serial monogamy (see DDM 27), symptoms of inbreeding may manifest over time when too many dykes in a community have been in relationships with each other. The consequences of inbreeding include a drop in the collective lesbian socio-emotional intelligence, a loss of fertility manifest as lack of creativity in cultural productions resulting in the production of dull poetry and uninspired romance stories, as well as an increase in all of the disorders described in this manual. If there are 100 lesbians in a community, and they have an average relationship length of 2.57 years, then within ten years, all the dykes have been with each other, unless there is an active effort to encourage immigration into the community to keep the bloodlines more varied. In these circumstances where risk for inbreeding is high, extensive lesbian recruiting strategies are recommended. Dyke communities are clear: no walls are wanted. Immigrants to the community are welcomed and celebrated.

LESBIAN EPISODIC INFATUITIS

The scientific literature contains little information about this problem that is characterized by confusion, impairment of judgment, irrational or even positively delusional beliefs, and mood swings from extreme euphoria to the deepest despair in a matter of minutes. Rather than a dykignosis, this condition seems to be an almost universal experience of lesbians. Physical symptoms include increased heart rate, irregular breathing, profuse sweating, sudden wetness, and nipple-erection. There may be disturbing sensations in the lower abdomen that lead to physical restlessness and sleep disturbances. The symptoms may appear suddenly and the duration of the disorder ranges from hours to months, or even years. This chronic condition is known in the field of dycology as Episodic Infatuitis (EI), or in lay terms, the crush. Although this affliction has plagued womankind for centuries, scientific study of the disorder has been lacking until recently.

History of Episodic Infatuitis

Accounts of Episodic Infatuitis can be found in the earliest writings of lesbian-kind, and there is evidence that crushes predate written languages. In 2011, a well-preserved skeleton of a woman clutching a female fertility symbol was unearthed in northern Africa, dating to 8000 BCE. Some anthropologists speculate that Neanderthals showed little evidence of Episodic Infatuitis and suggest that fact may explain their demise. The crush may be the missing link, the quality that separates woman from ape. Cave drawings in France show an entwined double women symbol, suggesting the first example of lesbian fusion found in human history.

In early Greek culture, Sappho had a chronic case of EI, with multiple relapses. Some historians believe that the island of Lesbos may be the original source of the infectious agent or mutant gene that causes the disorder; the ground zero of the lesbian crush. However, recent feminist scholars reject this idea and insist that Lesbos was the inspiration for bad lesbian poetry, not the crush. The Dark Ages brought about persecution of the afflicted woman, and crusades were launched to stamp out any evidence that women could be sexual beings. The condition became hidden out of sight by a devoted secret sisterhood. The cult kept the crush alive by retelling the stories of ancient women's crushes and ecstatic secret relationships, huddled together in dark caves and remote forest glens. These stories were re-discovered in the 1950s and were translated into lesbian pulp fiction.

Social conditions of the 1960s allowed Episodic Infatuitis to flourish above ground once again. Songs glorified the crush for women and men alike, and romanticized the symptoms with lyrics such as "Whenever you're near, I hear a symphony" and "Going out of my head over you." Lesbian songwriters acknowledged the timelessness and chronic nature of the crush, as in k.d. lang's "constant craving has always been." The gay liberation movement of the 1970s brought lesbians out of the closet, and into much more public and visible crush behavior. For example, the crush on the gym teacher in high school is a common coming of age experience of young lesbians.

Causes of the Crush

The causes of the crush are still unknown. Once thought to be a mental illness, recent research suggests that it is a normal phenomenon. Research in the 1980s suggested that Episodic Infatuitis is similar to the herpes simplex virus. That is, once infected, the afflicted woman carries the crush virus for life, dormant for months or years at a time. But once triggered, the crush symptoms re-emerge suddenly. For some afflicted dykes, the trigger is related to a physical trait like a beautiful smile or graceful shoulder blades. For others it is a personality trait like nurturance or neediness. For yet others, it might be a skill, such as a slide into third base, expertise with power tools, or the ability to accessorize.

Subtypes of EI

Research in the dycology laboratory in San Francisco reveals multiple subtypes of Episodic Infatuitis. Type I, the "Fatal Attraction" is the most severe. The victim is stricken suddenly and within days loses all sense of reality. She devotes her life to the crush object and plots chance meetings. In extreme cases, she parks outside the crush object's house in a U-Haul. Sleeping and eating patterns may be adversely affected, and the physical symptoms may become quite incapacitating when the victim is near the crush object, and sometimes first aid is necessary. The afflicted woman must be assisted to place her head between her knees, or someone else's if circumstances permit, to avoid swooning. The Fatal Attraction crush may have a long and agonizing course with periods of true psychotic breaks. Fortunately, full recovery is the rule, but occasionally a Fatal Attraction lasts for years, to the frustration of the

46

victim's friends, who grow weary of hearing the same tale of unrequited love over and over.

Recently, the advent of websites such as MyLife may be responsible for an upsurge in re-triggering of old crushes. If an unsuspecting lesbian should ever, in a weak moment, search for her crush object on one of these websites, she will be plagued for years thereafter with email messages proclaiming that the love object has been found. These frequent, repeated messages can be quite embarrassing if the woman has moved on and is in a relationship with another woman.

Type II Episodic Infatuitis, the "Moonstruck" crush, is short-term and self-limiting, like the common cold. It may strike suddenly, but lasts only a few hours or days. It often has its onset in a bar, at a dance or a softball game, or in the middle of a women's music festival, frequently under the influence of lesbian mania generated by a room full of uninhibited dyke energy. Lesbian mass mania has a similar effect to the love drug, ecstasy. Unlike Type I, which is connected to one very specific crush object, the Type II crush might have multiple objects, such as the entire cast of *The L Word*, the whole band, or the entire basketball team. Most commonly, however, the object of the crush is a stranger on the dance floor. Alcohol seems to lower resistance to this type of crush, as does excessive reading of Katharine Forrest novels. It may be intense, but is typically short-lived. The danger of this type of crush, if it is not nipped in the bud quickly, is that it can progress to the U-Haul Syndrome, often creating months or even years of misery.

Type III Episodic Infatuitis, the Celebrity crush, occurs when the object of the crush is a national or local celebrity, and the symptoms are based entirely on fantasy rather than reality. Over the years, famous lesbians or stars who played lesbians, such as Aphrodite, Sappho, Eleanor Roosevelt, k.d. lang, Jodie Foster, Suze Orman, Melissa Etheridge, Helen Shaver, Rachel Maddow, Angelina Jolie, Sharon Gless, and many others, have had "groupie lesbians" who are devoted to them, swooning at concerts, tattooing their names on their asses, and obsessively stalking them whenever possible. Celebrity crushes are based on the iconography of the lesbian (a phenomenon also called Dykonography), not the actual woman, because, of course, most ordinary dykes have not had the opportunity to witness these celebrities in the types of behaviors that often kill crushes, such as poor table manners, narcissistic tendencies, or excessive flatulence. In the absence of these reality checks, a celebrity crush can last for many years, but they are typically harmless, except for the annoyance factor for friends who must listen to the afflicted dyke obsess about their crush. In rare cases, the celebrity crush can progress to dyke stalking syndrome, a form of serious pathology that requires professional intervention. Regrettably, sometimes law enforcement interventions are required.

Epidemiology of the Crush

Crushes are virtually universal in lesbians worldwide, affecting over 99%. Those who deny ever experiencing a crush are likely suffering from Episodic Infatuitis Occulta, a form of crush repression. Once a dyke has experienced a crush, she is vulnerable to repeat episodes in the future. The average lesbian has 12.4 crushes in her lifetime, with a range of 1 to 142 crushes.

The manifestation of Episodic Infatuitis depends on many factors. For example, the introversion/extroversion personality difference has a profound effect on how a crush is expressed. An introvert may have a quiet, secret crush for years that the crush object never discovers. Extroverted dykes, however, are more likely to publically declare their crushes in grand dramatic gestures, such as tattooing the name of the crush object on her arm or announcing her crush over the loudspeaker at the pride rally. In the past, it was thought that Episodic Infatutis aged out in women, leaving older women with more mature forms of love. Recent research, however, shows that the symptoms only weaken slightly, and the onset of a Fatal Attraction crush in a woman over 70 may create a regression to adolescent behaviors in a matter of days, no matter how wise the woman was pre-crush exposure. Some proclaim crushes among old lesbians to be "undignified" but this attitude is an example of ageism. Old lesbians have the right to act just as foolish when they are in love as younger lesbians.

There are also geographic variations in crush symptom manifestations. Lesbians in rural areas may repress crushes more often than urban lesbians, who are able to find a new social network if she is ostracized or rejected because of the crush. Rural lesbians have been known to implode because of unexpressed crush symptoms.

Treatment for EI

Mutual crushes generally require no interventions and can blossom into real love, but unrequited cases may be quite debilitating and warrant supportive therapies. Sadly, there are no cures, but symptoms can be reduced by dark chocolate infusions and binge watching of bad lesbian movies. Harm reduction programs may help to reduce the pain and suffering of severe forms of EI. One experimental treatment involves transference of crush symptoms to inanimate objects such as dolphin or rabbit shaped vibrators. However, high intensity sex toys with significant wattage are needed for this type of therapy, and the expense of replacing batteries daily may make the cost of this therapy prohibitive.

In conclusion, crushes have afflicted lesbians since pre-herstory. The symptoms are variable, but the disorder affects most of the lesbian population at some point in the lifespan, and the majority of dykes have multiple episodes. The crush is the most common underlying cause of lesbian dysfunctions such as the U-Haul Syndrome and fusion disorders, and deserves dedicated funding to find preventive strategies. Research has identified some of the subtypes of Episodic Infatuitis, but has not been helpful in addressing the central philosophical question: Crushes: blessing or curse?

LESBIAN PERSONALITY TYPES

There is growing research on lesbian typologies and one of the most promising systems is based on the idea that lesbians can be classified by their home décor. When further research has been conducted, it is likely that these types will be related to clusters of dyke dykignoses. Thus far, ten types or styles have been identified in the United States.

Traditional Lesbian

This is the original lesbian style, dating to the early 1970s and is organized around Georgia O'Keefe flower prints, bricks and boards bookcases filled with lesbian separatist literature and dyke poetry, and eclectic furniture purchased at Goodwill and decorated with women's symbols and labryris'. Stone or wooden carvings of Venus/goddess figures dot the shelves. Photographs of Rita Mae Brown and Cris Williamson are typically found in the hallway and there is always a portrait of a naked woman in the bedroom (tastefully done, of course). Ladyslipper catalogues and ancient, crumbling blue mimeographed copies of *The Ladder* grace the coffee table. Lavender is the preferred wall color and essential oil infusers permeate the house with the scent of patchouli.

Contemporary LGBT

This style centers around the theme of pride, with a particular use of the rainbow and pink triangle motif, often initiated when lesbians and gay men share housing. Framed Keith Haring posters are often found in this interior design style. Rainbow flags are a common accessory, on the front of the house of out and political lesbians, and in the fenced backyard or basement rec room of those more closeted dykes. The furnishings come primarily from IKEA, with half of the furniture assembled and the other half still in boxes awaiting attention from the DIY household member (or handy ex). More prosperous contemporary LGBT homes are furnished from Pottery Barn.

(Post) Modern

Modern style is typically stark and minimalist, with use of bold colors. The (post) modern style eschews the bright colors and tends toward excessive use of black with occasional purple accents. Bookshelves are lined with postmodern feminist and queer theorist writers. In the home of the academic (post) modern, there is typically a shrine to Judith Butler or Gertrude Stein. Furniture is arranged into conversation pits, where intense debates about feminist theory versus queer theory may occur on a regular basis. Uncomfortable furniture is deliberately selected so that guests do not get too comfortable with their assumptions.

Shabby ButchChic

This is the style preferred by single butch lesbians, with comfortable overstuffed sofas, recliners, and large screen TVs for superior sports viewing. Accessories include assorted power tools and electronic toys, softball gear, and home remodeling books. There are no frills, lace, or non-utilitarian baubles in the Shabby ButchChic home. The kitchen is equipped with mis-matched dishes, but not in the fashionable way. More attention is paid to the garage workshop than the interior of the house, with gleaming tools arranged meticulously on the walls. Posters of the butch dykes' favorite *L Word* character and neon beer signs make up the wall-hangings.

Retro Queer

Popular among the artistic and trendy lesbians, retro queer style uses poster prints of lesbian pulp novels, photos of 1940s and 50s gay bar scenes, and kitchy knick knacks like lawn jockeys and muscle man magazines in an effort to be ironically out of date. Oscar Wilde books and slogans may be found throughout the home in the more gay-identified retro queer, and posters of possible lesbians from history in the dyke-identified home. These lesbians often quote Gertrude Stein, much to the puzzlement of other dykes who think they are speaking a foreign language.

Country Dyke

Back to nature and eco-feminist dykes often prefer the country dyke style, with heavy, rustic homemade furniture, milkmaid paintings, and domestic animal prints, most commonly of their own companion animals. Back rooms may be equipped with goat-milking apparatus and a minimum of five bins for various recycling and compost activities. The country dyke estate may or may not include a barn or a pseudo-barn (a shed). This home is scented by an indoor herbal garden for culinary (and occasionally, recreational) purposes. Hot tubs for pagan rituals are found in the backyard.

Art Dyco

This style typically has hardwood floors laid out in triangle patterns, lacquered bright furniture pieces embossed with the lambda sign, and homemade stained glass windows with rainbow motifs. Arched doorways and angular furniture are common. Art Dyco dykes may attempt to create a prairie style home out of a 1960s split level suburban house, to varying degrees of success. These dykes may idolize architect Julia Morgan as their dykon (see DDM 2).

Early American Vet

This is the style preferred by cat and dog fetish lesbians (see DDM 1). Their homes are organized around their companion animals, with furniture pieces chosen for animal comfort and ease of cleaning. The household furnishings consist primarily of cat climbing towers and dog beds. There are no curtains, because the cats have torn them down. There is a noticeable mélange of aromas, with the scent designed to cover up kitty litter or wet dog smells often overpowered by the sheer number of pets in the home. The main accessories are cat or dog throw toys, casually strewn across the living room to emulate a casual lived in look.

Dyco-matrix

In this style, common to the S&M lesbian, erotic photographs line the walls, and furniture is selected for durability and ease of cleaning after orgies. Accessories include whips, paddles, handcuffs, slings, and leather items of every size and shape. Often, the basement has been transformed into a dungeon. There may be a discrete display case of dildos of different sizes, shapes, and colors. The aroma is that of scented lubes and rubber. It is best for the faint-hearted to avoid dropping in unannounced at the home of a dyco-matrix.

Lez-eclectic

This is the most common style of lesbian home décor, particularly among those with no training in fashion or the arts, such as those on the neutral to butch side of the gender continuum. Lez-eclectic is a combination of all the other styles, sometimes by room (a Shabby ButchChic living room, retro queer dining room, traditional bedroom, and LGBT bathroom, etc), and sometimes each room is a conglomerate of styles with a dog bed center piece in the living room and pink triangle quilt on the wall. This style has emerged from the lesbian serial monogamy pattern, whereby lesbians collect different furniture and home accessory styles in different relationships, resulting in the eclectic pattern when they merge yet again with a new partner and combine households.

Conclusion

There is a pressing need for collaborations among dycologists and lesbian interior designers to discern the significance of these home décor patterns, and identify their links to lesbian dykignostic categories. In addition, the common addiction of some lesbians to Home and Garden TV and home remodeling shows are altering these patterns. The latest trend toward tiny homes among lesbians may alter the U-Haul pattern of rapid cohabitation. Instead of needing to load and reload a U-Haul, an afflicted lesbian may pull up to her girlfriend's house in a Tiny House, ready to move in immediately.

RESEARCH EVIDENCE FOR THE DDM

As noted earlier, this manual is the result of years of systematic study of dyke behavior. The dykignostic categories in this manual were derived from several sources including extensive field notes accumulated over a period of over 30 years by a professional lesbian (the author) living as a participant observer in many subcultures of the U.S. lesbian community in two different geographical regions, one rural and one urban. Detailed field notes were taken at such diverse sites as lesbian brunches, concerts and music festivals, meetings of lesbian collectives in women's centers, behind the bleachers at softball games, at queer studies conferences, in bathrooms in gay bars, at gay pride organizing committee meetings, during dyke walking or hiking group events, book clubs, and at hundreds of lesbian potlucks and game nights. At these events, some of the richest data were collected from overheard conversations between partners or ex-lovers. Additionally, in-depth interviews were conducted with hundreds of lesbians over those 30 years, usually over coffee and often focusing on crushes, new relationships, and/or breakups. Focus groups were conducted with lesbian therapists, both the professionally trained ones and the lay therapists.

The field notes are supplemented by quasi-experimental studies conducted in several dating and relationship situations. On rare occasions, the author was able to observe lesbian sexual behaviors directly as a participant observer of the phenomenon under study. Lesbian census data were reviewed to identify demographic profiles of lesbian communities and to map community assets and deficits. Finally, the author completed qualitative thematic analyses of lesbian romance novels and lesbian online dating profiles to verify the research. The results of this diligent research using ethnographic observations, qualitative analysis, and quantitative experimental methods are reported in this manual. Each dykignostic category was carefully fact-checked by an expert panel of dykes from around the world to verify their accuracy, thus establishing the reliability and validity of each dyke drama generator.

Organization of the DDM IV

As noted earlier, the DDM is modeled after the Diagnostic and Statistical Manual (DSM) of Mental Disorders used to make psychiatric diagnoses and bill for services in the general population. The DSM was first published in 1952, originally had a total of 106 mental disorders, and underwent revisions in 1968, 1980, 1987, 1994, 2000, and 2013. The DSM is organized into five dimensions or Axis categories. Axis I includes clinical mental disorders such as depression and substance abuse; Axis II contains personality disorders such as narcissism and anti-social personality; Axis III refers to brain injuries and physical health problems that contribute to psychological adjustment difficulties; Axis IV includes the psychosocial and environmental factors that contribute to an individual's dysfunctions; and Axis V is a global assessment of functioning.

The DDM has the same general structure as the DSM, but unlike the DSM, the DDM includes suggestions for treatment. The DDM is still under construction, and it is likely that future editions will deviate from this format. If heterosexual people have five Axis categories for mental health, no doubt lesbians will find them too limiting and come up with 23 or more categories and hundreds of diagnoses in the near future. Some dykes may object to the axis structure similarities to the DSM and will accuse the author of aping heterosexual norms. This may necessitate creating an entirely different, non-hierarchical classification system. Others, however, will continue to resist labeling, and some will organize protests about this manual and publicly chastise the author. Yet, for the sake of science, the DDM Academy will persist even in the face of protest and shaming, to expose the dykignoses that underlie dyke drama.

AXIS I DYKE DYKIGNOSES

Axis I conditions stem predominantly from environmental situations such as misapplication of heterosexual and gender-based socialization patterns to lesbian relationships and social organizations. These triggering conditions can include pressure from parents to date boys or act more "girly," lesbo-phobic messages in the mainstream media, experiences of rejection and discrimination, misinformation obtained in the girl's bathroom at school, broken hearts, and other traumatic life events that ultimately create dyke drama and dysfunction. Axis I conditions may also stem from living in a dyke-dismissive world and from the traumas inflicted on young emerging lesbian identities by negative experiences with parents, peers, roommates, teachers, ministers, and others who make lesbian life intolerable at times. These traumas and family/societal dysfunctions combine with genetic dyke (sometimes referred to as genetdyk) vulnerabilities to affect lesbian relationships and communities, and create unique pathologies that manifest differently in dyke communities than in the population as a whole. Virtually every lesbian will experience at least one of these conditions in her lifetime, and she will surely encounter most of the conditions in other members of her dyke communities. Each category is described in terms of its major signs and symptoms, frequency in the lesbian community, etiology, and finally, the most effective methods of treatment and prevention. Case examples from the author's extensive files about deviant behavior in exes are offered to illustrate each disorder.

DDM 1: Lesbian Fetishes

Overview

The definition of a fetish is a sexual arousal caused by some object or situation that is not generally thought of as sexual. In the general population, common fetishes include leather, rubber suits, women's lingerie, women's footwear (particularly high-heeled shoes and argyle socks), money, Sears catalogs, and Barbie dolls. Gay men may also exhibit fetishes for Martha Stewart cookbooks, pink poodles, and Abercrombie catalogs. Some people afflicted with a fetish are only aroused by highly specific body parts, such as elbows or shins, or by body ornamentation such as tattoos and piercings.

Because there were so few openly lesbian role models for dykes to observe when they are in their formative years, many lesbians focus all of their pent-up passions into various non-human objects of affection, such as pets and inanimate objects that do not judge, discriminate, or call them evil or immoral. The repressed desires may manifest as a fetish, or unusually strong, almost erotic, attachment to the object of affection. This manual describes five common variations of this syndrome, but there are probably many more yet to be recognized. For example, lesbians may develop a disorder that on the surface appears to be similar to a heterosexual person's fetish, such as an obsession for shoes. Rather than high heels, however, the dyke fetish in the 1970s might have been for the Birkenstock, in the 1990s, for Doc Martens, or in any era, the cowgirl boot. Similarly, heterosexual men may fetishize nurse or schoolgirl uniforms, whereas lesbians are more likely to develop fetishes for UPS or softball uniforms. Recently, there has been an unhealthy upsurge in dyke fetishes for orange prison jumpsuits, paralleling the popularity of *Orange is the New Black*. These fetishes for fashion or cultural trend come and go, but the five disorders reported here have been relatively stable over the past 50 years.

DDM 1a. The Femi-Feline Fetish

Having and loving pets is not inherently pathological, however, some lesbians are excessively involved with their cats, spending more time, energy, and attention on their felines than on potential or actual partners, thus qualifying as a fetish. Afflicted lesbians talk obsessively about their cats, cancel dinner parties when their cats sneeze, annoy their friends by posting daily updates of their cats' antics on Facebook, and tweet friends with messages such as "precious coughed up hairball today." Their holiday cards depict the cat in some type of costume, and their online moniker or password is their cat's name. A key sign of the disorder is the orgasmic zeal by which the woman talks about her cat. Femi-Feline Fetishists are rarely cat-monogamous, and typically have polygamous feline relationships with two or more cats. Some practice feline serial monogamy.

Femi-Feline Fetishists may spend a significant portion of their often meager incomes on items related to their cat(s), and their home is typically cluttered with cat toys (that the kitty mostly disdains), scratching posts, climbing towers, and kitty heating lamps. At least one entire kitchen cabinet is devoted to cat foods, treats, grooming products, medications, and other health care items. Some afflicted dykes with cat dander allergies must take immune-suppressors and antihistamines along with emergency inhalers to be able to live with their cats, but they would rather endure the high cost of medical visits, medications, and the side effects of the drugs than give up their feline fetish. In some dyke households, humans are strictly prohibited from using certain sofas or chairs that are reserved only for cat use. In very extreme cases, the dyke fuses her identity with her cat(s) rather than a partner, creating a loss of personal identity and a taking-on of cat personality traits such as arrogance, love of catnip, frequent napping, and a tendency to rub her head against her girlfriend's shoulder for attention. The high prevalence of Catwoman and Hello Kitty costumes at lesbian Halloween parties is evidence of the pervasiveness of this condition among dykes.

Case Example

Jesse is a downwardly mobile dyke of age 34, who had six cats in a studio apartment; two were diabetic and needed daily insulin injections, and one had a rare skin disorder requiring daily mineral baths and ointments. She took all six cats to the holistic health vet for kitty acupuncture once a month. Jesse complained to her hairdresser, Sasha, that she was tired of being single. However, she related to Sasha that she spent all of her leisure time at the Animal Shelter petting and grooming cats or shopping for the one and only gourmet cat food that her elitist cats would eat. More than 80% of her conversations with Sasha were centered on her cats' antics and 10% regarding her concerns about dating and relationships (the other 10% was spent on negotiating the sliding scale fee for the feminist dyke hair salon). Jesse reported that she had been attracted to one woman in the past year, but did not pursue it, because the woman was allergic to cats, thus, a totally unsuitable partner.

58

Another woman she met at lesbian speed dating said that she found cats a bit haughty—Jesse found this statement so disturbing that it was her primary topic of conversation for the next eight weeks.

DDM 1b. The Dog Park Cruising Zone

The second variation of the displaced affection fetish syndrome is the lesbian preoccupation with dogs. Again, the disorder is not related to a normal affection for dogs as pets, but an obsessive focus on dogs rather than people. Curiously, this condition rarely co-exists with the Femi-Feline Fetish (for the exception, see DDM 1d). There are so many afflicted with this disorder that dog parks have become lesbian cruising zones. Gay men may seek out dark corners of parks for a blow-job, but afflicted lesbians are sexually aroused when parading their canines at the dog park. Dog parks in densely lesbian neighborhoods resemble a Kennel Club dog show with both the dykes and the dogs competing for "best in show." In fact, the film *Best in Show* may be partly responsible for an upsurge in the lesbian dog fetish prevalence, related to Jane Lynch celebrity crushes (see DDM 2). The dog park cruising lesbians climax when others fawn over their dogs. For those unfamiliar with this disorder, the appropriate etiquette when meeting an afflicted lesbian on the street, on the way to or from the dog park, is to pet the dog rather than hug the dyke. Lesbians who want to avoid a dog park cruising girlfriend should be advised to check out the profile pictures on lesbian online dating sites. If the dog appears in the profile picture with the woman, there is a 65% probability that this is a dyke dog fetishist. If the dog appears alone, there is a 90% probability that the woman has a dog park cruising fetish. There appears to be a preference for large dogs among some afflicted dykes, because dainty small dogs are considered the domain of gay men or ultra-femme lesbians, but this preference may be more geographical than universal. One enterprising dyke with a Labrador, a dog considered highly prestigious among the dog park cruisers in her local community, considered making a living by renting out her dog. She reported that dykes with dog park fetish proclivities, but who could not own dogs because of rental agreements, allergies, disapproving partners, or other barriers, regularly begged her to borrow the dog for cruising on a hilltop lesbian dog park or frolicking at the beach because the dog was a potent dog-dyke magnet. After careful soul-searching, she decided to loan out her dog to needy dykes as a public service to her community, rather than profit off those afflicted with a dykignosis.

Finally, there are a growing number of Jewish dog dykes who are having Bark Mitzvah's for their pooches, and earth mother dog dykes who seek crone ceremonies for their aging dogs. Many lesbians in their communities who are invited to these events are perplexed about the protocol, and do not know whether to bring gifts or even whether to take the invitations seriously. For the afflicted lesbian, these are solemn events, not to be made fun of, so invited dykes must accept the invitation with the appropriate alacrity.

Case Example

Leslie, a 40 year-old rural dyke, lived on an acreage with 24 miniature poodles, all of whom had human names like Bobbie Jo, Vicki Sue, and Joanie Lou. Leslie, who called herself Sparky, an ironically dog-sounding name for a woman whose dogs had human-sounding names, had a girlfriend briefly. After dealing with the smell and chaos of the two-dozen dogs in one small house for a month after the lust had worn off, the woman gave her an ultimatum—"It's me or the dogs." Being afflicted with this disorder, Sparky chose the dogs. Sparky once caused a public scene at a lesbian brunch (more about this later), when someone said, "What's that noise?" The conversation died down and the brunch participants could all hear the ear-splitting high-pitched sound of yapping little dogs. Sparky had brought all 24 dogs to brunch in her Honda Civic, and proceeded to bring them one by one into the restaurant to introduce them to the brunch dykes, until the restaurant manager threatened to ban the lesbian brunch for the next year.

DDM 1c. Teddi-lezzies.

Readers may be anticipating that this condition is about the lingerie called a teddie, and it might be if the manual addressed cross-dressing heterosexual men. In dykes, however, this category refers to the teddy bear, the prototype of the stuffed animal. Many lesbians, like heterosexual people, own a stuffed animal or two. They are a poignant reminder of the innocence of childhood, a testimony to skills at the carnival, a source of comfort like the "blankie" of childhood, or a gift from a special friend. But stuffed animals can also be objects of fetishistic obsession and displaced affections. For some lesbians with pet dander allergies, stuffed animals take the place of actual cats and dogs in their fetishistic obsession.

Case Example

Celia, a femi-feline fetishist of age 43, once met a young upper middle class professional couple, Celeste and Anne-Marie, at a lesbian community fundraiser for the free medical clinic. They were new in town, and had just emigrated from France. They seemed very nice, so when they invited Celia to dinner to tell them more about the local community, she accepted the invitation. When Celia arrived, she noticed the dining room table was elaborately laid out with formal table settings for six. She asked politely, "Who else is coming to dinner?" Celeste answered, "No one, it's just us," and indicated where Celia should sit. At that moment, the other hostess, Anne-Marie, emerged from a bedroom carrying three large teddy bears. Celeste dashed into the kitchen and returned with three high chairs. The two carefully arranged the bears each in a differently colored highchair at the three vacant places and introduced Celia, "This is Mopsy, Bear, and Pooh." Celia did not know the appropriate response for this type of introduction, so she merely said, "Oh." Then Celeste brought out the appetizer and they proceeded through dinner, with the hostesses putting small servings on the plates of these three mute dinner guests. Celia had to contain her growing panic through dinner and escaped as quickly as she could after the honeycomb dessert was served. She thought that Anne-Marie and Celeste were probably perfectly harmless, but she felt completely freaked out. In her youth, she had viewed too many horror movies with innocent looking children or dolls that turned into evil monsters. That night Celia dreamed that the three bears lured her into a "build it yourself teddy bear" store, where they proceeded to stuff her into a bearskin. She thought that perhaps their teddy-affliction came from cultural factors related to their non-U.S. background, but other friends assured Celia that they had also met similarly affected dykes from the U.S.

DDM 1d. Lesbian Polyanimalry

Like polyamory, a condition where a lesbian chooses not commit to a monogamous relationship with only one woman, this dyke declines to commit to being a cat lover or a dog lover. Instead, she has a dog, at least two cats, a parrot, an albino rabbit, a guinea pig, and if she lives in a rural area, a mule, pot belly pig, and a herd of pygmy goats. The house and yard closely resembles a wild animal park or a petting zoo, depending on the general personality of the afflicted dyke. Introverts tend toward the wild animal park to scare away visitors; extroverts tend toward cute and cuddly animals to lure in strangers. Lesbians with pet dander allergies and this polyanimalry tendency must satisfy their lust for animal contact via zoos and excessive watching of Animal Planet on cable TV. Dykes who have been in relationships with polyanimalry-afflicted women report that they get an occasional petting or grooming, and get taken for a walk once a week, but do not get quality time and attention from the zoo-keeper.

Case Example

Paula is a 62-year-old impoverished lesbian who lives in a cabin by the river of a small college town. She worked as an assistant to a vet and was president of the local dog, cat, and raccoon rescue groups. Her living room was reduced in size by half by a 150 gallon aquarium, filled with dying fish, as Paula weekly visited local pet stores and took in all of their sickly fish to her aquatic hospice care center. Indoors, she had three longhair cats, two dogs (a golden retriever and a sheepdog), a pair of iguana, and a collection of every beanie baby ever made, lined up on a shelf in the living room. Outside in the shed she erected for this purpose, she raised llamas, geese, and banty hens, and she had two goats that she milked for her own cooking and cheese making. She put out food to attract beavers and river otters to the riverbank near her cabin. Her backyard was dotted with 26 small gravestones of past pets where she held weekly memorial services and regularly put flowers on the graves. The local lesbian community complained that when Paula attended events, she was covered in animal hair and exuded various animal aromas. In addition, she was always asking lesbians for donations to her various rescue activities, contributing to the excessive length of the announcements prior to lesbian events (see DDM 19). Paula had never had a live-in relationship with another woman, although she had been out as a lesbian for 32 years. She had experienced an 18 yearlong relationship with a tortoise, however.

DDM 1e. Butch Power Tool Fetish

Fetishes among lesbians can extend beyond companion animals or their symbols. Butch lesbians, almost by definition, gravitate to power tools, making it quite difficult to discern when the condition lapses into disorder. Some of the telltale signs of disorder include wearing a tool belt in inappropriate situations, such as at her partner's family Sabbath dinner or to a lesbian women's music festival. She has a drawer in the kitchen filled with batteries of every imaginable size, stemming from her irrational fear of loss of power sources for the tools. Finally, she engages in an obsessive collecting of (mostly unread) home repair books and has an addiction to remodeling shows on HGTV. When selecting sex toys, this affected dyke is drawn to the vibrators with the most buttons and settings, and the highest wattage. Other signs of disorder are the use of disproportionately large and complex tools for simple tasks, and preferring the company of her power tools to the company of her girlfriend. Granted, routers do not need to process every situation and miter saws do not make demands, but when the butch dyke gets more sexual pleasure from a reciprocating saw than her partner, the tool issue has become a fetish. Some more technologically savvy dykes may also have a fetish relationship with their electronic devices. For example, if one is on a first date, and the other woman is texting to friends on her smart phone, posting on Facebook on her iPad, and filming the date on her flip video camera, she just might have a fetish. These Tekkie lezzies are not to be confused with Trekkie lesbians who have a Star Trek fetish (and many have a concomitant celebrity crush on counselor Deanna Troi).

Case Example

Sandy once had a key snap off in a small padlock on a gym locker and asked a power tool fetish butch friend to loan her a tool to cut the lock. Jamie disappeared into her workshop, to return moments later dragging a 40-pound, four-foot long bolt-cutter. When Sandy asked to see her workshop (hoping to find a bolt cutter that she could actually carry to the gym), Jamie proudly showed off her collection of power tools. This included five different models of drills, six types of saws, five electric sanders of various sizes, eight nail guns, and an entire wall of neatly organized wrenches, metric and U.S. She also had a riding lawn mower for her 12 by 12 yard, three types of weed whackers, and four sizes of chain saw. When Sandy inquired about her girlfriend, Jamie said that they had broken up because her ex did not want the bathroom remodeled for the third time in two years, and was tired of parking on the street because Jamie's workshop had expanded to take over the entire two-car garage. Ultimately, the trip to the workshop was successful, because Sandy discovered that Jamie had ten different sizes of bolt cutter and was able to find an appropriate one for the task at hand.

Prevalence and Etiology of Lesbian Fetishes

Cat and dog fetishes are by far the most common forms of dyke fetish. Femi-feline disorder afflicts 19.3% of lesbians with cats, about double the rate of heterosexual women, and 15.2% of dykes with dogs are dog park cruisers. Polyanimalry is less common, with 6% of the lesbian population affected to some degree. The prevalence of the teddie-lezzie is unknown, because the condition is easier to hide. Finally, 9% of butch lesbians have a fetish relationship with one or more power tools and the power tool fetish is virtually unheard of in femme lesbians at 0.01%.

Although the underlying cause of dyke fetishes is the same regardless of the particular manifestation (cat, dog, teddy, tool, etc.), there are slight differences among the subtypes. All of them stem from lack of lesbian socialization in youth resulting in repressed and displaced sexual feelings, but there is growing evidence that lesbian femi-feline fetishes are also caused by a deep-seated anxiety about relationships. Cats represent the unavailable lover, as they tend to be standoffish and aloof, and no matter how hard she tries, the afflicted lesbian cannot totally win their love. Dog fetishes are related to an underlying need for unconditional love that can never be realized in a human relationship. The dog represents what the afflicted lesbian really wants---someone to look adoringly at her 100% of the time, fetch, and never talk back or want to process her feelings. The polyanimalry dyke has a multiple ambivalent fetish personality disorder, vacillating between wanting to be adored and wanting to be left alone. She may have had an obsession with zoos as a child. The tool fetish dyke wants a partner who always satisfies and never runs out of energy. As mentioned earlier, teddy-lezzies are often dykes with pet dander allergies who must express their fetishes with hypoallergenic objects such as stuffed animals or American Girl dolls. They may suffer from fear of intimacy, so that those in couple relationships put their affections on the objects rather than each other. The teddy bear rarely makes cutting sarcastic remarks or begs for greater vulnerability in the relationship.

Treatment Considerations for Lesbian Fetishes

Fetishes are notoriously difficult to cure, so some experts propose that rather than seek treatment, which may require years of lesbianalysis, afflicted lesbians should consider strategic pairing approaches. For example, femi-feline disordered women should seek out only other cat lesbians for relationships and dog park cruisers need only consider other dog lovers. These pairings are by no means free of problems, because in addition to the potential compatibility of the two humans, one has to consider pet compatibility. Far too many cats and dogs are the product of broken lesbian relationships and suffer the pains of custody battles that may rage for years after the end of the relationship. In addition, step-pet sibling rivalries can create chaos in new blended dyke families. For financial reasons, lesbians with polyanimalry syndrome should seek relationships only with veterinarians or dykes who work in pet supply stores and have employee discounts. An exception to the strategic pairing treatment is the polyanimalry condition. Dykes with this disorder should be actively discouraged, even banned, from partnering with another polyanimalry-afflicted woman. If two lesbians with polyanimalry syndrome develop a relationship together, they are likely to show up on the nightly news after being arrested and charged with being animal hoarders. Butch power tool fetishes are relatively harmless, and at times serve a useful function in their relationships and communities, so are best left untreated. House flippers make ideal partners for these dykes.

Finally, the teddi-lezzies need phased behavioral exposure therapy to acclimate them to human interactions, beginning with brief exposures to cartoon depictions of people. The gay teletubbies are an excellent start, as they are cute and nonthreatening and a cross between human and animal. Next they are exposed to humans in film, such as episodes of *The Real L Word*. Lastly, therapists guide them through actual in-person communication practices with surrogate friends to wean them from the dependence on the stuffed animals. Some teddie-lezzies seek allergy treatments during the critical periods of this behavioral therapy and ultimately are at high risk for succumbing to a femi-feline or dog dyke fetish over time.

In some communities, there are support groups for lesbians without pets because pet owners so often treat them with scorn and/or deep suspicion. Pet fetish lesbians in treatment may benefit from attending these sessions to learn strategies for living without dependence on their cats, dogs, or guinea pigs. Facilitators of the group must approve of the pet fetish lesbian's visits, however, to avoid violating the charter of these groups and distressing the actual non-pet dykes.

DDM 2: Lesbian Celebrity Groupies

This syndrome also arises from the lack of lesbian role models while growing up, but in this form of dysfunction, the displaced affections are placed on celebrities. Even today, there are only a few openly dyke role models in the media or in positions of power in local communities. When a celebrity comes out, she takes on superstar power and immediately becomes a Dykon (lesbian icon). Some "ordinary" lesbians develop unhealthy attachments and obsessions with these stars. This syndrome is highly context-specific, and the exact manifestations change with the times, of course, depending on who has emerged as the latest lesbian celebrities. Lesbian celebrity groupies have an interesting combination of symptoms of a dyke crush (e.g., intense emotional involvement and sexual longing occurring after only one or two meetings or viewings) with celebrity groupie behavior. The symptoms include displaying an irrational attachment to a complete stranger coupled with idealization of the celebrity stranger. The afflicted lesbian demonstrates obsessive behaviors in regards to the celebrity, such as attempts to email, text, tweet, blog, write fan letters, or camp outside of her house in hopes of catching a glimpse of her. When the addiction is for a celebrity performer, the afflicted lesbian may deplete her life savings to fly around the country to attend every concert or appearance. Friends will report that the afflicted dyke talks incessantly about the celebrity, often as if the celebrity were a close personal friend. This section provides a few contemporary examples of celebrity groupies, but these are constantly evolving as new dykons emerge and others fall into obscurity.

DDM 2a. Rachel Rachel

One of the contemporary lesbian icons, Rachel Maddow, soared to the top of the lesbian heartthrob chart in record time in late 2008. Objectively, she is attractive, intelligent, has a wicked sense of humor, and is extremely accomplished, with her own TV show as a well-respected news commentator, so admiration and respect are understandable. However, those lesbians who idolize her, talk about her incessantly, and cancel dates with actual women so they can get home in time for her show, even though they tape every episode, are showing signs of Rachel Rachel celebrity groupie-dom. They listen to her on the radio every day, check out her website and Facebook page at least three times a day, write a blog about her every move, and have extensive online discussions about what she wore that day. They search the internet for new Rachel information multiple times each day. Whereas some experts believe that Rachel is a better role model than some other celebrities, for example, Lindsay Lohan, ultimately celebrity crushes can be problematic, as they far exceed viewing the celebrity as mere role model. However, lesbian groupies may ultimately discover Rachel's DDM diagnoses and become disenchanted, forcing them to replace their Rachel obsession with another celebrity dyke crush.

Case Example
Georgia is a 31 year-old lesbian who is engaged in multiple and complex Rachel conspiracy theories, most of them focusing on her hair, and why she had to change it to a more "girly" style. She was convinced that it was a homophobic plot of the conservative and powerful news media conglomerate (there is some validity to her claim), but the fact that this woman had an ongoing blog entitled "Rachel's Hair" is a sure sign of crossing the line to a fetish or addiction. If Rachel was not on the air unexpectedly one day, Georgia attributed it to some conservative plot to remove her voice from the air waves, or a lesbian-phobic attempt by Glen Beck to get her fired because of her lesbian hair. In June of 2017, when Rachel had the flu, Georgia started a "Where in the world is Rachel?" facebook page, attracting millions of followers in a few hours. Georgia's therapist had worked for three months using a reality therapy approach to help her see that Rachel might take a day off now and then without it being related to catastrophic circumstances, and helped her to find ways to cope with her debilitating withdrawal symptoms on weekends when Rachel's show did not air.

DDM 2b. *The L Word* **Junkie**
Even though *The L Word* is no longer on the air, it continues to impact dyke mental health. While it was on Showtime, a subset of lesbians was seriously addicted and they changed their hairstyles or accessories to emulate their favorite characters, planned their entire week around Sunday nights, and exhibited serious withdrawal symptoms and anxiety during the months of hiatus of the series. Lesbian communities organized their fundraisers and social events around *L Word* viewings. Financially strapped lesbians had to choose between food for the table and a subscription to Showtime. Some lesbians continue to show serious withdrawal symptoms now, years after the series ended. Some of the dangers of this obsession with *The L Word* are similar to a preoccupation with any soap opera. That is, none of the characters are responsible and

respectful people that anyone should want as role models. For example, some dykes worshipped Shane, the commitment-phobic party dyke (see DDM 9), who had unsafe sex night after night, smoked, drank, used a variety of illicit drugs, and flaunted a painfully anorexic body as something to which all lesbians should aspire. There were never any negative health consequences to any of Shane's excesses. Even years after *The L Word* ended, one can find Shane Syndrome and Shane Impersonation in young dykes around the world. Some observers have noted that there are as many Shane impersonators in dyke communities as there are Elvis impersonators in Las Vegas.

How about Bette Porter, the museum curator/art school dean? Superficially, she seemed to be a better role model than Shane as a highly educated, cultured, professional woman. But on closer inspection, Bette was the poster child for conflict avoidance. For example, she had an affair while her partner Tina was trying to get pregnant instead of talking openly and honestly about her dissatisfaction with Tina's obsession about having a baby. She led Jody on for months after she realized she was still in love with Tina, instead of having a hard, but honest discussion about her feelings. She had sex with a student when she was dean of the art school, and she abducted the child that she and Tina co-parented. Lesbian public opinion polls suggest that Bette killed Jenny in the final season, adding murder to her list of character qualities. Lesbians who identified with Jenny, the character who came out of a heterosexual relationship with Tim because of the powerful influence of her next door neighbors Bette and Tina, are pure evil and wreak havoc in their communities. After criticisms that *The L Word* did not realistically depict lesbian communities, particularly, lower middle class and poor lesbians, the show inexplicably introduced Helena Peabody, an extremely wealthy daughter of a philanthropist. Helena impersonators are fairly rare in lesbian communities because 99.99% of dykes do not have the adequate income level to realistically emulate Ms. Helena. Those drawn to Alice Piasecki express their celebrity crush by engaging in excessive gossip. Soap operas can be a guilty pleasure, but lesbians must put them in context and resist thinking that the lesbian world should or does look like *The L Word* World.

Case Example

Lynn, a downwardly mobile, highly educated lesbian who worked for a struggling community nonprofit agency, reported an encounter with an *L Word* junkie she met online. Helena was a corporate lawyer from a wealthy family. Lynn discovered that her real name was Shirley, but she had changed it during Season 3 of *The L Word* after she developed a deep sense of connection with the Helena Peabody character. Lynn and Helena chatted online for a month about common interests in books and movies, and they seemed pretty compatible, so they decided to meet for drinks at Helena's favorite neighborhood bar. Lynn arrived at the upscale bar a little early, and internally moaned at the drink prices, wondering how could they get away with charging $15 for a glass of house wine. She bit the bullet and ordered the $16 dollar glass so Helena wouldn't think she was cheap, but it became apparent within a few minutes that they came from different worlds. Upon meeting, Helena gave Lynn a head-to-toe scathing glance, not in a sexual way, but in a dismissive manner. Lynn assumed it was because of her wardrobe, which came mainly from LL Bean, but it could also have been related to her love handles, or the fact that she could not pass as straight. Helena was dressed in designer labels, tastefully accessorized, and her conversations were about all the famous and influential lesbians she knew. Helena casually mentioned that she was a member of the *Different Daughters of the American Revolution*, as well as president of the local LGBT chamber of commerce. After Helena drained her wine glass, she fled the bar and Lynn never heard from her again. She concluded that A-list lesbians do not want to be seen with B or C list dykes.

DDM 2c. Gleesbians

A newly emerging phenomenon is the growing dyke fascination with *Glee,* especially since Season 2 and the plot line hinting about an open lesbian relationship between two cheerleaders who were formerly heteroflexible, then bi-curious, and at the time of the DDM-IIIR when first discovered, seemed to be on the brink of turning full blown dyke. Other dykes migrated to *Glee* with Jane Lynch as she transformed from high-powered dyke lawyer on *The L Word*, to vicious bitch jock Sue Sylvester. Although Sue is portrayed as straight on the show, she clearly fits the lesbian gym teacher stereotype and triggers or retriggers adolescent fantasies in many dykes. Sue Sylvester obsessed lesbians dress in nylon tracksuits and make nasty jokes about curly hair. Serious research by Fox News network has shown definitively that watching Glee causes viewers to turn queer, suggesting that it is one of the largest environmental factors contributing to dyke (and other queer) identities in the U.S. If Glee is not cancelled, by 2021, 51% of women in the U.S. will be dykes.

Case Example

Jordan is a 25 year old newly out lesbian who is a graduate student in social work at an east coast women's college. She accidently watched the first episode of *Glee* one evening when she was hung over from partying all weekend and could not reach her remote control. She was hooked from that moment on. Jordan was totally obsessed with the cheerleader Santana and spent hours of each day on chat sites speculating whether Santana would come out publicly and win Brittany's heart in season 3. Jordan joined a lesbian cheerleading squad so she could get the uniform, and wears it every week when she watches *Glee*. She has a tendency to spontaneously break into 1980s pop tunes, seriously annoying her coworkers and classmates.

Prevalence and Etiology

The majority of dykes (86.8%) have at least one celebrity crush or addiction in their lifetime, however, the object of lust of lesbian celebrity groupies varies by age, race, ethnicity, economic status, location on the butch-femme continuum, and geographic region. Over 60% of lesbians over 40 own the boxed set of Season 1 DVDs of *The L Word*, and 43% have the entire six seasons, putting them at high risk for *L Word* obsessions. *The L Word* is partly responsible for a heightening of class distinctions in many lesbian communities. Thus far, the DDM Academy has not encountered any cases of addiction to or fetishizing of *The Real L Word*. It appears that this spin-off does not have the same appeal as the original series. Lesbians, like straight people, appear to prefer fantasy to reality. Rachel Maddow crushes are not quite as common as *L Word* and *Glee* celebrity obsessions, because not all lesbians have extended basic cable subscriptions, and political news programming does not appeal to all segments of the dyke population. Glee celebrity obsessions escalated in Season 3 as dykes anticipated the public coming out of Santana, but are nearly nonexistent now a few years after the series ended.

Celebrity crushes may be on actual celebrities, or the characters they portray in movies or TV, whether the actual person or the character is a lesbian. The author must admit to a "Christine Cagney" crush in the 1980s, but rest assured that the author was not Sharon Gless's lesbian stalker in real life. Older lesbians may have had (or currently have) Meg

70

Christian, Holly Near, Cris Williamson, Rita Mae Brown, Catherine Deneuve, or k.d. lang obsessions. Middle-aged lesbians might be more likely to manifest crushes on Ellen Degeneres, Ani DiFranco, Xena, Wanda Sykes, Melissa Etheridge, Suzie Orman, Jodie Foster, or Rosie O'Donnell. The expert panel members for this manual were all over 50, therefore, there is no data yet available about the object of celebrity crushes for younger women, but it is likely that Ellen Page, Ruby Rose, and Kristin Stewart are objects of lust for some young dykes. These data are currently being collected and will be revealed in the DDM-V, scheduled for release in early 2021.

Academic dykes may have intensive crushes on their theoretical heroines, such as Audre Lorde, Judith Butler or Teresa de Lauretis (see the description of the LezBorg in the Emerging Disorders section of the manual). Academic crushes differ somewhat in their manifestations, with less chance of physical stalking, but higher chance of becoming academic conference groupies and exhibiting an excessive tendency to quote their favorite academic celebrity. For example, some lesbian's signature line on email proclaims, "Gender is performative," indicating their Judith Butler crush.

Celebrity crushes arise from a need for attention, and a fear of intimacy with real women. They are most common prior to coming out, but can afflict dykes of any lesbian-developmental phase. In fact, celebrity crushes may re-appear at times when relationships are getting stale and one or both partners are vulnerable to crushes because of the absence of lusty desire in their current relationship. Sometimes the crushes help dykes through the rough times, and sometimes they contribute to break-ups if the woman expects her partner to be like the celebrity.

Treatment Considerations for Lesbian Celebrity Groupies

In moderation, celebrity crushes are relatively harmless, and can even be pleasant distractions from life stressors. Treatment for more severe celebrity groupie behavior that negatively impairs the daily life of the afflicted dyke is aimed at helping the sufferer to see their idols as real people. For example, repeated watching of *Flashdance* can impress upon Bette Porter groupies that the actress is indeed heterosexual. Behind the scenes footage from *L Word* out-takes show a drunken Shane puking her guts out, getting meth mouth, and losing her teeth, and may deter some lesbians from emulating this lifestyle. For Rachel Maddow groupies, viewing of home videos made by her ex-girlfriend and available on

YouTube, reveal the star burping the alphabet with Budweiser, squeezing the toothpaste from the middle, and refusing to clean up her mess in the kitchen. These reality checks are typically sufficient to reduce or eliminate these crushes. Gleesbians are mostly hopeless, but the obsession will most likely pass as the glee club students graduate and the show ends. For most dykes with celebrity crushes, relationships with real women may relieve or eliminate the need for these obsessions with celebrities. For others, a shared celebrity crush by a couple may help to break them from the bondage of lesbian bed death.

DDM 3. Lesbian Fusion Syndromes

Overview

To fuse is to combine or blend. It refers to a couple, triad, or whole community who melt or merge together into one relatively unified being. In the heterosexual world, it is rare to find the degree of relationship fusion that exists in many lesbian partnerships. Heterosexual couples rarely synchronize their monthly cycles or think of themselves as one unit rather than two separate beings. Whereas heterosexual couples may finish each other's sentences, fused lesbians may speak whole monologues for each other. Few heterosexual women keep their ex-husbands as best friends and confidantes, and rarely does a straight man present every new potential girlfriend to be interrogated by his ex-wife before deciding whether to date her. Some lesbians, however, fuse for life, with unusually close relationships. This fusion, like the nuclear fusion process in nature, can often occur almost instantaneously upon first meeting. Once fused, the bonds are strong and difficult to break. Fused lesbians often cannot give up ex-lovers, no matter how painful the relationship or the break-up was. Many lesbians have learned that sex may not last forever, but an unhealthy emotional dependence certainly can. There is nothing inherently pathological about staying friends with exes, but the experience of having to undergo a grueling qualification exam to convince a critical woman of one's worthiness to date her ex is often painful and cruel to the new partner.

Lesbian fusion disorders manifest differently while the fused pair is in a relationship than when they transform into exes. Signs and symptoms of this disorder in the initial relationship phase include rapid attachment and fusion (this process that might take months or years in a heterosexual couple occurs by date number three in most lesbians); difficulty telling the two partners of a relationship apart; and an inability for the afflicted dyke to make a decision on her own. All decisions, no matter how small, are made by the fused unit, such as what shoes to wear to work today, what to eat for a snack when one of them feels peckish in the afternoon, or whether to buy the 6- or 12-pack of toilet paper. When the relationship ends, and the ex-lover phase begins, the main symptoms are an excessive need for approval from the ex (or exes); an inability to make decisions without input from the ex; and chronic, episodic re-experiencing of the break-up every time one of the members of a former relationship dates. The over-involvement in each other's lives makes it difficult to determine when, if ever, the relationship is actually over, or when the relationship transitions from lover to ex-lover status. There are three major subsets of lesbian fusion disorder, discussed next.

DDM 3a. Simple Lesbian Fusion Disorder
Although some think that lesbian fusion is a myth or a stereotype, a significant number of lesbian couples do develop an unusually close relationship, merging personalities, behaviors, and sometimes even physical characteristics. They may get the same hairdo, wear identical clothing, take up the same hobbies, display identical mannerisms, use the same slang terms and expressions, and finish sentences for each other. They do everything together and are in serious distress when separated. They spend many of those moments physically apart on the phone, texting, or emailing. Sometimes those communications are curiously devoid of content, such as texting, "What U doing?" every ten minutes, making their correspondence much like an ongoing twitter feed of two. Interestingly, an unusual speech characteristic often develops; an inability to say the word "I." This couple becomes a "we," rather than two separate I beings. This disorder represents an almost complete lack of boundaries. Mild forms of simple fusion disorder are relatively common in the first 6-12 months of any relationship, but most couples maintain or at least re-establish separate identities as the relationship matures. In some cases, the fusion is permanent, and the couple operates as one unit for the entire length of their relationship.

Case Example
Sue and Susan have been together for 22 years. The first eight months of their relationship, they were never separated and in fact, rarely left their bedroom. Their menstrual cycles synchronized within 48 hours of meeting each other (see DDM 15). They bonded so deeply that they are like symbiotic twins with their own unique language that others do not understand. At lesbian brunches or concerts, they always sit together and go to the restroom together, and one never accepts an invitation that does not include the other. When friends call them on the phone, they can never tell which one of the pair they have reached, because they now sound so much alike, having the same cadence of speech and common phrases. They go to the same hair stylist for the lesbian mullet with braided tail that they have worn for 20 years, and buy their clothes from the same stores. Although they started out quite different body types, they now wear the same size. They consider each other as soul mates and

are determined that they will be together forever. When they must be separated during the day for work, they spent at least six of those eight hours apart on the phone or emailing each other. In the local lesbian community, they are known merely as "The Sues."

DDM 3b. Simple Lesbian Ex-Lover Syndrome

When fused lesbians break up, as they often do, they have considerable difficulty letting go of the attachment to each other. Being fused is not a predictor of a successful long-term relationship, but fused couples have more difficulties with breakups than do non-fused lesbian couples. They have spent so much time pledging to love each other forever that in spite of extreme incompatibilities, they are determined to stay best friends. Whereas the relationship totally lacked boundaries, the breakup may institute some hints of limits and boundaries, but they tend to be semi-permeable, making them extraordinarily confusing. Sometimes this couple continues to live together years after their breakup, further delaying any relationship grief processing and moving on. Simple lesbian ex-lover syndrome generally occurs only after the first breakup, and thereafter DDM 3c, the multiple fusion disorder subtype is the most appropriate dykigonosis.

Case Example

Phung, a 39 year-old lesbian librarian, once went out to dinner with Joyce, a 35-year-old gym teacher. They had a pleasant time, so they decided to see each other again. Joyce invited her to a lesbian Pictionary party the following week. When they got there, the party consisted of Phung and Joyce, and the hostesses, both of whom were exes of Joyce. Joyce had introduced them to each other when she recognized that they had complementary dysfunctions. They were cordial for the first ten minutes, and then began a rapid-fire interrogation of Phung. "Do you have cats or dogs?" "How many partners have you had?" "What went wrong in your last relationship?" "Have you ever cheated on a girlfriend?" "How much do you drink?" (At this point, she desperately needed a gin and tonic, but was afraid to say so). "Are you looking for a committed relationship?" "Do you want children?" "Have you ever had or acted on an attraction to a man?" "What kind of relationship do you have with your exes?" "What sign are you—Zodiac and Chinese?" "Are you into S&M, BDSM, or any type of water or land sport?" They never got to the Pictionary, and Phung was exhausted by the end of the evening. She went out with Joyce only once more after that date. At the end of the evening, Phung asked her if she wanted to go to a lesbian dance with her the following weekend. When Joyce said she would have to ask Pat and Sally before she could commit, Phung decided that she wanted a woman who could make up her own mind about dating and she gave up on Joyce and the exes. Incidentally, Joyce, Pat, and Sally represent that classic form of triad in the lesbian community, consisting of the current couple and an enmeshed ex-lover of one or both of them.

DDM 3c. Multiple Ex-Lover Fusion Syndrome

In some communities, this condition is known as Dyke eX-Factor. For many affected lesbians, the ex-lover situation is compounded by concomitant multiple serial monogamy disorder (see Axis II disorders, DDM 27). This dyke may have five or more ex-lovers and ex-lovers of ex-lovers with whom she is trying to maintain intimate ties, as well as the children, pets, and shared properties or belongings of the earlier relationships. The song, "All my exes live in Texas" was originally a lesbian ballad about the trials and tribulations of ex-lover fusion syndrome. The complexity of these relationships can be mind-boggling. New lovers may be subject to a virtual gauntlet of qualifying exams with three or more critical ex-lovers before the new relationships is authorized by all the exes and their current partners. The extended ex-family can sometimes take on features of a cult, with multiple inside jokes, family secrets known to some but not all members, and creative and convoluted custody arrangements. For example, when household items are bought together, such as a food processor, one member of the ex-couple may have possession of the item and the other have visitation rights. The new partner of the one who has custody of the food processor may not be allowed to touch it. Dykes with ex-lover fusion disorders may claim to be committed to monogamy, but in reality, they are in polyamorous, or at least poly-emotional relationships.

Case Example

Barb once spent six months of her life in therapy, not for couples' therapy to save the relationship, but instead to foster the transition into ex-lover status with Tracy, a woman with whom she had been fused for four years. Barb's ex-once-removed, Gloria and Gloria's new partner, Joan, as well as Tracy's three past lovers, Ann, Makela, and Aisha were all involved in this group therapy. The counselor focused on finding ways for all the exes to maintain their social and relational ties in spite of jealousies and strong dislikes among some of the extended family members. Ann had given birth to a child while with Tracy, whose brother had donated the sperm. Tracy was considered the primary co-parent, even though Ann's current partner, Jackie, was the stay-at-home Mom with their daughter. The child, now age 6, had the daunting task of learning all the complex family relationships, including having to learn to distinguish between Mother, Mom, Mommy, and Ma, as well as a laggle of aunties. A further complication was the complex pet custody arrangements that were made for the dog that Barb and Gloria had adopted together, and that Tracy had co-pet parented. Barb and Gloria had bred the dog eight years ago, and distributed ten puppies to various exes, creating a complex extended pet family as well. The lesbian therapist in this case had to bring in a dyke para-legal and a vet to help them sort out all the custody and social arrangements, such as what couples got to keep which lesbian brunches and game nights, who could play on what softball team, and who had visitation rights with which dog(s). The messy ex-lover extended family also had to seek out individual therapists in a tri-state area, because it would not be ethical for any one therapist to take on all of these women as clients. In fact, two women in the extended ex-network were therapists, and they had to carefully screen new clients to avoid working with anyone who had a relationship or friendship with any woman in the network. This task was inordinately complicated and required extensive bookkeeping to keep track of all the network's liaisons.

Prevalence and Etiology

Over one-third (34.9%) of lesbians have some degree of fusion disorder in at least one relationship; when those fused relationships end, they frequently lead to ex-lover fusion disorder (63.1%) and a subset progress to multiple ex-lover fusion syndrome (existing in 22.2% of dykes). The average lesbian has two ex-lover/best friends who have undue influence over them. This can cause much dyke drama if the exes give conflicting advice to the afflicted dyke—which one does she heed?

As noted earlier, fusion is not a predictor of relationship success, and the rate of breakup of fused lesbians is 52.5% compared to a break up rate of 49.8% among non-fused lesbian couples. The causes of fusion are varied and complex, like the ex-lovers, but fusion disorders often stem from co-dependency tendencies in at least one partner, a mythology about lesbians bonding for life, and the resultant inability to ever let go of a relationship. The onset of this condition is usually during the pre-oedipal stage of development, when the young girl experienced a close bonding with or intense crush on a nurturing female figure. The affected dyke spends the rest of her life trying to re-create that closeness. In one subset of the disorder, the cause is a passive personality style. For this passive dyke, it is simply easier to let a lover or an ex-lover run her life and make decisions for her, than to exercise an independent personality. It appears that many lesbians are completely averse to the idea of a "clean break" after a breakup, and are overly attached to a mythology related to "she is the only one that gets me."

In rare cases, dykes may fuse with their pets and suffer ex-pet fusion disorder when the pet is lost to death or break-up. This afflicted lesbian pines for the lost pet for years, may keep the ashes of the pet(s) in her living room, and carries pictures of the pet in her wallet like mothers and grandmothers carry baby photos.

Treatment Considerations

Mild fusion disorders are relatively harmless in the early stages of intact, long-term lesbian relationships although they can be disconcerting or annoying to others in the community. Friends may complain when a dyke enters one of these relationships, because she is virtually lost to the community. Fusion disorders cause the most damage when a fused couple breaks up. In those cases, drastic measures are needed to avoid future dyke drama that may impact entire extended communities. Boundary therapy is useful, as are lesbian self-identity restoration camps aimed at regaining a dyke's sense of autonomy and agency after a break-up, so that she does not let an ex-lover make all of her decisions for her. All lesbians should be mandated to attend at least three months of this type of therapy after a break-up, so that they can rediscover their own likes and dislikes, establish new routines, and emotionally disentangle from the ex. Paralegals and counselors may need to collaborate to work out appropriate custody arrangements for children, pets (or ashes of past pets), best friends, stuffed animals, favorite lesbian detective books, and beloved sex toys. In some cases, a court-appointed guardian may be necessary to help a particularly co-dependent ex to make decisions until she has had enough therapy to think on her own.

Ex-lovers should not be allowed to meet potential dates of their former partners until the new couple have had at least six dates (typically they are living together by then). The exception is when a dyke suffers from U-Haul Syndrome (DDM 7) and needs the group support of her exes to keep her from calling the rental agency too soon the next time and creating yet another ex-lover situation to add to the already confusing ex-network. A national support and advocacy group modeled after PFLAG (Parents and Friends of Lesbians and Gays) has been formed to help ex-lover triads and laggles. This group, the Parents and Helpers of Ex-Lovers League (P-HELL) has recently begun to establish local chapters to help ex-lover communities to survive and thrive, smooth relationships in lesbian communities with complicated ex-lover configurations, and to educate the clueless heterosexual community about the dynamics of these relationships. For example, parents and siblings of lesbians are often quite perplexed by the relationship dynamics in their dyke family member, and pamphlets and discussion groups hosted by P-HELL can be helpful educational tools.

DDM 4. Lesbian Infantile Regressive Disorder

Overview
Some vulnerable dykes regress to behaviors more characteristic of young children or baby dykes when they first develop a dyke crush or enter into new relationships. This syndrome might not be unique to lesbians, but is a common source of annoyance at lesbian events, enough so to classify it as a significant pathological condition. The symptoms manifest early in a new relationship and affect mainly voice and somatic postures. The voice disorder is characterized by three symptoms: 1) a high-pitched, rhythmic cadence, 2) a defect of articulation, and 3) a severe limiting of the vocabulary to a preschool level. The afflicted dyke seems to constantly forget the name of her loved one and thus reverts to simplistic alliterations or rhymes to compensate for the memory loss, calling the girlfriend "boo-boo" or "honey-bunny." Body postures and gestures are also affected, and may include an unusual tendency to drape one's body over another's in public. It also involves a child-like naming/touching of body parts, as in "What a precious little ear lobe you have." It typically affects both members of a new couple relationship and all members of a new polyamorous relationship. There are several physical manifestations as well; the affected couple act as if they are Siamese twins connected at the hip and are unable to go to the bathroom alone. They also exhibit frequent public displays of affection, at times appearing like a pair of teenagers whose braces have locked together. This behavior may be an early manifestation of a fusion disorder, or a short-term acute condition that resolves after two or three months.

Case Example
　　　　Nikki, a 37-year-old certified public accountant, met her friend, Sam, for brunch. Sam brought her new girlfriend, a woman she had met the weekend before this brunch, and described as the new "love of her life." The two of them sat on the same chair with arms around each other's waists and fed each other. Their conversation was conducted in a sappy, high-pitched, singsong voice, "You are the cutest baby" and "No, you are the sweetest smoochie-woochie." At one point, Sam said to Nikki, "Doesn't you just w-ove her w-ittle nose?" Nikki reported that she finds this type of speech objectionable enough with an actual baby or pet, but finds it intolerable in adult lesbians. She found the conversation with Sam, who had a PhD in molecular genetics, to have deteriorated to the first grade level, and Nikki left the restaurant feeling disgusted and sad

about losing her intelligent friend. Ironically, the new girlfriend was a distinguished judge---pre-relationship intelligence is not a protective factor for infantile regressive disorders and the disorder can affect women of any profession, level of maturity, or degree of seriousness prior to the crush. Intense crushes appear to erase all shreds of dignity from those afflicted.

Prevalence and Etiology

This condition affects 37.3% of lesbians in the first three months of a new relationship, and then declines thereafter, although a small subset of dyke couples continue to display this irritating behavior for months or even years. It can progress to full-blown lesbian fusion disorder (see DDM 3) in some cases. This condition is most likely caused by an overpowering of the rational centers of the brain by pheromones and lust-related chemical reactions in the central nervous system, short-circuiting the adult language centers of the temporal lobes of the brain. This chemical reaction resembles the effects of a mood-altering drug, causing a euphoric state of being. There is also a concomitant impairment of rational reasoning skills, leading to a condition much like the "beer goggles" phenomenon of heterosexuals. Beer goggles syndrome typically leads to one single night of regret, but because of lesbians' tendencies to form strong emotional bonds within seconds of meeting, lesbian beer goggles (and resultant infantile regressive disorder) may last for weeks or months. In middle aged and older lesbians, this phenomenon is known as lesbian bifocals. This older dyke is paradoxically both far-sighted and near-sighted in regards to her own relationships. In extreme cases, a hysterical blindness can occur. This phenomenon is the origin of the phrase, "love is blind."

Treatment Considerations for Infantile Regressive Disorder

The condition is not life-threatening, is typically short-lived, and resolves spontaneously by about month six for most couples. Those dykes who repeatedly display these behaviors in public should be given a warning. According to the Lesbian Rules, public displays of affection are always welcome, as long as they are conducted in a mutually consensual, adult fashion, but infantile regressive behaviors are strictly prohibited. After two warnings, the couple is banned from lesbian events for a period not to exceed one month. If it progresses to lesbian fusion disorder, this doomed couple may cycle between fusion and ex-lover fusion disorders for the rest of their lives.

Footnote from the Editor: Members of the expert panel have suggested that the author of the manual may have a DDM dykigonsis that caused her to create this dyke drama generator out of jealousy. In fact, the expert panel could find no evidence of lasting harm caused by regressive infantile behavior symptoms, and no long-term impact on intellect or relationship satisfaction. The expert panel members have suggested that in the next revision of the DDM, this disorder be replaced with Dyky-Dovey Aversion Syndrome, placing the onus on the one who is annoyed by lovers' behavior rather than blaming the lovers.

DDM 5. The Lesbian Papparazzi

Overview

There are gossips, voyeurs, snoops, manipulators, and drama-chasers in every community, but most lesbian communities are so small, so packed with exes and soon-to-be-exes, and so much interchanging of partners in complex ex-lover social (and anti-social) networks, that gossip exerts a disproportionately malignant influence. The lesbian papparazza incessantly pries into the lives of others. She appears on the surface to be a gregarious social butterfly, showing up at any and all lesbian events— the weekly brunches, tea dances, softball games, *L Word* parties, book club meetings at lesbian coffee houses, Women's National Basketball Association (WNBA) parties, ladies nights at the gay bars, and Rachel Maddow viewing parties. The papparazza is particularly drawn to group therapy, support groups, and dyke hair salons where lesbians are likely to reveal personal information that she can use for her own personal gain.

She engages in conversation with everyone. At first glance, she may seem to be genuinely interested in others, but she is actually gathering dirt, to be shared with malicious glee at her next stop or in her weekly gossip blog. If she does not get some actual gossip, she will fabricate information from her overzealous imagination. She is a shrewd observer and has a diabolical skill in turning innocent events into dyke drama. She does not care about verifying her observations or ascertaining the truth; she gossips to gain power. Jenny, as manifest in the final season of *The L Word,* was the prototype for this lesbian rumormongering and manipulation; Alice displayed milder symptoms of this disorder.

Case Example

Cassie is a 45 year-old lesbian in a small rural community. Cassie had a bad reputation in the local lesbian community and was thought to be personally responsible for at least ten break-ups in the past two years. When she entered therapy, she was able to hide her symptoms during the intake. Her therapist initially diagnosed her with a lesbian event addiction (see DDM 8) because of the sheer number of events that Cassie attended every week, and had initiated therapy to attempt to wean her from her out-of-control brunch attendance schedule. Then in the third therapy session, Cassie shared that she was convinced that the therapist's partner was having an affair. She provided carefully documented evidence including two blurry, dated photographs. The partner, Jane, had been seen three times at different coffee shops and restaurants in intimate conversation with the same other woman. Luckily, the therapist knew her partners' schedule well and recognized that the other woman in the photographs was Jane's mother. She then corrected her dykignosis to lesbian paparazzi and changed the course of the therapy. Before Cassie was cured of her affliction, she outed two lesbian nuns and leaked information about several lesbian crushes on dyke community leaders, causing major drama in the current relationships of the crush-afflicted lesbians. Cassie was responsible for approximately 26% of the dyke drama in her small community until she developed a sense of lesbian ethics with the help of her therapist.

Prevalence and Etiology

Every dyke community has at least one papparazza, making the prevalence about one in two hundred. This condition is related to power and control; a pathological need to create drama for one's own amusement. Often affected lesbians get an erotic thrill from manipulating other people's lives. Typically, they are single frustrated women, but they can also, on occasion, be coupled frustrated women. A lesbian papparazza who is romantically involved creates an inordinate amount of drama in her relationship, so usually these are short-term couplings. Ultimately, she must seek out her drama thrills from the larger lesbian community when her own relationship ends. During a breakup, she frequently attempts to make the larger dyke community choose her side by concocting outlandish negative stories about her ex to create sympathy for her victimhood. When the lesbian papparazza has a co-occurring fusion disorder, she often reveals all the vulnerabilities, DDM dykignoses, and secrets of her exes to the whole lesbian community. Alternatively, she may threaten to reveal secrets as a means of lavender mail, an insidiously evil form of emotional blackmail in lesbian communities.

Treatment for Lesbian Papparazza

Because of the high rate of gossip in society in general, dykes are given three chances with only a warning before more drastic measures are taken. A common form of treatment is shunning, typically consisting of a month-long ban on attendance at any lesbian brunch, or whatever event is the most desired in her community. If the woman continues to exhibit this aberrant behavior, she may be branded with the Scarlet L so that her affliction is made visible and other lesbians can avoid her or dismiss her gossip as unsubstantiated rumor. All lesbians should be educated to avoid these women, particularly if they aspire to public office and have any actual skeletons in their closets that may ruin their reputation if the papparazza discovers them. To be fully re-accepted into a lesbian community, a papparazza in recovery must obtain a clean bill of health from a certified dyke counselor.

DDM 6. The Lesbian Mother Superior

Overview

Every lesbian community, and often each sub-community within the larger dyke realm, has its unwritten Lesbian Rulebook, including the ten commandments of lesbian conduct. The rules vary from one group to another, and depend highly on factors such as whether there is a strong separatist or radical feminist lesbian faction in the community. These essentializing forms of lesbian feminism typically have many more rules than do social constructivist or postmodern approaches to feminism, thus are more likely to spawn mother superiors. The postmodern varieties of theorizing too often lead to the paralysis of individuals and organizations. This is because the postmodern theoretical interventions' emphasis on deconstructing terms and unpacking assumptions renders them unable to find a name, create a mission, or take an action. The postmodern Lesbian Mother Superior is critical of everything, and her rules are constantly evolving along with the historical, political, and socio-cultural context. She rarely has any followers because of the lack of any consistency in her philosophy.

Other factors that contribute to the density of lesbian mother superiors in any region include the average age/generation of the community, and the strength and influence of the women's music and women's land subcultures. A dyke who becomes a lesbian mother superior is self-appointed, and may or may not be accepted by the larger community as the leader/spokesperson for the community. She considers herself responsible for the moral conduct of lesbians in her gaggle, and often sits in judgment over her community members. The problem is not so much with the rules, although obviously some of them are too limiting or rigid, or any of the trappings of the Mother Superior's home or lifestyle, but with the zealous and righteous fervor by which some LMSs adhere to the rules they have created, and their tendency to severely judge those who do not comply. It is quite difficult to be a perfect lesbian, but the LMS does not permit any slight indiscretions or minor violations of the rules.

Case Example

This example is specific to the 1980s feminist lesbian, rural community in which the author came out. Carolyn was a 52 year-old, radical feminist, separatist lesbian, and became a mother superior when she took a job as the director of the women's center. She came out at the age of 35 in the middle of a feminist consciousness-raising group, when she fell in the love with the woman who was demonstrating how to squat over a mirror to see one's own cervix. Carolyn honed the lesbian rulebook over the next several years. Here were the rules of the community that she monitored and enforced during her reign from 1982 to 1993:

1. Lesbians shall be womyn-born womyn who only have relationships (and sex) with other womyn-born womyn (wimmin-born wimmin are also acceptable) who socialize primarily in women-only space. Note: Carolyn was a member of the Michigan Women's Music Festival organizing board in the early 1980s.
2. A lesbian shall be a separatist lesbian feminist who must memorize every product and company to boycott; and she shalt not buy a book from a corporate bookstore or a non-union grape at the grocery store. All music must be ordered only from the Ladyslipper catalog or purchased from a lesbian feminist bookstore.
3. A lesbian shalt not purchase a sex toy that resembles a penis; only a cute, lavender, preferably endangered animal-shaped toy is acceptable (however, other Lesbian Mother Superiors may dispute this point, for example, those who adhere to rules regarding animal rights may be concerned about the trafficking of innocent animals into sex toy work). Dolphins and rabbits are favored.
4. A lesbian must never confess to an attraction to anyone other than another real lesbian (see commandment number 1). Fantasy, behavior, and identity must be completely aligned. No bisexual or transgender women need apply to belong to this segment of the lesbian community.
5. The home of a lesbian must contain at least one record album or CD of Cris Williamson, Holly Near, Meg Christian or the Indigo Girls (younger readers: google "record album").
6. The home of a real lesbian must also contain a copy of *Claire of the Moon* (book and video) and the companion video, *The Making of Claire of the Moon*. Dykes preferring the books of Danielle Steele or movies with Julia Roberts are to be publicly humiliated.

7. A lesbian shalt not carry a purse, the evil accessory of a sexist, capitalist, misogynistic society. Backpacks and fanny packs are acceptable, but wallets on a chain hanging from the back pocket are not. Androgyny was the goal of all fashion statements in Carolyn's lesbian community.
8. A true lesbian must not stray more than two points from center on the butch-femme continuum. Make-up is out, and so is the Harley-Davidson. A lesbian who strays beyond these parameters is accused of "aping heterosexual norms."
9. A true lesbian must belong to at least one lesbian feminist political collective that shall spend 98% of each meeting processing the feelings of all members, and they shall make every decision, not matter how small, as a result of consensus (see DDM 17 for an example of how the collective can become dysfunctional).
10. The lesbian uniform consists of 100% cotton (now it would probably be bamboo or hemp), flat utilitarian shoes, work boots in winter, and Birkenstocks without socks in summer, with socks in fall.

Lesbian Mother Superior Carolyn had a Georgia O'Keefe vulva-like flower poster hanging in her bedroom, and a well-worn copy of Mary Daly's *Gyn/Ecology* in the place of honor that a Christian home has a Bible. Her phone answering machine greeted callers with Cris Williamson's "filling up and spilling over." Her bookshelf was lined with only womyn-born womyn writers, mostly lesbians or suspected lesbians. She had a labyris hanging in the bathroom, and a crystal rock in place of the deodorant bottle. Carolyn and her partner had a baby girl by parthenogenesis (i.e., virgin birth) so as to avoid any male taint in their home.

Prevalence and Etiology

Fortunately, most lesbian communities have only one lesbian mother superior, making the prevalence about one in two hundred lesbians. The disorder is latent in approximately 18% of lesbians. They are judgmental, but may not express these thoughts out loud on a regular basis. Some humans, including dykes, need the structure of rules to feel safe in the world. The Lesbian Mother Superior is insecure at heart and feels adrift by a lack of a guidebook for negotiating lesbian life, so she creates and zealously enforces rules for her own community, and may secure many followers who also feel the need for rules. Many LMSs in the past were separatist lesbians, as described in the case example in this section. The contemporary lesbian mother superior may be more influenced by utopian lesbian fiction, identity politics, the Butch-Femme Manifesto, lesbian vampire stories, LGBTQQAID2SSGL inclusive politics, or *The L Word*. Naturally, these affinities result in quite diverse, sometimes contradictory sets of rules. In some academic communities, there is a hint of an emerging form of the disorder tentatively called the Post(pissed)modern Dyke, who deconstructs any and all rules, resulting in communities always already rife with anarchy and historically and culturally specific traumas and dyke dramas.

Another etiological factor in the development of the LMS is a sublimated desire to be a nun or the strict teacher of some sexual fantasies. Those with more libertarian sexual views may become a dominatrix whereas those who are less overtly sexual settle in as Lesbian Mother Superiors.

Treatment for the Lesbian Mother Superior

As she has no actual power in most lesbian communities, it is typically safe to merely ignore the rules that emanate from the Lesbian Mother Superior, although timid or insecure lesbians, especially those in the fragile early coming out years, may be traumatized by the chastising behavior of the Mother Superior. In extreme cases, it may be necessary to conduct a public de-frocking of the lesbian mother superior's habit, along with humility training and a feminist lesbian version of the hair shirt, which involves being forced to wear polyester for two weeks. When a community has LMSs of competing political ideologies, then separate but equal social structures, such as parallel but non-overlapping brunches, might be needed to avoid escalating hostilities in the community. When the de-frocking or shunning are not effective, Lesbian Mother Superiors may be encouraged to seek jobs as prison wardens or Catholic school principals where they can satisfy their urges to control at work instead of in their lesbian communities.

DDM 7. The U-Haul Syndrome

Overview
This is the most well-known of all lesbian pathologies. It is one of the few lesbian conditions to have its own entry in Wikipedia, and even many in the heterosexual community know the answer to the question, "What do lesbians take on a second date?" There is a fairly large subset of the lesbian community with a devastating impairment of the cognitive skills needed to distinguish between lust and love. In fact, the disorder is so wide spread that every twenty minutes in the United States, two afflicted lesbians encounter each other and trigger the onset of the symptoms. When two U-Haul lesbians meet under the right circumstances, they can progress from first date to committed relationship, from stranger to soul mate, and from just meeting to living together, within an hour. Lust is a powerful emotion, and much like alcohol or drugs, intoxicates the senses and impairs the brain, reinforcing a delusional belief that the couple has an unusually close emotional connection. For example, two women who each have these tendencies may discover on the first date that they both like Lady Gaga, and they leap to the assumption that they are soul mates. The aroused state of the physical body appears to activate some pre-programmed romantic fantasy that over-rides the logical part of dyke brains, for example, leading to thinking that having the same dentist is a sign that they are meant to be together for eternity.

As noted in an earlier section, this condition may share some features with the heterosexual diagnosis of Beer Goggles, but in a much more protracted state. Women with this affliction overlook warning signs, misinterpret cues, and refuse to look at reality. They live in a delusional state of euphoria during this early phase of the disorder. This syndrome may underlie the majority of lesbian break-ups, because disillusionment often follows the lust stage, rather than enduring love. Undoubtedly, for a few lesbians "love at first sight" does happen. But for many, after the glow of the "lust at first sight" wears off, the relationship sickens and rots rather than blooms. Then they must face all the trauma and drama of re-dividing the household, and having to hire the U-Haul again (the Re-Haul phase). The aftermath of U-Haul syndrome is plagued by the need for conversations about such issues as, "Whose copy of *Desert Hearts* is this?" and "Did you buy the pink bunny vibrator or did I?" That is when the break up is amiable. In a less than cordial breakup, one partner may abscond with the DVD's of Season 1 through 6

90

of *The L Word*, or sell all the estranged partners' power tools on eBay. One irate ex removed all the batteries from her partner's toys and tools, a fact that she only discovered weeks later at a time when she really needed that turbo-charged, water proof rubber ducky, and it was still and lifeless, like the relationship.

The U-Haul Syndrome has both physical and emotional manifestations, with the physical components involving actually renting the U-Haul, or similar vehicle designed for or temporarily used for the purpose of merging households. Some lesbians do not physically merge their households, but suffer from the Emotional U-Haul Syndrome, and merge their psyches instead of their belongings. This merging of physical and emotional lives can progress into Lesbian Fusion Disorder (DDM 3) if allowed to proceed unchecked by reality. Break-ups of U-Haul relationships are devastating, whether the disorder has manifested physically, emotionally, or in both ways. In addition, U-Haul inclined dykes are susceptible to opportunistic partner-hunters from both the lesbian community (see DDM 10, Desperately Seeking Susans, and DDM 25, Late Onset Lesbians), and from the heterosexual community. A recent phenomenon reported by regulars in dyke bars is the POW (pussies on welfare), the derogatory name given to heterosexual women who in economic hard times are looking for a dyke to support them. POWs prey upon U-Haulers and get them emotionally involved before they realize that this will be a nonsexual relationship. POWs often target alcoholic U-Haulers who are even less discriminating in their initial attractions to other women when they are under the influence, and can sometimes be persuaded to merge households after the first date. For women with severe forms of the disorder, a rapid-repeat cycle can result in three or more U-Haul experiences within a three-year time span.

There has been some speculation as to the origins of the "U-Haul" name to refer to lesbians' tendencies to cohabitate prematurely. Some suggest that it is related to the successful marketing campaign of U-Haul as the most recognized of the moving companies. Yet others believe that it is related to the lower socioeconomic status of most lesbians that requires using the do-it-yourself moving method of U-Haul. Lesbians of greater economic means may show the same symptoms, but never have to resort to the U-Haul and can hire a more upscale moving and packing company. In countries without the knowledge of, or access to, the U-Haul option, the condition manifests as a simple love addiction, often without the dramas of the moving in and out of physically living together.

Case Example

Carmen is a 50 year-old professional lesbian in both senses—she holds a professional type of job and she is a professional lesbian academic, studying lesbian behavior. She is very intelligent and mature in every aspect of her life except for one: love and relationship. In the past ten years, Carmen, has announced to her potluck group on 14 different occasions, "I found the one! This woman is the love of my life." She would then relate that she had a date with a woman, in person or cyber, and that they connected immediately at the deepest possible spiritual level, usually within the first fifteen minutes. By the second week/date, they were in love; and by one month, were in a committed relationship. Only on five occasions did they actually employ the U-Haul and move in together, but in every case, Carmen experienced the emotional version of the U-Haul Syndrome. The sad consequence of being afflicted with this disorder was that Carmen had to experience soul-mate loss 14 times in ten years, and each breakup was as traumatic as the beginning of the relationship was dramatic and euphoric. Over the course of ten years, she rented a U-Haul ten times, far exceeding the national average usage rate of 1.6 rentals per decade.

Prevalence and Etiology

Well over half (58.9%) of lesbians have experienced the U-Haul Syndrome at some point in their lifetimes. The rates are highest among those who are in the baby dyke or adolescent lesbian years (typically the first five years after coming out), regardless of their chronological age, and first lesbian loves/attractions are particularly prone to advancing to U-Haul Syndrome. One cause may be over-exposure to lesbian romance novels in those critical first three months after coming out. This unrealistic romanticizing of lesbian love is combined with overactive dyke lust hor-mones (see glossary) and lesbian community pressures to couple, fuse, or merge.

Another possible contributing factor is a lesbian-specific form of bipolar disorder that is directly tied to lust feelings. This condition causes a lust-repulsion cycle. When two dykes with U-Haul tendencies meet in a lust state often enhanced by a mood-altering substance such as drugs, alcohol, or chocolate, they immediately merge in euphoric lust-driven mania, but as this phase gradually wears off over the next three to six months, a sense of depression, despair, and repulsion for the partner or the relationship sets in, and the relationship ends. In a few cases, the end is mercifully quick, but in the majority of U-Haul relationships, the breakup is prolonged because of shame, guilt, and doubt. A common feature of the U-Haul Syndrome is that the break-up phase lasts at least twice as long as the lust/love phase of the relationship, often because of attachment to beliefs such as "I thought this woman was 'the one.'" Some dykes are so convinced that their initial lust was evidence of deep-seated love that they stubbornly continue the relationship for months or even years after the relationship should logically have ended, rather than admit being wrong.

Treatment Considerations for U-Haul Syndrome

The very high prevalence of this condition in the lesbian community calls for drastic measures. U-Haul Syndrome has had emotionally devastating effects on the afflicted couple as well as the friends of the couple who have had to help their friends pack and unpack the U-Haul far too often. U-Haul syndrome is largely responsible for the high prevalence of chronic low back pain among lesbians. On the other hand, an unexpected positive consequence of U-Haul Syndrome is that some lesbians become skilled in the art and science of packing and can use those skills to benefit their communities and for gainful employment.

Some experts propose instituting lesbian dating permits that apply U-Haul delay tactics such as restricting both partners from uttering words such as "I love you" for at least a month, and preferably six months. The permit requires at least 40 hours of serious conversation (and not just about *The L Word*) before anything sexual can occur, and absolutely prohibits any signs of Lesbian Infantile Regressive speech or behavior (see DDM 4). The permit will strictly prohibit access to U-Haul for at least one year, at which time the permit can be upgraded from a dating permit to a probationary relationship permit. After another year, the couple may be eligible for an upgrade to a full relationship license, or where available, a marriage license for those who desire it. For some lesbians, participation in Lesbian Love Addicts Anonymous is helpful in those critical first few weeks and months of a new dating relationship, and participation in the group may be mandated for repeat U-Haul offenders. For chronic, rapid-repeat U-Haulers, a chastity belt may be a treatment of last resort.

Promising treatments that may be available in the near future are under study at the FDA (Federal Dyke Administration), including a vaccine, a protocol for aversive therapy that pairs pictures of Rush Limbaugh with the U-Haul van, and trained lesbian chaperones for dating. The DDM Academy is also experimenting with lesbian slow dating events, that includes hours of assessment and treatment for DDM dykignoses before matching potentially compatible women.

As a preventative measure, lesbian dating and relationship education classes will be mandated in high school. Much like driver's education, the young dyke will have to take an intensive course of study for a semester and then pass a test of logical relationship reasoning skills to get a lesbian-dating permit. In addition, lesbian scientists have been pilot-testing a lust versus love detection device, similar to a pregnancy test. Newly enamored lovers must (separately) urinate on a stick that would light up red for lust or purple for real lesbian love. These tests will be available in vending machines alongside tampons and placed in all lesbian venues. U-Haul contracts might be made contingent upon receiving a "true love" reading on the stick. In fact, it might be helpful for communities to create local chapters of the Healthy U-Haul Group (HUG), a dyke-run community grass roots agency that monitors U-Haul use in the local community, raises community awareness of the disorder, and refers severely afflicted lesbians to therapy. In some larger cities, HUG has crisis centers located in U-Haul rental agencies and performs screening examinations before lesbian couples are allowed to sign the contract for the truck.

DDM 8. Lesbian Event Addictions

Overview

Most dykes report that they experienced a euphoric rush the first time they attended a lesbian event. That event was often their first exposure to a "community" that they did not previously know existed, and to a plethora of openly lesbian women all in one place in their dykiest glory. Many lesbians chase this high for the rest of their lives, trying to recreate that magical first time. Lesbian events have an addictive potential because of their novelty early in the coming out process, their role in social support against a lesbian-phobic culture throughout the lesbian lifespan, and as places to meet girlfriends. But like anything, too much of a good thing can lead to an unhealthy dependence. Different events may create somewhat different symptoms depending on social context and trappings of the event, but they are merely manifestations of the same underlying causative factors. Signs and symptoms of all the lesbian event variations include an obsessive need to attend, arriving 15 minutes early to secure the best seat, or in more drama-prone dykes, arriving 30 minutes late to make a grand entrance. If one source of event is lost because of a breakup or a move, the afflicted dyke compulsively searches lesbian newspapers, listservs, and websites for a replacement event. The disorder is characterized by a loss of control over lesbian event attendance. Afflicted dykes may spend an inordinate amount of time scheduling, planning for, attending, and cleaning up after these events, to the detriment of their partners, pets, and friends. Like other addictions, tolerance can be built up over time, so that an affected lesbian needs to attend more and more events to get the same buzz or relieve her craving for lesbian company. Over time, however, her relationship is to the brunch, not to the people there, as the addiction takes hold of her life.

DDM 8a. Lesbian Brunch Junkie

Many lesbians show addictive symptoms related to brunch, that oddly timed meal that supposedly falls somewhere between breakfast and lunch, but in most lesbian communities, happens inexplicably at noon or even later. In some communities, so many lesbians are afflicted that they cannot have social gatherings at other meal times. They are paralyzed by the idea of meeting in non-food venues such as a park in the middle of the afternoon or taking an early morning walk on the beach. Instead, virtually all of their social life revolves around the brunch. One differential dykignosis for the brunch junkie is the lesbian who never actually dates one-on-one, but only socializes at weekly or monthly lesbian brunches. She may be afraid of intimacy, or maybe she merely likes the huevos rancheros they serve, but the brunch is her only social life. She is not a true addict.

Brunches are typically held at noisy and inexpensive restaurants to accommodate dyke downwardly mobile salaries, but the restaurant must have a wide choice of menu items to cater to all the different dietary needs of lesbian communities, that contain a disproportionate number of vegetarians, lactose intolerants, hypo-glycemics, gluten allergies, diverticulosis, colitis, GIRD sufferers, nut allergies, and leaky gut syndromes (see also, DDM 13, Dykochondria). Brunch addiction may be one of the most important causative factors in the higher body mass among lesbians than heterosexual women, because lesbians attend three times more brunches than do heterosexual women. The brunch menu might also contribute to this elevated rate of overweight among lesbians. For example, at one lesbian brunch in a northwestern location, the most commonly ordered menu item was the calorie-laden lumberjack special, because of the picture of the sexy plaid-shirted woman with the axe on the menu. There appear to be subtypes of brunch addictions based on socioeconomic status and political affiliation, although these are not yet well studied. Higher income lesbians may attend the $50 brunches with mimosas, whereas recovery oriented and lower income level dykes gravitate toward the dive diner with daily specials and no alcohol.

Case Example

Robin reported that she met her first lesbian brunch junkie a few years ago when she was dabbling with the lesbian personals and meeting potential dates online. She had exchanged a number of interesting emails with Carol, so they made arrangements to meet. Carol suggested brunch one Sunday morning. They had a pleasant conversation and were beginning to get better acquainted, so near the end of the meal, Robin suggested that they consult their calendars and get together again soon. Carol pulled a huge datebook out of her purse, and started flipping through the pages. Even looking at the book upside down from across the table, Robin could see that she had four or five brunch dates every week. Robin suggested that they meet for coffee one Friday afternoon that appeared to be open on her calendar, but Carol looked at her in horror. "I only do brunch," she said. That was their first and last date. Incidentally, Carol represents a rare dyke condition, the Lesbian Luddite, who believes in conspiracy theories about the role of cell phones in causing dyke drama, brain tumors, and world hunger. Carol was one of the few lesbians in 2009 who did not own a cell phone, PDA, laptop, or iPod. Robin later found out that Carol had Lesbian Mother Superior tendencies (DDM 6), so Robin was relieved that they did not have a second date.

Note: Lesbian-hosted brunches for singles are a unique kind of addiction, and there are very specific dycological characteristics that go with these brunches that newly minted lesbians should be aware of before attending. The following case study outlines the common issues.

Case Example: How many dykes does it take to pay the check?

One foggy day in San Francisco, 12 mature, urban lesbians gathered in the entryway of a popular queer-owned restaurant for a 50s plus singles brunch. Among the group were three lawyers, two teachers, a corporate executive, three dog-walkers, a free clinic receptionist, and a pagan priestess and palm-reader. Only three of the women had ever met before. There was one dog, which meant that they had to be seated on rickety chairs in the chilly outdoor patio instead of the more comfortable indoors. The brunch began with stressful decisions about placement and food. Each woman had to ask herself questions such as: Where should I sit? Should I try to get next to that outgoing dyke with the wonder woman tattoo? Do I want to sit near the end so I can make a fast getaway if things do not go well or I get bored? Each woman quickly scanned the group to see who she should avoid. Who had the traits that she found annoying or gave off visual or olfactory signals that were off-putting? Was that vaguely familiar woman a friend of her ex? The one woman with cat allergies furtively surveyed the other women's clothing for telltale signs of cat hair, and quickly noted that she needed to take an anti-histamine before sitting down because there was not one other dander-free dyke.

Once each woman had selected the woman she most wanted to sit next to or near, she had to physically jockey for position and settle into her seat, hoping she made the best decision. Four women competed to sit near the dog-walker who exuded a sexy flirtatious confidence. The lawyer with the bad knees had no chance, the Wiccan priestess who got a frigid look from the desired brunch companion gave up and dropped out of the competition, and the final two competitors tried to sit on the same chair. The sportier dyke of the duo won. Some women looked deflated already because of their inferior position at the table and started brunch at a disadvantage.

Now each woman had to consider the menu. Was this a beer or a mimosa crowd or would she immediately be dismissed as a possible date if she ordered a drink? Should she order the hamburger she really wanted, or try to impress the cute vegetarian teacher across the table? Should she eat the garlic fries that she loves? What if the attractive woman sitting next to her was put off by the garlic breath, and she lost her chance with her? The special of the day was bean soup. Could it be risked? Would the intestinal effects begin to percolate before brunch was over? The waiter was bombarded with questions about the menu. Was the tomato soup vegan? Did they have gluten free bread? Was the chicken free range? Was there corn sweetener in the lemonade? Could she order something that was not on the menu? Once the questions had been answered, orders were placed. Nine of the dozen women modified their orders: dressing on the side, cottage cheese instead of fries, poached eggs instead of scrambled, and a flask of hot water so that one dyke could steep her own herbal tea and supplement drink that she pulled out of her purse.

These initial agonizing food and drink decisions made, and the orders taken care of, the brunch proceeded with awkward silences, stilted conversations, strained laughter, and occasional disapproving looks. Some women seemed to connect and had pleasurable conversations; other more introverted dykes waited quietly for someone to talk to them. One woman reacted badly to a joke that she thought was offensive to animals, and sat with her arms crossed and lips pursed for the remainder of the brunch. After about 45 minutes, the food had been consumed, and the wait staff removed the dishes and brought the check. The listserv advertising this brunch had clearly noted that the restaurant refuses to separate the checks, so one bill would be rendered. Women were urged to bring cash to simplify the process of paying for their meals. How did this group of highly educated professional women figure out who paid what? Here is what ensued for the next 45 minutes:

- One woman left early, leaving only enough money to pay for her omelet, but did not add the tax or gratuity (minus $3.45).
- Another, the offended animal lover, slipped out the back door without leaving any money to pay for her meal (minus $12.95).
- Two dykes began a loud discussion about the audacity of restaurants that refuse to issue separate checks, embarrassing the other remaining women at the table.
- One launched into a lecture about class privilege and money issues in dyke communities, railing against the convention of

98

splitting the bill equally, because it unfairly advantages the woman who ordered mimosas and appetizers with her meal and cheats the poor dyke who only ordered a bowl of soup. The risk-taker who ordered the bean soup was then embarrassed to protest splitting the check equally, but was even more humiliated by being made the example by the woman who started the conversation, who ironically had ordered the most expensive meal. She nervously awaited resolution of the check so she could escape the restaurant before the beans escaped her body.

- One complained that the bill had gratuity included, whining that the service was poor so she did not want to give the wait staff 15%. She left a 10% tip on principle (minus $1.00). Predictably, she was the one who asked for the most substitutions, was the one who brought her own tea concoction, and had the most complicated order, which the staff accommodated with only slight eye-rolling.

- Three agonized about whether someone might get stuck paying too much and anxiously asked each woman what she had to eat. They stood up and paced up and down the length of the table, looking at the cash in each person's hand, hovering over the table in a cloud of anxious energy.

- Three of them had no cash, even though the email invitation to the brunch clearly requested that all women pay for their meals with cash. The restaurant would accept only two credit cards on any check, so the three of them had to negotiate who got to pay by credit card, and who had to borrow money from a complete stranger. Luckily, the one who had to borrow money was the sexy-confident dyke who had sparked the seating frenzy, so three women quickly volunteered to loan her money so that they could give her their phone numbers.

- One brought her dog, who ate another woman's fries when she was not looking, and a discussion ensued about who should pay for those fries. The dog dyke angrily declared that it was not her problem, because she was only guardian, not the "owner" of the dog, who makes her own decisions. Unfortunately, the dog was not in the habit of carrying cash.

- One pulled a calculator out of her backpack and tried to compute each person's contribution, but the women at the other end of the table were not listening to her, so she did not know what they ate. She gave up in frustration.

One woman finally got fed up and gathered together the cash on the table, counted it out, divided the cash between the two women who are supplying their credit cards, and handed the check and two credit cards to the waitress. She was the alpha dyke of the group. She wisely passed on the missing money to the two miscreants who did not read the email, or worse, did read the email and decided to flagrantly disregard the instructions.

By this time, the process of paying the check had taken twice as long as ordering and eating the meal. Exhausted by the mental and emotional labor required to complete this task, the 12 lesbians went their separate ways to nap, drink off the experience, or call a best friend/ex-lover to process the experience. One developed post-traumatic check disorder (PTCD) and needed a year of lesbianalysis to recover. The stress of paying the check had wiped out all thoughts of dating and the 12 lesbians left the brunch still single.

Understanding the Case Study

Lesbian mass hysteria reactions, such as the one recounted above, have not yet been well-studied, but are probably responsible for a fair amount of dyke drama in any given lesbian community. Some speculate that the root causes are competing dyke pheromones or clashing menstrual or peri-menopausal symptoms that impact the entire group. Interactions of DDM dykignoses when lesbians band together, may create potentially explosive combinations of dyk-function. Situations like this one where potential romances may begin, are particularly ripe for drama. Friendship groups or gatherings of stable couples that have acclimated to each other only rarely experience such trauma when they dine together.

DDM 8b. Lesbian Potluck Addiction

Another variation of the lesbian event junkie is the dyke addicted to potlucks. Scientific research shows that lesbians have more potlucks than any other slice of the U.S. population, except perhaps for Lutheran church ladies. Lesbian Lutheran church ladies spend the majority of their time planning and attending potlucks. Potlucks can be anxiety-provoking events, as participating dykes may feel considerable pressure to bring just the right item, one that everyone can eat, is all organic, homemade, and politically correct according to the Rules of the hostesses and other guests. These rules may be extensive if the hostess is a lesbian mother superior (see DDM 6). The choice of container can also be critical...plastic bowls are verboten at many potlucks. One bad choice can get a dyke banned from potlucks for years. Like brunches, potlucks are class-based events. A dyke invited to a new potluck must do extensive research on the hostesses before deciding what type of dish to bring and in what kind of container. Some working class butch potlucks consist primarily of store bought chips and dips whereas potlucks at a Bette Porter impersonator's house may require a home-made dish created from a recipe from Bon Appetit magazine that necessitates trips to five different stores to find the right exotic ingredients.

Case Example

Sal and Joan have been together for 18 years, and their home is the hub of a long-standing lesbian potluck in a small rural community. This potluck is held on the full moon of each month and approximately 20 dykes show up each time from the pool of 56 members. Sal suffers from potluck variety anxiety disorder, and always has back-up food in the refrigerator. In fact, they had to purchase an additional refrigerator to place in the garage for this express purpose. Sal feels compelled to prepare one item from each food group in case no one brings a main course, or the potluck is short on desserts. Joan resents the extra money and time they must spend on food preparation to relieve Sal's anxiety, and she has asked that they receive couple's potluck counseling from their regular dyke chiropractor. They are both experiencing potluck hosting fatigue syndrome, but are terrified of experiencing withdrawal if they go cold-turkey on the potluck after all these years. They also worry about the emotional status of their potluck guests, many of whom rely on this potluck to meet their social needs. Their chiropractor, who happened to be one of the potluck regulars, helped them to develop a plan to gradually wean them off the potluck over the course of a year. The chiropractor also graciously offered 10% discounts to all the other regulars for cranial adjustments to help them reduce their potluck cravings as they withdrew. With this critical support, the entire network was able to withdraw from this potluck habit and each member found other outlets for their social needs, with only two having a rebound Brunch addiction.

DDM 8c. Over Counseled Dykes (OCD)

Some lesbians appear to become addicted to therapy, although many experts suggest it may be more similar to obsessive-compulsive disorder (hence the name OCD) than an addiction. Women with the condition seek individual counseling at least twice a week and attend group therapies another 3-4 times a week. In addition, they are prone to spending long hours sitting at the hair salon or vet's waiting room to talk to others about personal issues. With friends, the OCD's conversations focus half the time on the issues that she is discussing with her therapist, and the other half analyzing her friends' behaviors. The OCD likes to engage in dykignosis of others. She speaks in a psychobabble jargon language that varies depending on the type of therapy to which she is addicted. For example, she may accuse friends of sublimating their sexual desires for a celebrity into excessive eating of ice cream cones (psychoanalytic), or tell her co-workers that she is not responsible for the mess in the break room because she has low self-efficacy for cleaning the microwave (cognitive behavioral). The bookshelves of the OCD afflicted are full of lesbian psychology and counseling books as well as generic self-help manuals. She keeps several journals; one for processing her daily experiences, one for her dreams, which she reviews in great detail with her therapist, and another for collecting her favorite psychological terminology and theory. Other journals may record her insights about her coworkers' behaviors or diagnoses of her lesbian community and network. The lesbian afflicted with OCD is prone to claiming to be a lay therapist, to the detriment of her friends and coworkers.

Some speculate that the addiction is caused by the excessive amount of Kleenex used by this dyke during therapy sessions, rather than the therapy itself, thus the disorder should be renamed Therapy Kleenex Overexposure (TKO). There is simply not enough scientific research to determine whether OCD and TKO are two separate disorders or subtypes of the same underlying addiction. There is growing anecdotal evidence, though, that toxic chemicals used in the Kleenex factory production line may induce acute episodes of dyke drama and thus, facilitate the development of addictions to therapy.

Case Example

Marj, a 68-year-old retired nurse, has been going to therapy for over 40 years. She started after her first disastrous U-Haul relationship a year after coming out, and has been a regular ever since. She prefers psychodynamic types of therapy, and casually intermingles psychoanalytic jargon into her conversations with acquaintances, including projection, castration anxiety, rationalization, Electra complex, and primal scene. She is trying to reach her ego Ideal. She has the entire collection of Sigmund and Anna Freud's writing. These dog-eared books

102

are her most priced possessions. In spite of her years of intensive therapy, Marj has at least five DDM dykignoses, including DDM 1a, 6, 7, 27, and 30. Unfortunately, her current therapist, a bartender who she pays $15 per hour to listen to her on her off hours, has not recognized her OCD disorder, that probably manifested around 1988. Marj now has few friends because of her complex and intersecting pathologies, so she uses group therapy sessions to meet her social needs. She is currently in a relationship with her cat, Fluffy, and they are about to celebrate their fifth anniversary. She once had a partner for 18 months in 1993-94, but Marj claims that the relationship did not work because of Deborah's reaction formation to lesbian sex. Marj is also addicted to TV talk shows, reality shows, and programs like *Intervention*. She has been a member of 27 different brunch and potluck groups over the years, but typically after about three months of exposure to Marj, the brunch or potluck mysteriously disappears. The members regroup later at a different venue.

DDM 8d. Miscellaneous Lesbian Event Addictions

There are many regional, generational, and gender-related variations of the event addiction. For example, some lesbians are addicted to lesbian game nights, lesbian golf leagues, women's sports (basketball, softball, soccer, rugby), country-line dancing, women's music festivals, talent shows, book clubs, meet-ups, or happy hours. There are reports of a growing number of dykes addicted to Rachel Maddow's blog site, suggesting a hybrid DDM dykignosis that combines the celebrity crush with a lesbian event addiction. These other events, like brunches and potlucks, have the addictive quality created by the adrenalin rush that impacts brain chemistry and lesbian collective consciousness.

Prevalence and Etiology

88% of lesbians have experienced at least one episode of lesbian event addiction in their lifetimes, making it the most common of the dyke drama generators, and 22% have chronic potluck or brunch addiction that results in severe withdrawal symptoms if ever the event is cancelled for a month. Nearly 14% of lesbians have experienced an addiction to therapy (OCD) in their lifetimes, and 6% are currently OCD or TKO.

For many lesbians, deep-seated anxieties about intimacy underlie the event addiction. Brunches, potlucks, group therapy sessions, and game nights are group activities that are less stressful than dates. Couples may seek out these activities when they tire of each other's company but are conflict avoidant and do not talk about their relationship dissatisfaction. The game night dyke addict may differ somewhat from the brunch and potluck dependencies. These women may have a thrill-seeking nature that gets aroused by, and eventually addicted to, an exciting game of Pictionary or Scattergories. In a recent turn of events, however, many feminist dyke communities have boycotted Pictionary for introducing the new version of the game, Pictionary Man. Once again dykes must rise up against the patriarchy and challenge the sexist use of "man" to stand for all people.

Some lesbians get addicted to the event that marked their "first" entrance into a lesbian community, and like a heroin addict, they are chasing the high associated with that first time. Lesbians addicted to therapy have a compulsive need to talk that is not satisfied by their friends, partners, or pets. The OCD afflicted may find that the unconditional listening capability of many therapists is a powerful reinforcer and satisfies narcissistic needs.

Treatment Considerations for Dyke Event Addictions
The key to surviving lesbian events is to pace oneself, schedule lesbian events in moderation, be vigilant about over-indulging, and thus, avoid slipping into addiction. Some smart phone apps will sound a warning tone if the number of events per week exceeds the healthy limit. According to the National Institute on Lesbian Wellbeing, safe levels of lesbian event attendance have been determined to be once a week. Twice a week denotes a level indicative of dyke event abuse, and three or more events per week signals a full-blown addiction. Once a lesbian enters into the addictive level, she needs a full intervention, involving going cold turkey from all lesbian events for a period of no less than two months. This woman needs to be monitored, lest she attempt to illicitly Skype her way into an event before she is properly de-brunched. If she is a game addict, she must purge her home of all the board games. Internet games may also be addictive, but are a different etiological entity than the lesbian game addiction, thus are not discussed here. Those in couple relationships need to have supportive therapy so that the non-afflicted partner does not have to suffer from lesbian event deprivation while her partner is in the two-month abstinence phase. Finally, OCD or TKO lesbians need to be slowly weaned off of therapy sessions. If she returns to therapy at a later time, to avoid a relapse, she must not attend more than one session, group or individual, per week, and take frequent

scheduled therapy breaks. She should also be counseled to use cotton handkerchiefs rather than Kleenex for emotionally charged sessions, to avoid the toxic exposure to Kleenex, as well as being more ecologically sensitive. For severe cases, lesbian event detoxification units, located in shopping malls and grandmother's houses, may be needed.

Choosing a brunch venue with a wireless connection allows women to have lesbian community without the stresses of ordering from the menu. It also may help to avert the dyke dramas that often accompany paying the check in restaurants that will not provide individual checks. Many lesbians have suffered financial and emotional burdens when they are stuck with the check and several members of the group have underpaid. Group checks at restaurants appear to inhibit the computational centers of dyke brains, resulting in forgetting to add tip and tax or forgetting what they ordered. The one holding the check at the end must often add an additional $5-25, depending on the size of the group, leaving her resentful and accusatory. If a lesbian papparazza (see DDM 5) is present, she will carefully observe how much money each dyke puts in, and report the ones who short-change the bill to the whole community.

In short, lesbian brunches, potlucks and other events are often positive community-builders and provide considerable social support to participants, but like any mood-altering substance or situation, can be addictive.

DDM 9. The Party Dyke

Overview

There are excessive partiers in every community, but this disorder primarily manifests in a lesbian community in the social set that revolves around the lesbian bar, the Dinah Shore weekend, Olivia Cruises, ladies nights, or other places where two key elements converge: alcohol and dancing. Although on the surface, this condition may appear similar to the lesbian event addiction, potluck and brunch addicts rarely show a "party" lifestyle, providing evidence of different etiological factors. Since *The L Word,* a large subset of young party dykes around the world have been found to emulate the behaviors of Shane, a character written with the party dyke prototype in mind. Shane Syndrome, a party dyke subtype that emulates the looks and behaviors of Shane is to be distinguished from mere Shane impersonators who copy the appearance but not the drinking, drug use, fear of commitment, and casual sex.

Obviously, there are class differences in how the party dyke syndrome manifests, as only the affluent lesbians can indulge in the cruises and Club Med trips regularly, but there are similarities even across the class lines. The conversation of a serious party dyke revolves around drinking ("I got so wasted last night…"), excessive frivolity ("I laughed my ass off"), and hang-overs ("I need mimosas for brunch"). There are impassioned debates about the best beer or lager (at working class dyke parties) or the finest California wines (at upper middle-class lesbian parties). The party life leads to short attention span, need for constant stimulation, severely impaired judgment toward the end of the evening, and limited conversational skills when sober. Alcohol kills brain cells—the only evidence needed to confirm this fact is to go to a party sober and listen to the conversations of the party dykes. They have mastered the art of superficial and meaningless talk. These women's lives often revolve around the happy hour. Sadly, some cross the line into drug or alcohol addiction and a true DSM disorder.

Side effects of the party dyke condition are unfortunate couplings, such as the "relationship" that begins as a casual sexual encounter at the bar when both parties are inebriated. That one casual encounter can take months to resolve if one of the parties equates sex with love with relationship (see DDM 7 U-Haul Syndrome). In fact, alcohol is one of the most powerful underlying factors in the U-Haul Syndrome when lesbians meet, fall in love, and move into together, all before the buzz of those three mojitos has worn off, and before they can see relationship warning signs. Dykes who suffer from the Shane Syndrome subtype of party dyke typically are not U-Haul lesbians; in fact, they fear and flee from committed relationships and show considerable commitment phobia.

The primary signs of party dyke syndrome include: inability to have a normal conversation, hearing loss resulting from repeated exposure to pulsing disco beats (substitute electronica, country rock, hip hop, ska, salsa, square dance, R&B, or electric boogaloo, depending on the dancing/music preferences of the afflicted dyke), presence of frequent and short traumatic relationships, dance frenzies, and inability to schedule any events before noon. In fact, the high frequency of lesbian brunches in many communities may be originally related to the fact that party dykes could not arise before 11 am, so no lesbian social event could begin before noon.

Case Example

Deborah is a 32 year-old party dyke, who came out when she was 17. In recovery from drug addiction, she continues to go to bars every weekend to drink and dance. She rationalizes her heavy drinking by stating that she had a problem with cocaine, not alcohol. She never misses "ladies night" at any of the four bars that offer them in her urban community, and goes after hours to gay men's bars because "they are more fun" than the lesbian events. Deborah is painfully thin and meticulously styles her hair into a "bed head" look. She spends an hour every day in front of the mirror creating a hairdo that looks like she just crawled out of bed, and wears highly sexualized garb such as very tight tube tops and low cut jeans revealing her eight belly button piercings. Every time her therapist asks how she was doing that week, or what she did on the weekend, she says "I danced my ass off," "I met this unbelievably incredible woman," "I got this crazy tattoo but do not remember why I chose this design," and "I can't remember much about it…" Although she mostly has casual sex, Deborah had six relationships in a two-year period. Two of them lasted only a weekend, but were notable for their drama…one woman left Deborah's apartment after drunken sex and stole her car, another showed up on her doorstep the next day with her suitcase and her three cats, intending to move in. In addition, Deborah had five different jobs in ten years and cannot decide what she wants to do with her life. She would really like to be a lesbian gigolo, but found that most dykes do not have the income level to be able to support her lifestyle.

Prevalence and Etiology

Whereas many lesbians spend some time in lesbian bars and parties in their youth, it becomes a way of life for only about 10% of dykes in their young adulthood, and 4% of lesbians over the age of 40. The causes of the party lifestyle are varied, some of them similar to the etiology of alcohol and drug abuse among lesbians, but one uniquely dyke causative factor is the Shane Syndrome subtype. Some lesbians over-identified with the Shane character on *The L Word* and glamorize the idea of a party lifestyle with drinking, drugging, and frequent casual sex. Shane Syndrome is associated with a highly specific look: the carefully crafted messy hairdo, a boyish appearance, and a painfully anorexic body. Younger dykes who came out after the heyday of *The L Word* may suffer from Lezzie Gaga Syndrome instead. Their wild outfits, constantly changing hairstyles and color, and penchant for bad romances can distinguish them. Their anthem is "Born that way." The party dyke condition may stem from an underlying fear of intimacy or commitment, or anxiety over lesbian sex and/or relationships.

Treatment Considerations

Many party dykes have actual DSM substance use disorder diagnoses and must be treated accordingly. However, when the party dyke condition is identified early enough, before it becomes an addiction, it can be treated via a number of dyke drama harm reduction strategies. For example, concerned friends can facilitate finding a replacement dependence on a lesbian brunch or potluck, which are less harmful addictions. Harm reduction activities aimed at delaying inopportune couplings resulting from premature physical contact include changing from high-level physical contact dances to country line dancing with no contact. Another environmental preventative measure might be to re-design the lesbian bar with alternative conversation pits serving green tea, and with "get-acquainted" card games to direct the dialogue to deeper connections prior to frenzied sexual dancing episodes.

Lesbian dating classes in high school need to address lesbian sex and intimacy issues to prevent dyke party syndrome. The Department of Lesbian Public Health has proposed that communities assess the ratio of lesbian or gay bars to coffee shops, and strive for a shift to more coffee outlets than alcohol outlets to improve the general public and pubic health of lesbians. On the other hand, dyke community leaders must be aware that an excessive number of lesbian coffee shops pose potential dangers as well. If party dykes merely substitute caffeine drinks for alcoholic beverages, the community is faced with a different set of problems, and the crazed hyperactive behavior of heavily caffeinated dykes can cause almost as much drama as alcohol or cocaine. Recently, hostilities broke out between a small group of dykes at a lesbian dog park in Houston, when a coffee addict frenetically ran after tennis balls tossed by other lesbians for their dogs' entertainment. They were not amused when the coffee-addled dyke intercepted the ball, frustrating their dogs, and they attempted to eject her from the park.

If harm reduction strategies are not effective, and women progress to party dyke status, then treatment interventions must be instituted. Therapy for the Shane Syndrome involves victim empathy treatment, whereby the afflicted woman must watch video clips dramatizing the emotional impact of Shane's commitment phobia on all of the women she rejected over the six year run of the show. Many counselors find that showing the sequence of episodes focusing on the relationship between Shane and Carmen, and their disastrous wedding day will cure most Shane Syndrome dykes within three sessions.

DDM 10. Desperately Seeking Susans

Overview

Every community has some of these unfortunate women, but they are particularly noticeable in lesbian communities. They lurk on the fringes of lesbian events, such as lady's nights and softball games, and stare longingly at anyone they perceive to be single, and sometimes pursue partnered dykes as well. Their personal ads exude angst "Looking for someone to complete me," "I NEED you," "Are you my soul-mate? Let's find out," "I crave a partner," "Inconsolably single and in dire need of girlfriend," and "Looking for love in all the wrong places." At brunches, parties, and bars, they anxiously try to lock eyes with desirable lesbians, and their body posture begs for attention. These are dissatisfied, morose women who have bought into the myth that only the coupled can be truly happy. They cannot stand their own company. This syndrome is not limited to the lesbian community, but even in the lesbian supposedly-superior-to-heterosexual world, there is still tremendous pressure to be coupled. Friends often view other dykes with concern when they are single for too long (for example, if still not dating two months after a break-up), and with great suspicion if they seem to be happily single. This intense pressure to be coupled is what creates the aura of desperation that surrounds DSS lesbians.

DSS dykes often lack a strong friendship network. Couples avoid them for fear of the drama they may bring to their relationships, and single friends avoid them because the low lesbian self-esteem leads them to act like pity-party dykes. DSS lesbians also avoid each other because they fear the competition.

Case Example

Chris, a 38-year old plumber and musician once knew a woman whose name actually was Susan, a 33-year old receptionist at a vet's office. Susan had a long-standing crush on Chris that went back about 10 years. Susan had co-occurring lesbian disorders (besides DSS, she was also a brunch addict and had paparazzi tendencies), and Chris had been avoiding her for years. Occasionally, however, Chris would let her guard down and answer the phone without checking caller ID, or get distracted from her usual vigilance, and be forced into a painful encounter with Susan. For example, Chris reported that several times in a coffee shop, she looked up from her book to find Susan across the table from her. At these times, Susan would begin a rapid-fire monologue, never taking a breath or pausing so that Chris could politely extricate herself. With each sentence, she moved closer to Chris. Susan's body language trumpeted DESPERATE! LOVE ME! One day Chris was home alone rearranging furniture the day after her partner had moved out. Only Chris's best friends knew about the breakup, yet the doorbell rang and Chris unwittingly opened the door to find Susan on the front porch with a bouquet of flowers and box of chocolate. Before Chris could blink, Susan said, "I knew she was not good enough for you and you would leave her eventually. Let me take care of you." It took Chris nearly 30 minutes to talk herself out of this situation and keep Susan from entering her home during that vulnerable time immediately after her breakup.

Prevalence and Etiology

This condition seems to be most common among lesbians in their late 30s and early 40s, for whom instinctual evolutionary urges to nest combine with general societal pressures to couple and lesbian community peer pressure to fuse. This combination of factors creates an unbearable physical and emotional desire to have a mate. About 30% of single lesbians have an acute episode of this condition during that critical time period, but another 12% of lesbians have a chronic case, relapsing into desperate despair with each break-up. The condition stems from deep social conditioning that one only has worth if in a relationship. This delusional belief system creates lesbian communities where only couples are acceptable and single lesbians are pariahs in the social network outside of the bar or party scene. In fact, in some lesbian communities, the major organizing framework of the community is around S&M. Lesbian Community S&M does not refer to the common use of the term, sadomasochism, but instead is an organizational structure in some dyke communities that segregates Single and Married dykes. These communities have social networks for singles that are completely separate (but equal) from the social networks of married or coupled dykes. DSS dykes, once in a relationship, fear intrusions from other DSS single lesbians, and jealously and fervently defend their relationships. They may cut off all ties with former single lesbian friends.

There is emerging evidence of a subtype of DSS that manifests not as desperation for a partner, but as desperation to be a mother. These Desperately Seeking Motherhood (DSM) dykes can be single or partnered, and have exaggerated biological clocks ticking loudly. They may also have a genetdyk variation in the maternal gene that causes an intensive longing for a baby. More research is needed to sort out the relationships between DSS and DSM.

Treatment Considerations

This condition is 100% preventable. Lesbian communities desperately need extensive and serious singles educational programs, therapy approaches to promote healthy relationships with self, and multi-faceted campaigns to free dykes from the unhealthy preoccupation with couple-dom that fosters the Desperately Seeking Susan Syndrome. This insidious idea that everyone must be coupled to be healthy underlies many other DDM diagnoses as well, but is most evident in the DSS. Dyke community efforts to force lesbians into pairing up must be halted, such as the lesbian speed-dating phenomenon, and resources should be put into helping women find their inner dyke hermits. Actually, given the dyke penchant for rushing into relationships too quickly, lesbian speed dating should be banned entirely, because speed is the enemy. A DSS dyke almost always suffers from a concomitant U-Haul Syndrome because if she does find a willing woman, she jumps into relationship far too quickly. The singles therapy should focus on societal de-programming combined with lesbian self-love therapy and empowerment strategies. For example, some women relate well to the words of modern day philosopher, Madonna, "Don't go for second best baby...respect yourself." Some afflicted lesbians have found that chanting this mantra ten times a day for 60 days rids them of the desperation.

In addition, reading this manual may be sufficient to frighten lesbians into choosing singlehood. The sheer number of lesbians with some underlying pathology is staggering, and the chances of meeting a completely sane dyke are less than one in ten thousand. The DDM should serve as the primary textbook for any course on lesbian relationships and dating, as both an educational intervention and a scare tactic.

DDM 11. Dyke Sexual Performance Anxiety

Overview

This syndrome may be in decline with the advent of sexually explicit lesbian films, lesbian internet porn, and cable TV, but older generations of lesbians, Amish lesbians, and others without cable TV or good internet connections may be prone to this disorder that stems from a lack of education about lesbian sex. A woman first coming out is confronted with many confusing questions about sex that were never addressed in teen slumber parties, on the afternoon talk shows, or in Cosmo magazine. Heterosexist media still puts the onus for sexual initiation on men, and rarely provides any useful input for the budding lesbian. In fact, much of the heterosexually oriented sexual education materials continue to express puzzlement over what lesbians might do in bed. Heterosexual magazines that focus on "best pickup lines for men" and "hairstyles that scream sex" are typically not helpful in the lesbian world of sexual relationship.

If a newly out dyke dares to pick up an anthology of lesbian erotica, she is faced with S & M, BDSM, role-playing, vampire dykes, threesomes, strap-ons, vibrators, tribadism, anal plugs, dyke daddies, nipple clamps, double dildos, clit piercings, and the whole gamut of sexual activities, but often not the answers to very practical questions. A trip to the local sex toy shop is also daunting. Baby dykes may be confused by the selection of 49 different types of harnesses, 106 varieties of dildos that differ in size, shape, and color, and 26 types of lube. Vibrators come in a dizzying array of options. Does one stick with the simple two speed plug in model, or the rotating head, vibrating, pulsating device with three motors and 27 settings? Lesbian erotica and sex toy shops constitute advanced sex education; the newly out dyke needs beginners lesbian sex 101, to address questions such as:

- Should I leave the lights on or turn them off?
- Shave my legs or not?
- Get a bikini wax, yes or no?
- Where do I get information about safer sex for lesbians?
- Dental dams or saran wrap? If dental dams, where the hell do I find one if not dating a dentist?
- Do all lesbians use sex toys? How do I ask my partner about her preferences?

- Condoms on sex toys? If so, ribbed or plain, lubricated or not?
- Astroglide or KY?
- How do I start the conversation about sexual histories with a potential new partner?
- How is HPV spread?
- How do I negotiate sex during a heavy menstrual flow?
- What is the polite way to remove an annoying pubic hair from my teeth during sex?

It exerts a lot of pressure on someone who is a baby dyke, or newly single after a long relationship with a limited sexual repertoire. Older lesbians who are forced into the dating pool again after a breakup may re-experience dyke sexual performance anxiety even if they were accomplished lovers in their youth. Arthritis, sensory impairments, chronic belching and uncontrollable gas that often come with normal aging processes can create significant anxieties about sex with a new partner.

The lesbian media does not help matters. The older lesbian movies are full of meaningful glances and innuendo, but no real sex. When anything beyond kissing occurs, the camera focuses on the face of the one partner who is on the verge of orgasm. Dykes learn what orgasm looks and sounds like from the neck up, but not what leads to it. Heterosexual-male-oriented pornography mostly shows artificially large-breasted young women sticking their tongues out at each other. The expert panel members agreed that none of them had ever witnessed this type of behavior among lesbians in situ.

Lesbian-made erotica is a little better than mainstream lesbian romantic film in depicting lesbian sex, but all filmed sex is staged, edited, and made to look so much more smooth and easy than it really is. Thus, filmed versions of sex can be quite misleading and unrealistic. Lesbian romance novels may be explicit about the specific behaviors that may lead to orgasm, but some women find that reading 26 pages of overblown, flowery descriptions of a sexual activity that actually takes about four minutes is so exhausting that it removes any sexual desire that may have been present at the onset. Some others actually find these written sexual accounts dull, although they would never state this fact out loud at a lesbian public event.

Case Example

Gloria came out at age 42, after being in a heterosexual marriage for 18 years, and having had sex only with men. She was never very attracted to men and she had always played a passive role in sex. Now, as a newly out dyke, she is beginning to date and having anxiety attacks about physical intimacy. Her first foray into dating was checking out the craigslist page for women seeking women. The first two ads she read were:

> I'm looking for a girlfriend to have fun with in and out of the bedroom for me and my husband. You should be outgoing, adventurous, and attractive. I am attractive, tall, and shaven. He is clean cut, muscular, and very well hung. We are very laid back and encourage creativity!!! If you're interested send naked pictures. Please put your zodiac sign in the subject line.

> Gender queer boi dyke seeks kinky BDSM, for buying kale at farmer's market, fisting after dessert, water sports on the kitchen floor...I'm the masochist and you're the sadist. Me, BBW, you, have a big clit to worship. 420 friendly, have a daddy side.

Now she was even more confused--she was pretty sure she didn't want the first one, as she was ready to give up sex with men involved in any way forever, but the second posting scared her. It took 20 minutes of internet research to translate all of the words in the message, and she still was not sure whether "buying kale" was code for something sexual. And how big did a clit need to be to be worthy of worship? She did not know lesbians were into size like men were. By this time, Gloria was considering the convent.

Prevalence and Etiology

99% of lesbians experience some degree of dyke sexual performance anxiety at some time in their lives, and 35% have relapses of sexual performance anxiety every time they start a new relationship. The primary cause is lack of education, although some dykes experience performance anxieties when dating a woman with a different level of sex drive than herself or whose craigslist or other dating profile indicates potentially high or unusual expectations for sex. Some dykes hint at these sexual proclivities in their profiles rather than state them specifically, leaving too much to the imagination. For example, one woman's screen

115

name on a dating profile was "kindapervy," leaving the potential viewer confused and wondering whether to "wink" at her or not. This imprecision of language is undesirable when one is seeking out a partner, and it is better to know ahead of time precisely what is meant by "kind of pervy," rather than find out in the heat of the moment.

Treatment Considerations

Clearly along with the lesbian dating classes, schools need to develop an advanced seminar on lesbian sex. Much like driver's education, lesbian sex school needs to address the dead ends, the blind spots, the speed limits, and illegal left turns, instruct the student on how to identify the stop signs and avoid road rage, and teach the penalties for parking and speeding violations. Similar to driving a car, initiating a sexual encounter involves turning on the motor, achieving a consistent speed for a comfortable ride, and avoiding sudden turns, jerks, and stops. Requirements to pass sex school would have to include a written anatomy quiz. Every budding lesbian must be able to identify all the erogenous zones—if the student cannot find the clitoris, she must repeat the course. She must also pass a "hands-on" test to assess for adequate dexterity and technical skills. There is a great need for lesbian sex coaches with advanced training in dyke sex education for older lesbians who need refresher courses, and for newly out women who need re-training or updating of skills after years of heterosexual sex. A glossary of euphemistic terms for sexual parts and activities, and a guide to internet dating sex slang, would be a highly beneficial resource for all lesbians, but is beyond the purview of this manual and sadly, beyond the expertise of the author.

DDM 12. Hypoactive Lesbian Desire Disorder

Overview
Hypoactive lesbian desire disorder refers to having a low or absent sex drive for female sexual partners in general, for dyke sex toys, or for one's specific partner. This condition has a primary and a secondary form. In both cases, sexual desire is low enough to cause concern in the afflicted lesbian and/or her partner. The definition of "normal" sex drive is obviously rather subjective, so the definition used here is a sex drive that is satisfactory to the woman and her partner(s), if applicable, regardless of whether others consider it high, low, or just right. Primary hypoactive disorders are present before the onset of a relationship, whereas secondary hypoactive desire disorders develop after a period of mutually satisfying sexual activity in a relationship. Hypoactive lesbian desire disorders create considerable dyke drama in relationships and are a primary cause of unfortunate affairs.

DDM 12a. Primary hypoactive lesbian desire disorder
This disorder occurs in the lesbian and the occasional straight woman who wants to be emotionally (or financially) nurtured by a dyke, but who does not want sex, even at the beginning of a relationship. She wants to cuddle endlessly, rub her partner's back, and get emotionally entwined with another woman, but is not interested in sex. There is absolutely nothing wrong with this, as long as the potential partner has been duly informed of this non-sexual tendency. Many unsuspecting lesbians have been enticed into relationships with women who promised that they just needed time to learn to trust her, and then she would be a sexual tigress. Sadly, it rarely happens. Sometimes this condition is confused with laziness or self-centeredness rather than lack of desire. Some women just want all the attention focused on themselves, and then promptly go to sleep, leaving their partners awake and frustrated. The technical term for this phenomenon is "being a pillow queen." This is a completely different dykignosis than the hypoactive dyke disorder, and is one of the most common differential diagnoses that therapists must rule out.

Case Example
Dina was a 29-year-old lesbian graduate student. She hit it off with a straight classmate, Christina, a beautiful German exchange

student, and they began spending a lot of time together. Christina confided that she was attracted to macho bad-boys who were not very satisfactory as partners, and that she preferred the company of women to meet her social and emotional needs. She was very physically affectionate with Dina. After they had known each other for about a month, Christina started showing up late in the evening with a bottle of wine, and the two would drink a bit too much. Christina would start to cry about some man who was treating her badly, Dina would comfort her, and they would end up in bed together kissing. Christina would stop any behavior beyond kissing. Christina told Dina that she loved her and wished she was a man, but could not be in a lesbian relationship. Dina kept seeing her with the irrational belief that if Christina really loved her, eventually she would see the light and they could be together. Dina stopped dating, abandoned her friends, and devoted her time and energy to winning Christina's love. After eight months, Dina felt frustrated and totally used, but had a strong emotional attachment to Christina that she found difficult to give up. Christina, on the other hand, had a condition closely related to the POW, or pussies on welfare, but in this case, she did not require financial support, just emotional intimacy and affection from another woman.

DDM 12b. Lesbian Bed Death

Another manifestation of hypoactive lesbian desire disorder is the secondary form of the disorder, or in lay terms, Lesbian Bed Death. This is a well-known problem, but is rarely openly discussed within lesbian relationships. The phenomenon of Lesbian Bed Death resembles what Oscar Wilde said about homosexuality: "the love that dare not speak its name." In this case, often the love quite often speaks its name, just not the sex. This disorder typically occurs after the first blush of a relationship has worn off, and the sex begins to diminish. One common scenario among lesbian couples is that after too many weeks or months without sex, each member of the couple is afraid to bring up the topic, so the cycle continues and each one gets more and more worried. In some couples, one or both partners begin to look for excitement and sexual arousal elsewhere as soon as the sex diminishes in their primary relationship, rather than do the hard work of examining the reasons for the loss of sex and intimacy in their lives. It is easier to get a new partner every few years than to heal from a DDM dykignosis, however, afflicted dykes should be counseled to address these issues, because frank

118

discussion of sex and intimacy could avert 65% of dyke drama within couple relationships.

Case Example

LaShonda and Ty, both in their late 30s, have been together for four years. They met each other at work and came out of heterosexual relationships together. The first year, they had sex about four times a week. In the second year, they had a baby, began to seek out lesbian community as a couple (a weekly brunch for lesbian moms and a monthly potluck for lesbians of color) and as individuals. LaShonda joined a lesbian cheerleading team and Ty took dyke DIY classes. In their third year, they started breeding Chihuahuas and joined three lesbian dog clubs. Their sex life declined even more, to about once a month because between the baby, the dogs, and the lesbian events, they had no time or energy for each other. They sought advice from a friend who had been in the same relationship for 23 years, concerned that in another year, they would not have sex at all. Unlike conflict avoidant lesbians, they successfully staved off lesbian bed death with a little help from their friend and a few visits to the local sex toy shop for some spicy variety in their sex life.

Prevalence and Etiology

The rate of hypoactive lesbian desire disorder is similar to rates of hypoactive desire in heterosexual women, but is doubled in impact because of the increased likelihood of both partners in a relationship having the disorder in lesbians compared to heterosexual couples. Even though more frequent than among heterosexual couples, the overall rate of lesbian bed death is relatively small, affecting 12% of couples who have been together for three or more years. The causes are many and varied. For some lesbians, the hypoactive desire stems from too much time spent at lesbian events, particularly lesbian collectives, which are notorious for draining energy. For others, the cause is U-Haul Syndrome (see DDM 7), and is related to getting into a relationship before determining basic compatibility. When the lust wears off, there is nothing left to sustain the relationship. Another underlying cause is Lesbian Emotionally Exhausting Processing (LEEP) (see DDM 30), a condition that also drains the couple of physical and emotional resources, and has a dehydrating effect on body fluids. Finally, over-use of animal-shaped sex toys can also have negative consequences on sexual behavior in relationships, including decreased desire for one's partner. This is because the sex toy is often more reliable than the partner and never argues, whines, fails to please, or runs out of energy. If it does, it is easier to change the battery than to have to process with a partner about a topic so sensitive as sex.

Treatment Considerations

In the case of an underlying U-Haul Syndrome, the afflicted couple needs to break up and undergo treatment for the U-Haul problems before commencing a new relationship. If the cause is excessive lesbian events, more careful scheduling can reduce the symptoms dramatically, but if there is an underlying lesbian event addiction, that dependence must be addressed first. Finally, lesbian sex school with homework is an excellent way to revive a boring relationship, as is access to good lesbian erotica. Unfortunately, good lesbian erotica is exceedingly rare, as shown in popular media when the couple in *The Kids Are All Right* had to resort gay male porn to treat their lesbian hypoactive desire disorder. Government resources need to be allocated to the making of dyke sex education and enrichment films and other materials created in age-appropriate formats. Lesbian sex education should begin in the third grade and continue throughout the rest of the dyke-cycle (not to be confused with the dyke-sicle, an important aspect of lesbian sexuality that might need some attention in those whose sex life has become stale). Finally, the myth of lesbian bed death as the inevitable end of lesbian sexuality must be de-bunked by public media campaigns to correct this misconception and stop the self-fulfilling prophecy. Many lusty young women have been hesitant to come out because of this myth. Careful research shows that the term lesbian bed death was most likely coined by a heterosexual sex researcher in the late 1970s, and may have had to do with lack of understanding of lesbian sex. Sex researchers tended to focus on the number of times a couple has sex, and not the duration of the sex. Some research found that heterosexual couples sex lasted on average about four minutes; the DDM Academy's sex lab showed that lesbian sex lasted on average for 60 minutes in the first year of a relationship, and 40 minutes in the 10th year. As dykes, we need to claim quality over quantity.

DDM 13. Dykochondria

Overview

Hypochondriacs, people who have symptoms of physical health problems that are caused by irrational or neurotic thoughts, exist in all communities, but the manifestations can differ among lesbians. In fact, the most common manifestation among dykes is the claim of having at least five un-diagnosable allergy and/or fatigue syndromes. They also tend to have phobias about germs and carry hand and body sanitizers that they may spray indiscriminately on unsuspecting others at dyke activities. This condition can dramatically affect lesbian events, such as potlucks and game nights, and puts all dyke potluck hostesses and lesbian event organizers on edge. In some communities, serious rifts are found between the cat and dog fetish dykes who bring their pets to every event and the dykochondriacs (and the actual pet allergists) who threaten anaphylactic shock if the dog gets within six feet of her. Dykochondriacs are self-diagnosed for allergies to animals of all sorts, molds, dust, many types of food (mostly the ones she does not like), scents, and plants, plus she exhibits symptoms of at least two other rare chronic fatigue syndromes.

Case Example

Ana, the lesbian potluck hostess queen for her urban community had invited a visiting celebrity dyke, Shirley, to a potluck at her house to celebrate the winter solstice. The local dyke community revered Shirley because of her seminal role in women's music and politics, so Ana was ecstatic that Shirley was coming to her party. Her joy was greatly deflated, however, when Shirley said that she would be happy to attend if Ana sent out a notice to all the other guests to:

- Wear no cologne and do not use scented shampoo, moisturizers, deodorant, toothpaste, mouthwash, or douche for at least 24 hours prior to the event;
- Bring no foods with sugar, gluten, nuts, MSG, red meat, white meat, brown meat, dairy, fat, artificial sweetener, food coloring, or flavor, leaving only freshly made hummus and quinoa pita chips on the table;
- Bring no drinks with alcohol, caffeine, sugar, or carbonation; and please, no plastic bottled water;

- Do not clean the house with any cleaning product except for apple cider vinegar, and do not wash towels with scented detergent or fabric softener;
- Have a room where she can sit with no carpets, upholstered chairs, or venetian blinds that may hold dust or mold spores;
- Have a cat-dander and dog-hair -free, scent-free, quiet place where she can nap halfway through the party because of her chronic fatigue syndrome, Lymes Disease, fibromyalgia, gluten intolerance disorders;
- Require that all cat, dog, and hamster owners coming to the party be vacuumed at the front door to remove any pet hairs;
- Have the air ducts vacuumed and a mold inspection of the premises completed at least one week prior to the event;
- Have no fresh cut flowers, flowering plants, or photographs of flowers anywhere in the house.

Prevalence and Etiology

Not all people with allergies, chemical insensitivities, or symptoms of fatigue are hypochondriacs, but lesbians seem to disproportionately report multiple symptoms of these disorders. Contemporary research finds that three times as many lesbians as heterosexual women report multiple allergies. Fortunately, the condition is fairly rare, with fewer than 2% of dykes having pan-allergy conditions, but even this small number has a huge impact on lesbian events. Milder forms of allergies are at the same rates as the general population, although cat allergies are under-reported because of the stigma in lesbian communities directed toward those without cats. It is not uncommon in some lesbian communities for femi-feline fetishists (See DDM 1a) to accuse some women of actually being cat-haters disguising their dislike of cats with a proclamation of allergies. These women, to avoid the public humiliation of being labeled a cat hater, will take massive doses of antihistamines in order to attend potlucks at lesbian cat houses undetected.

In less dramatic cases of dykochondria, sometimes a lesbian with a mild dog allergy and a high dyke drama quotient creates a hysterical scene to protest the dog dykes who want to bring their canine companions to every event. These are pseudo-dykochondriacs. Lesbians with Chronic Fatigues Syndrome, characterized by attraction to women in military uniforms, must not be confused with dykochondriacs. The cause of lesbian hypochondria may be a need for more attention. This dyke feels neglected or invisible in her community, thus creates a victim-identity for attention and/or drama.

Treatment Considerations

First, the lesbian hypochondriac needs a thorough physical exam by a certified dyke allergy specialist to distinguish real allergies from a need for attention. Once a dykignosis of dykochondria is established, behavioral exposure therapies can be applied gradually. For example, the afflicted lesbian can be assisted to first gaze upon a Georgia O'Keefe flower print for 20 minutes or until the anxiety passes, then move to plastic flowers and finally an actual flower bouquet. Next she is exposed to a photo of a cat, followed by a YouTube video of a cat playing the piano, then a stuffed cat, and finally, a real furry feline, if one can be found that will cooperate with this endeavor.

For true pan-allergists, lesbian event planners need to reserve a plastic bubble so these women can attend events. Lesbian potlucks and brunches need to provide guests with detailed lists of ingredients of all food items as well as air quality measurements for pet dander, dust and mold. All potluck homes must be equipped for Skype so that afflicted lesbians can attend in the safety of their own sterile homes, but still experience lesbian community. Skype is also a viable option for dykes with food limitations and restrictions who find the brunch menus incompatible with their digestive systems or budgets.

DDM 14. The Gay Male Lesbian

Overview

For some women who came of age in predominately gay male neighborhoods or bar scenes with an absence of a lesbian feminist influence, the opposite of the U-Haul lesbian may be found. In this condition, gay male stereotypes manifest in a dyke's body. This afflicted woman thrives on anonymous sex, open relationships, polyamory, narcissism, high fashion, disco dancing, campy humor, and Hollywood gossip. She watches *Project Runway* rather than *Orange is the New Black*, and *What Not to Wear* instead of *Flip That House*. She has the complete boxed set of *Queer as Folk* rather than *The L Word*. Instead of lesbian game night, she attends Hollywood award/red carpet viewing parties. She idolizes Joan Rivers instead of Wanda Sykes, Dolly Parton instead of Melissa Etheridge, Kathy Griffin instead of Kate Clinton, and Anderson Cooper rather than Rachel Maddow. This condition often co-occurs with the Party Dyke syndrome. Shane from *The L Word* is a classic example of the co-occurring party dyke/gay male lesbian. Shane was even mistaken for a gay man on several occasions, demonstrating how dykes can emulate gay male fashion and attitude and successfully "pass." Gay male lesbians often refer to themselves as "gay" or "queer," rather than lesbian or dyke, showing their primary allegiance to a broader sexual/gender minority community. Some dykes who are halfway between lesbian and gay male may be described as lesbigaggians, a true hybrid of these identities. The condition, similar to the hermaphrodite who is halfway between male and female, manifests as a blend between gay and lesbian physical appearance, behavior, and interests. The affected dyke may have a lesbian mullet, but wear a stylish scarf and sparkly accessories, and listen to a ballgame on her iPhone while at the opera. A gay male lesbian would find this book perplexing.

Being a gay male lesbian is not a disorder in communities that are large enough for them to band together and find community and partners. But it becomes a problem if the gay male lesbian moves to a small feminist enclave in college towns or rural areas where gay male lesbians may be mistrusted or even shunned. Relationships between gay male lesbians and certain types of feminist lesbians are unlikely to succeed, and the infrequent public encounters have historically led to conflict and drama at gay pride celebrations and lesbian dances.

Case Example

Pat reported that she met Liz, a hot, impeccably dressed dyke at lady's night at a gay bar. She discovered later that Liz usually hung out at this bar on weekends, and did not know that Wednesday nights were lady's night. When she went home with this gay male lesbian after the bar closed, she found that Liz preferred to make love to the pulsing beat of Sylvester rather than the harmonious tones of the Indigo Girls. Liz initiated a lesbian quickie on the kitchen table instead of the typical five-hour lesbian sex marathon in the more comfortable bed. Instead of cuddling the rest of the night, after sex Liz wanted to go to an after-hours party to dance until dawn. When Pat looked around Liz's living room, she found DVDs of old Bette Davis movies rather than *Claire of the Moon*, and books by Armistead Maupin rather than Katherine Forrest. Pat was amazed when she could not find a single dyke musician among Liz's extensive CD collection. Liz's closet was full of designer label clothing, with nary an item from REI, and her kitchen was fully equipped with a Martha Stewart gourmet cooking station. She had a freezer full of steaks, but no hummus. Pat felt dirty and a little ashamed when she left Liz's apartment, hoping that she had not tarnished her lesbian reputation too much if news of this scandalous one-night stand leaked to her community.

Prevalence and Etiology

More common in cities with large gay male neighborhoods and many gay bars, the prevalence of the gay male lesbian is fairly small, with only about 5% of dykes overall showing this syndrome, but rising to 11% in cities with a high density of gay male bars. They tend to be under the age of 30, and most of them have never heard of Holly Near, Audre Lorde, or Adrienne Rich. In communities with strong lesbian separatist feminist groups, the condition goes underground, as it is politically incorrect to identify with gay male culture. The disorder may cause intense psychological discomfort in affected dykes. This internalized gay-brother-phobia can create tremendous anxieties for the afflicted woman who gets most of her support from her gay male friends and feels guilt and shame about her lack of knowledge of lesbian history. The causes of the gay male lesbian condition are lack of exposure to a lesbian mother superior (see DDM 6), gay male best friends rather than lesbian best friends, absence of education on feminist ideologies, and not having attended an all-female high school or college. Alternatively, a few women consciously choose a gay male lesbian identity after suffering excessive dyke drama in the women's community. Sadly, they are merely exchanging one form of drama for another, as gay male communities have a completely different, but equally debilitating, set of pathologies.

Treatment Considerations

Lesbian education or re-education courses are recommended for the gay male lesbian. The curriculum may include mandatory reading of early lesbian feminists like Jill Johnston and Mary Daly, repeated viewing of *Entre Nous*, *Desert Hearts*, and *Go Fish*, listening to the music of Margie Adam and Phranc, and a subscription to LL Bean catalogs. Dykes who need training on lesbian fashion styles are instructed to watch a minimum of 20 hours of *What Not To Wear*, and to choose clothing and accessories from the items that the hosts declare are "not to be worn." If this does not succeed, she is to be locked in a small room with a lesbian mother superior for no less than four hours for reprogramming.

DDM 15. Lesbian PMS (Partner Menstrual Synchronicities)

Overview

It is a well-documented fact that any two women who live in close quarters together such as in dormitories or as roommates tend to synchronize their menstrual cycles. However, there is very little research available on how this synchronizing works in lesbian relationships. For example, how long does the synchronizing last? Is the synchronization only at the beginning of a relationship or does it run the course of the relationship? Do the cycles of each partner equally "compromise" into one new pattern, or does the partner with the more dominant personality have pheromones that force the less dominant partner's cycle into alignment with her monthly cycle? What are the consequences of menstrual synchronicities for dyke couples? Does a loss of synchronizing reflect the end of the relationship and therefore serve as an early warning sign of lesbian bed death? In spite of a lack of answers to these questions, there is clear indication that sometimes the synchrony can result in disorder. There are at least two variations of this disorder.

DDM 15a. Synergistic Premenstrual Syndromes (SPMS)

For a lesbian couple, having menstrual periods at the same time can have many benefits including having pads and tampons in the trash only once a month and experiencing messy sex less often. But there are many potential calamities, and the disorder may account for the relatively high rates of domestic violence among lesbian couples. Early lesbian feminist writers declared that there would be no violence in lesbian relationships because of the absence of a toxic male presence. These theorists obviously overlooked the potentially psychotic symptoms of PMS, a condition that can sometimes erupt into emotional, psychological, and even physical violence. PMS symptoms such as bloating, irritability, mood swings, confusion, memory problems, breast swelling and tenderness, and abdominal pain and cramping can turn the most loving partner into a snarling, angry, vicious stranger for a day or two a month.

Disconcordant PMS, when one member of the couple has PMS and the other does not, can create unique relationship challenges. If the non-afflicted partner cannot develop empathy and menstrual-specific coping skills for dealing with the irrational days with the one with PMS, the relationship is doomed. A general guideline is that if the non-afflicted partner has not developed appropriate coping skills after six consecutive months of living with a PMS-prone partner, the relationship will not last. Concordant SPMS may be somewhat easier for the couple, because they each can empathize with the other's condition, but in the throes of a SPMS episode, reason and rationality are sometimes elusive, and dire consequences may ensue. SPMS is not merely PMS doubled, but is PMS-squared in its effects on the relationship and the broader community when dual-PMSing partners attempt to interact in public. Even if both members of the afflicted couple manage to adjust to each other's SPMS symptoms, friends and family members should be warned not to schedule social events with this couple during their SPMS days of the month.

Case Example

Bette and Betty are a fused lesbian couple (see DDM 3) who met when they were both age 23 and they have been together for six years. They do everything together, including completing each other's sentences, brushing each other's teeth, and wearing the same clothes. Their menstrual cycles had synched by the second month after their first date. Bette had suffered from severe PMS prior to meeting Betty, who had only mild symptoms. Since Bette is the more dominant personality in the couple, Betty now has severe PMS as well. During those three SPMS days of the month, they sleep and live in separate rooms to avoid doing serious physical and emotional harm to each other, and friends mark their menstrual patterns on their PDA calendars to avoid inviting this couple to any events during their fused and exaggerated PMS phase. In fact, this couple is known in the local community for their wild mood swings, from showing DDM 4, Lesbian Infantile Regressive Disorder, most of the month, but anti-social and sometimes homicidal tendencies two or three days each month when they have Lesbian SPMS.

DDM 15b. Lesbian-Couple Menopause Squared

Menopause has two meanings in dyke communities. The first one, irrelevant to this dykignostic category, refers to women who are taking a break from men and explore sexuality with women, but typically return to heterosexuality within a year. The second meaning refers to a biological life transition that occurs in midlife and results in the end of the reproductive years. Lesbians have virtually the same physical course of menopause as heterosexual women, but those in couples may experience unique relationship difficulties during this time. Like the PMS subtype, menopause in dyke couples can be concordant or disconcordant. Disconcordant menopause may be another major cause of breakup in mid-life lesbian couples, when the woman not yet in menopause believes that her partner has lost her mind. Another sensitive issue can arise if the non-menopausal partner is still in denial that she will ever reach this landmark of aging, and thus downplays the significance of the menopausal partner's process to avoid triggering her own anxiety about aging. Concordant menopause may be the leading cause of lesbian spontaneous combustion, when hot flashes synchronize at night, turning the bed into a lesbian inferno. Research shows that the most stable and well-adjusted lesbian relationships are ones that are forged after each partner has completed menopause, thus there are no menstrual-related traumas to endure.

Case Example

Jeannie and Asha have been together for 20 years and at age 54, Asha is in full-blown menopause, while Jeannie at 46, has not experienced any symptoms yet. Jeannie suspects that Asha is having an affair, because instead of snuggling at night like they used to do, Asha pushes her away, complaining that she feels like a furnace. Asha is also forgetful and in the past six months, she missed several of their many anniversaries, events that they have been celebrating for years. She forgot the anniversary of their first date (April 6), the anniversary of their first kiss (April 7), the day that they declared their love for each other (April 10), the anniversary of the day they got their kitten from the animal shelter (May 1), and the day they moved in together (May 26). In addition, Asha bursts into tears at the slightest provocation, feels deeply wounded by Jeannie's accusations, and adamantly denies having an affair. Their family nurse practitioner was able to intervene and help Jeannie realize that all of these "warning signs" were indeed symptoms of menopause. The couple is now engaging in anticipatory therapy to avoid re-experiencing this drama again when Jeannie enters menopause. They are videotaping the therapy so that menopause-related memory lapses will not lead them to repeat the trauma.

Prevalence and Etiology

Mild symptoms of PMS occur in about 75% of women, so this means that lesbian couples who are both in their childbearing years are highly likely to experience some degree of Lesbian SPMS. Severe symptoms affect about 5% of women in the general population, so about 10% of lesbian couples will have at least one partner with severe PMS, and in rare cases, both members of a couple will have severe SPMS. There is anecdotal evidence that one of the few lesbian serial killer couples ever identified had severe SPMS. Bonnie and Clyda lived in the 1960s, and were thought to have murdered Bonnie's homophobic boss, Clyda's abusive ex-husband, and assorted obnoxious plumbers, cable guys, and fundamentalist evangelists who haplessly knocked on their door on the wrong day of the month. Ultimately, this couple on a really severe SPMS day drove their car off a cliff for a Thelma and Louise dramatic dyke ending.

Virtually all women go through menopause, making this an almost universal rite of passage in long-term couples that transition through mid-life together. Spontaneous lesbian combustion is a rare side effect, occurring in one in ten million lesbian couples, but aging dyke couples need to be warned of this rare occurrence so they can take precautions. These menstrual-related conditions are predominantly biological in nature, related to fluctuating hormone levels and the resultant physical and emotional symptoms, but the condition can be triggered and/or worsened by lesbo-phobic events in society or dyke drama at the local level. Stressful events, whether external or internal to a couple, triad, or laggle, will raise the ambient temperature of the dyke relationship, igniting PMS symptoms.

Other menstrual-related problems in lesbian relationships and communities can revolve around the most appropriate menstruation-management system. The politically green lesbian prefers the re-useable products that reduce stress and strain on the environment, whereas some squeamish dykes feel repulsed by these items. Culture wars have broken out in close-knit lesbian communities over this issue, and lesbian couples have broken-up over conflicts related to menstrual products and their disposal.

Finally, there is lesbian feminist debate over whether the terms menstruation and menopause are weapons of the patriarchy and perhaps were created by men to further oppress women. If we were to remove "men" from menstruation and menopause, would these conditions even exist? Obviously, we still have much to learn about these conditions.

Treatment Considerations

Mild to moderate cases of lesbian SPMS and menopausal conditions can be successfully treated via education on the effect of hormone fluctuations on behavior and mood. Supportive counseling may help the couple to adjust and to learn effective coping and appeasement strategies. One of the most important coping skills for a partner to learn is to never suggest to a woman in the throes of PMS that she is being irrational. In severe cases, couples need to have a padded isolation room in their home where the afflicted partner can be locked away for her own safety, as well as the safety and wellbeing of her partner and the community at large. In concordant cases of lesbian PMS, adjoining isolation suites with limited communication capacities and soothing music piped in might be needed. A neutral third party such as non-PMSing, or even better, a post-menopausal woman who will not be drawn into their menstrual synchrony is brought into the relationship to mediate on the days of SPMS. Older lesbians need to be counseled to purchase flame-retardant sheets and pajamas to prevent conflagration during simultaneous hot flashes. Discussions about whether they are compatible in their menstrual maintenance devices (i.e., tampons, menstrual cups, sea sponges, reusable rags, and so on) should be held no later than the fourth date.

DDM 16. Lesbian Softball-Related Dysfunctions

Overview

It is a well-known fact that there is a positive correlation between softball and lesbians. Even the conservative commentator Pat Buchanan, who is generally less than knowledgeable about lesbian issues, is aware of this fact. When pictures of then Supreme Court nominee Elena Kagan on the softball diamond were circulated in the press, on a morning news talk show Buchanan said "Women's softball has been associated with lesbians and being gay for a long time. That's been sort of a signal like two men sunbathing together on a beach, or something like that. The immediate implication is that they're gay, and I've known that for a long time." Of course, lesbians have known this fact for even longer.

Softball disorders originated in the fertile diamonds of rural geographic zones. Diamonds, after all, consist of two triangles, the universal iconic symbol of the lesbian. Although they have spread across the country, lesbian softball leagues are still far more common in rural communities than in urban areas. Anywhere that softball mania exists, it is SERIOUS business, and some dyke communities experience softball gang hostilities among opposing feminist teams, who wear color-coded uniforms, are identified by their team slogans, and socialize in different venues. They may aggressively defend their ideological turf. Lesbians with softball-related disorders typically belong to one of three groups, described below, although on rare occasions a hybrid condition, the Serious Softball Feminist, has been reported. In most of the United States, symptoms peak in the summer months.

DDM 16a. Serious Softball Madness

Usually associated with working class butch lesbians, the SSM manifests as a preoccupation with winning and with all things related to the softball experience. These can include practicing and playing in the summer and ritualistic oiling of the glove, repeated viewing of videos of the past season to analyze plays, telling of softball stories at bars and parties, and softball seasonal affective disorder in the winter. Bars, including predominantly straight bars, often sponsor serious Softball Dyke teams because if they want a winning season, they want dykes on their team. This sponsorship by bars means that SSM is also far too often associated with serious post-softball drinking, and occasionally pre- and concurrent-softball drinking. Because of this, SSM often occurs in conjunction with the party dyke syndrome. The exception is the Shane

132

Syndrome subtype of party dyke, because the Shane-type dykes are too concerned with their physical appearance to risk scars, sweating, or unintentional dishevelment. Serious Softball Madness is also characterized by dedication to practice, a willingness to slide into home plate with reckless disregard for skinned elbows and knees, and a particular love, approaching a fetish, of the softball uniform. The home of the SSM dyke is filled with trophies, bats, gloves, kneepads, catcher's masks, and other sporting equipment. A frequent topic of conversation in the household is the debate about the merits of wooden versus aluminum bats.

Case Example
Blue is a 31-year-old dyke in a rural mid-western college town. She drives a city bus for a paycheck, but lives for softball season. She belongs to a summer softball league with eight teams; six are predominantly dyke teams, and two are composed of mostly heterosexual female members of the local Harley-Davidson club. Blue has played shortstop since the 6th grade and proudly exhibits her many scars and crooked fingers resulting from softball injuries. For the past six years, she has been a mainstay of the Hilltop Lounge Dive-sters, a softball team sponsored by a rough bar on the outskirts of town that caters to a mostly straight, biker clientele. In the summer months, Blue goes to practice four days a week, plays in a game with her team twice a week, and attends all the other games in all four women's softball leagues in the county. She celebrates victories and commiserates defeats after each game at the local lesbian bar, RU12. Her girlfriend, Bree, is described under DDM 16c. Blue experiences softball seasonal affective disorder every year when softball season ends, and her partner has to toss the kitty ball at her for an hour every day to revive her spirits.

DDM 16b. Feminist Softball Pretenders
This condition is found mostly in rural college and university towns, particularly those with activist feminist groups and women's studies departments. Universities with strong radical feminist leanings tend to spawn these softball teams, as postmodernist dykes are inclined to challenge and deconstruct the rules, thus are too frequently ejected from the game to be reliable team-mates. The FSPs are distinguished from the SSM by being mostly white, middle class, highly educated, and they tend more toward the center of the gender continuum. FSPs have disdain for practice and often have long debates about whether they

should want to win, or play only for the political cache of women being athletic. Umpires are often intolerant of FSPs, shouting taunts at them such as "are you going to play ball or talk theory?" FSPs are less likely to risk concussion related to sliding home lest it affect their intellectual theorizing. They may engage in counter-intuitive practices such as the annual dress-up game found in some communities, events occurring when two mostly lesbian teams compete against each other in frivolous costumes that paradoxically compromise their athletic performance. Serious Softball Madness players sometimes secretly attend these events in disguise as spectators, but would not be caught dead participating in one.

Case Example

Suzanne is an English professor at a midwestern college town, and is the facilitator of the feminist softball team, called the Susan B. Antho(knees). They do not have a coach, because of their disdain for the hierarchal nature of most team sports. They formed a collective instead, with Suzanne as the temporary facilitator for the first half of the season. She is the one who sets the line-up for each game after listening to two hours of dialogue and theorizing about it; this intellectual processing often takes the place of physical practice. They exercise their brains rather than their bodies while they argue about the embodiment of gendered athletic oppression. The team members consist of four other faculty members (two from women's studies, one sociologist, one anthropologist in addition to Suzanne's English degree), five graduate students from women's studies, one dean of a college, and three university staff members. Among them, they have over 70 years of accumulated academic theorizing experience. Suzanne's dissertation was about the genre of lesbian softball fiction, and she has a tendency to lecture the graduate students about standpoint epistemological theory between innings, to the great annoyance of the opposing team. In the summer 2011 season, the Susan B. Antho(knees) were proud to sport a record of 15 losses and no wins. During the winter months, Suzanne has no thoughts of playing softball, although she writes constantly about it in her academic publishing and blogs, and teaches a course called "Diamonds are a girl's best friend."

DDM 16c. Softball Bleacher Narcissists

The final disorder related to lesbian softball is one that leads to the obsessive and often narcissistic diva of the bleachers. The SBN is typically a high femme lesbian, who holds court at all softball games, arriving in elaborate dress and accessories intended to attract attention. She is often highly sought out as a date by the softball players. She yells at the umpire, but her remarks are more often sexual than softball-related, and she generally does not know a triple play from a bunt. She is there to entertain and be worshipped in the stands. In fact, some lesbian community members attend softball games solely for the entertainment in the stands by the witty and urbane SBN, and ignore the game.

Case Example

Bree is a 36-year old self-proclaimed High Femme princess who is the undisputed SBN for the Susan B. Antho(knees), much to the chagrin of her serious softball dyke girlfriend, Blue, who plays for the Hilltop Lounge. Bree, however, does not like serious softball, but prefers the feminist version, which includes intellectual discussions, dress-up games, more frivolity, and making witty and ironic remarks from the stands. Bree wears 1940s vintage wear with hats and elbow length gloves, elaborate make-up and hairdos, and carries her Yorkshire terrier, Janie Austen, in her voluminous purse. She is known for her clever taunts of the umpire, a non-verbal butch woman who has a crush on Bree and blushes crimson whenever Bree talks to her. Several other femmes have attempted to upstage Bree and take over the top femme bleacher position, but thus far, none have been successful. Bree has ruled the stands for eight consecutive seasons.

Variations of Softball Madness

Occasionally, a dyke can be afflicted with the same general type of symptoms but attached to different sports, such as women's basketball, golf, rugby, or soccer. In the past few years, there has been a dramatic resurgence of roller derby madness among lesbians across the United States, partly fueled by Ellen Page celebrity crushes following *Whip It,* and afflicted dykes choose outlandish names for themselves such as Lesbolina Jolie, Lezberado, and Gaydzilla. These drag queen names are evidence of their derangement. On rare occasions, the syndrome may apply to lesbian game nights, with serious madness most often occurring with Pictionary, known to be particularly addictive to dykes. In some rural communities in the far north where summers are short, there are competitive team Scattergory leagues, known for their ruthless play.

Prevalence and Etiology

Lesbian communities in rural areas generally contain one softball dyke per each 105 lesbians in the community whereas urban communities contain only one softball-afflicted lesbian per 2000 dykes. Serious softball madness affects far more butch lesbians than femme, and feminist softball pretenders tend to dress all in black when not on the ball diamond. One can discern the SSM from the FSP by examining the parking lot next to the ball diamond. The SSM parking lot is populated with motorcycles and muscle cars; the FSP with Prius' and Subaru's. SBN dykes are almost entirely femmes, although some serious softball teams have retired butch lesbians who rule the stands, although they tend to behave more like a sideline coach than a narcissistic diva. Some cases of softball madness afflictions can be attributed to too frequent viewing of *A League of Their Own*.

Treatment Considerations

Given the seasonal nature of softball in much of the United States, these conditions tend to ebb and flow and, therefore, not cause any long-term negative consequences. On the rare occasion when they become a form of lesbian event addiction (see DDM 8), steps need to be taken to wean the afflicted dyke from softball gradually. Most lesbians eventually give up softball voluntarily after years of knee injuries, rotator cuff tears, new relationships that take their time away from the diamond, and breakups with a team member. Break-ups among team members are a particularly effective way of eliminating softball madness, because one partner typically has to quit the team, be forced to retire, or join an opposing team. Often the animosities between teams created by varying feminist or activist philosophies make joining an opposing team nearly impossible for FSPs, although SSM dykes switch teams as readily as some dykes switch partners. Break-ups with umpires are particularly devastating to the serious softball dyke. Umpires are nearly as sought after as partners as are vets, particularly in rural dyke communities. Softball Bleacher Narcissists are hopeless. Any effort to wean them from the softball stands is generally unsuccessful, as they merely transfer their narcissistic performances to other dyke social formations, such as brunches. Encouraging them to channel their talents into dyke theater or becoming potluck hostesses best serves them.

DDM 17. Lesbian Collectivitis

Overview

Collectives are groups of 3 to 20 lesbians who coalesce around a common cause or purpose, such as event planning, health or social services, political actions, or book or journal publishing. This condition may be slowly phasing out from its peak in the 1970s, when lesbian feminist collectives proliferated in the United States. It is likely that even today, however, when groups of lesbians band together in common cause, even without calling themselves a collective, the same pathologies may manifest. Whereas lesbian collectives functioning at their optimal level can create wondrous new things such as a lesbian health center or a feminist bookstore, a dysfunctional collective will sap the life spirit from its members. Symptoms of lesbian collectivitis include an obsessive need to process even the smallest detail of the working of the collective (e.g., where they buy the organic free-trade coffee served at meetings), inability to arrive at consensus, and excessive meeting lengths related to allowing members unlimited time for check-ins. In fact, check-in and checkout may take one-half to three-fourths of the designated meeting time, leaving precious little time to accomplish tasks. The collective members often must process the same issues over and over, because they refuse to engage in patriarchal corporate business practices such as taking minutes of meetings or having a leader. Instead, they rotate the role of facilitator and rely on oral history. Relying on memory is highly problematic when the collective contains too many peri-menopausal members.

The members of the dysfunctional collective may experience chronic meeting fatigue syndrome as well as declines in lesbian self-esteem if they are unable to convince fellow collective members to follow their recommended political course of action. The world record lesbian collective meeting length was recorded in Madison, Wisconsin on April 4th of 1978, when a pride month meeting went for 16 hours without reaching consensus and three of the 14 members turned heterosexual the next day.

Lesbian collectives often move from functional to collectivitis when a mother superior lesbian (see DDM 6) decides that the group is moving too far from the rules, and performs a hostile take-over as "leader" thus corrupting the collective spirit. Other causes of the disorder are when two or more members become romantically involved, shifting the energy of the group, or even worse, when a couple in the collective break up, effectively splitting the collective into two opposing sides. This problem of romantic involvement and/or breakup is inevitable in lesbian collectives. Theoretically, any group containing five or more lesbians will spawn a new relationship within four months. Finally, some collectives devolve into collectivitis when two or more members develop competing political or theoretical ideologies that split the collective into factions.

Case Example

The Dyke Dog Park Collective of Mid-Central Ohio was founded in 2002 with a goal of creating a safe space for lesbians to cruise each other with their dogs (see DDM 1b). The original members were five single lesbians and one couple, with a combined total of 22 dogs. They were successful in creating the first lesbian dog park in their state, but then tensions arose when lesbians without dogs began to come into the space. The first big controversy to rock the collective was when one member posted a sign without consulting with the collective. The sign declared that the park was only for lesbian-born dog-lovers who currently had a dog, regardless of their past or future dog status. Other lesbians in the community were incensed by this rule. Some dykes with dog allergies wanted to be able to access the outer fringes of the dog park so they could satisfy their doggy longings, but felt unwelcome by the sign. Some potbelly pig owners protested that the policy discriminated against them and implied that their pigs were inferior to dogs. Their strident opinions about pigs being smarter than dogs upset the collective for months and led to much suffering from righteous indignation. The Dog Park Collective managed to weather this storm, but crumbled the next year when Jennifer, a femme lesbian with a cat on a leash, infiltrated the dog park to seduce Barb, an original collective member with a weakness for red-headed femmes. When Barb converted to femi-feline fetish disorder (see DDM 1a), the collective spirit was broken and it disbanded for good.

Prevalence and Etiology

Lesbian collectives are concentrated in cities, large or small, with strong feminist ideologies. In these fertile locations, collectives may flourish, and there may be 12 -15 active collectives at any given time. Most collectives that survive for two or more years suffer from lesbian collectivist at some point in their history, and this disorder is the leading cause of death of collectives. Lesbians join collectives for a variety of reasons, some noble and some more suspect motives. Less than noble causes that may set the stage for collectivitis are when women join purely because of a crush on another member, or a need for power in the lesbian community (such as the Lesbian Mother Superior types, see DDM 6).

There are many potential subtypes of lesbian collectivitis that have unique issues, depending on factors such as the type of interaction members have and the average number of DDM diagnoses among the members. For example, the lesbian softball collective may have collectivitis tinged with softball madness symptoms (see DDM 16) and a resultant inability to create a lineup. Having too many lesbian event junkies (see DDM 8) in any collective makes it difficult to identify meeting times. U-Haul lesbians are unreliable collective members and can cause discord by their frequent absences and demands on the collective to help them move. Finally, in all lesbian collectives, attention must be paid to menstrual synchronicities when planning important meetings, as it is possible for all of the members of a very close collective to synchronize their menstrual cycles (see DDM 15). Trying to make important decisions in a meeting where 14 individuals are collectively PMSing can have disastrous outcomes. Crone collectives must carefully guard against simultaneous peri-menopausal memory lapses, and require physical spaces with powerful air conditioning options. In some extreme cases, a lesbian collective devolves into a cult, and only de-programming can save the affected members.

Treatment Considerations

Luckily, larger lesbian communities have certified collective counselors; dykes who are specifically trained to work with collectives in dysfunction. As a side note, these collective counselors are also useful for lesbians with multiple ex-lover fusion issues (see DDM 3), whose extended family patterns can closely mimic a lesbian collective, although they rarely have a clear and consistent mission. Lesbian collectivitis can be prevented if membership requirements are enforced, such as: 1) Requiring five years of lesbianalysis to treat any existing DDM disorders prior to joining a collective; 2) lesbian self-identity strengthening training so that no member loses her individual identity to the greater collective; 3) dyke direct communication training to deal with conflict avoidance and passive-aggressive behavior in meetings; 4) absolutely no coupling with other collective members—new members must make a virginity pledge to remain dyke collective member abstinent while in the collective, and 5) no couples allowed. If both members of a couple want to belong, they must draw straws to determine which one can become a member. If two or more women in the collective have been lovers in the past, they may be asked to sign secondary virginity pledges.

If these rules are disregarded and a collective lapses into dysfunction, only extensive therapy with the whole group with a skilled lesbian collective counselor can save the collective. In some cases, a form of mass lesbian fusion disorder develops within the collective, and lesbian fission therapy is warranted.

DDM 18. Gender-Related Dyke Disorders

Overview

These disorders are linked to personality and behavioral traits that manifest along the disparate points on the butch-femme gender continuum, thus these disorders are more related to nuances of lesbian gender than to sexuality per se. As John Gray noted in the wildly successful (and completely sexist and heterosexist), *Men are from Mars, Women are from Venus* series, men and women are socialized differently. There are gender-based differences among lesbians as well, even if they are all women. The gender manifestations among dykes are much more subtle than gender expression in heterosexual women, and do not result in a "war of the sexes" as they do among heterosexual men and women. In lesbians, this phenomenon of gender variation leads to an intricate and fragile dance of the genders. As noted in the introduction to this manual, lesbian gender is a complicated phenomenon. Rather than only two points, butch or femme, various researchers have identified a wide range of different gender expressions along the continuum. Most often, a ten or eleven point (e.g., 0= very butch and 10= very femme) scale has been used, but one study of 38 lesbians found 38 different gender expressions. Obviously, the scale is not sophisticated enough to capture all the nuances of lesbian gender. Nor has there been sufficient study of gender variation over time, but anecdotal evidence suggests that fewer than one-third of lesbians have a consistent and stable BF number over time. The majority of dykes show shifts along the continuum across the dyke cycle, but particularly in the baby dyke phase, when women are exploring their gender, and in women with DDM 28, Multiple Dyke Personality Disorder, who are trying to fit a potential lover's expectations. Three gender-related dyke disorders have been identified thus far.

DDM 18a. Femme Gender Delusional Disorder

Many femme lesbians inexplicably declare themselves as butch, even when everyone who meets them, including complete strangers, can accurately identify their femme status. This delusional femme will gesticulate wildly with her well-manicured hands sporting blood red perfectly painted fingernails, and tap her high-heeled toes while insisting that because she once fixed the toaster (i.e., plugged it in), that she is butch. Afflicted femmes will insist that they are strong and assertive, thus butch. The delusion lies in equating being bossy with being butch.

In reality, bossiness is a common, maybe even core trait of the femme, and owning a battery-operated screwdriver or vibrator does not make them into a power-tool toting butch. Skill with a sewing machine does not make one a butch, unless she can take apart the apparatus, oil the parts, and successfully reassemble the motor. Whereas femmes often profess to be butch, butch dykes have never suffered delusions of femme-hood in over 30 years of epidemiological and ethnographic study.

Case Example

Diana was a 50 year-old highly successful professional woman in a ten-year relationship with Kay, who complained that Diana refused to accept her femme-hood. Kay felt that this delusional belief was negatively affecting their relationship. Kay scheduled brunch with a well-known lesbian gender expert in the community to discuss this dilemma. This expert, Jo, had been in four butch-femme relationships over the past 12 year and wrote a blog about gender for the local lesbian community website. Diana came to brunch dressed in a low cut sleeveless black dress with dangling earrings, three inch heels, dark mauve lipstick and nails to match, and her curly dark brown hair cascaded halfway down her back. She buffed her nails as Jo asked her questions about her interests, wardrobe, emotional reactions, communication style, and relational patterns. Diana revealed that in her spare time, she enjoyed watching *Project Runway*, collecting antique dolls, and making her own jewelry. Kay added that Diana's clothing and shoes took up three-fourths of their storage space, and that her hair products alone overwhelmed the available bathroom shelf space. Kay related that Diana refused to help her with the gardening because she might break a nail. When Diana was asked why she thought of herself as a butch, she replied that she rode a motorcycle and loved softball. Kay quickly added that the motorcycle was a pink Vespa scooter and that Diana liked to watch softball, not play it. Jo adroitly and quickly concluded that this was a classic case of femme gender delusional disorder and initiated gender reality training to help Diana embrace her femme-ness. This consisted of attending a butch-femme social mingle the following weekend. Diana was instructed to spend 15 minutes talking to a group of butches, and then 15 minutes talking to a group of femmes, and decide where she felt most comfortable. This simple exercise cured Diana of her femme-delusional disorder.

DDM 18b. Butch Conversational Deficit Disorder

One prototype of the butch personality is the strong, silent type, but this type can have a pathological side when taken to the extreme. The condition stems from a fear of femme-initity, or an irrational fear of being perceived as femme. The butch lesbian with this disorder has a unique language, consisting of monosyllables, flat tone, long silences, a tendency to mumble, and a restricted list of approved conversational topics. This list of acceptable topics might include discussion of sports (especially lesbian softball or women's field hockey), merits of light versus regular beer (or in upper class circles, Merlot versus Syrah), pet behavior, and cool cars. Taboo topics will include feelings, make-up, shopping, interior design, and fashion in any form. Bossy femmes who like to talk may be initially drawn to these non-conversational butches, and if they do not care if they get a response to their monologues, the relationship may work. Two non-conversational butches in a relationship together very closely resemble the cowboy duo in *Brokeback Mountain*.

Case Example

Chaz is a 32-year old butch lesbian from a working class family in the Midwest. She also suffers from lesbian event addiction and never misses a game of the local women's college basketball team or the women's national basketball association on TV. For the past seven months, she has been dating Shelly, an outgoing femme who initially found Chaz to be "mysterious" and a relief after her last girlfriend who suffered from Lesbian Emotionally Exhausting Process Disorder (see DDM 30). Now Shelly feels frustrated by Chaz's tendency to merely grunt when she asks her a question about her feelings. On several occasions Shelley proposed that they dine at Shelly's favorite Indian restaurant, and each time, Chaz said, "Cool." Later an ex-lover of Chaz' told Shelly that Chaz hated Indian food, but would agree to avoid a lengthy discussion about alternatives. Shelly insisted on going to therapy with a student psychology intern. When the student therapist asked Chaz why she was resistant to conversation with Shelly, who she appeared to love, Chaz replied, "Because." When the therapist pressed her to explain, she said, "Just because," and never returned to therapy. In fact, butch non-conversationalists are the only subgroup of the lesbian community who hate and actively avoid therapy. As Chaz said incredulously to Shelly, "Pay someone to complain? No way." It was the longest utterance of their relationship. Ultimately, they broke up and Shelly found a butch who was one point higher on the BF scale and correspondingly more communicative.

DDM 18c. Butch-Femme Fence-sitters

Some women manifest a delusional belief that they are exempt from the gender continuum. They adamantly refuse to label themselves along the continuum and abhor the labels of butch and femme, masculine and feminine, girly or boyish, or any gender-related language of any sort. The condition is a form of cognitive distortion or even delusional disorder. No matter what one says, no dyke can escape gender classifications on the planet Earth, and lesbians are particularly gender-obsessing creatures. She may resist labeling herself, but everyone around her pegs her along the gender continuum. This condition is not to be confused with a self-identified butch who is forced to wear more feminine attire and act more feminine because of job or family pressures. She is readily identified as a butch in disguise by other dykes. Another differential dykignosis is the butch in femme body, a condition whereby the outward appearance and physical body are highly feminine, but the personality and behaviors manifests as butch. This exceedingly rare condition is an example of a hermaphrodyke condition.

Case Example

Kim is a 63-year-old lesbian who came out in the heyday of the women's consciousness raising movement when androgyny was the goal. She is semi-retired and lives in a separatist women's land commune. She made a remark to a hostess of a lesbian potluck that butch-femme "role-playing" was a phenomenon of the past, and had been eradicated in the 1970s. When the hostess pressed her to explain why she thought that, she said that feminism had erased gender inequality for the majority of women, and that lesbians were above gender. The hostess then pointed out two couples at the potluck who were organizers of the local butch-femme conference, one trans-masculine guest at the party, a woman who regularly performed as a drag king, and three members of the Femme Fatales Barbershop Quartet group. Kim continued to deny the power of gender. She was dressed in jeans, work boots, and a plaid flannel shirt with a "dykes to watch out for" t-shirt under the flannel. Kim had very short hair, never wore makeup, and absolutely refused to carry a purse, making her girlfriend carry all of her necessities in a large satchel. When the hostess pointed out that Kim looked like a "soft butch," she was extremely offended and said she had no idea what the woman was talking about. Other women at the potluck concurred and gave Kim an average rating of 3.51 (range of 2 to 4.5) on the 0 to 10 butch-femme scale, confirming that she was firmly situated along the butch side of the continuum. In spite of this empirical evidence, Kim continued to deny that she was butch or femme, and continued to refuse to believe that butch/femme distinctions even existed.

Prevalence and Etiology

Gender-related dyke disorders are fairly common, with 38% of femme lesbians on occasion labeling themselves as butch. The condition may be related to a faulty belief that femme and feminine are the same thing, and the femme who claims a butch identity merely does not want to be seen as similar to a heterosexual feminine woman. Butch conversational condition increases in frequency as one goes farther down the masculine side of the gender continuum, with only about 9% of androgynous women so afflicted but 15% of moderate butches and 21% of extremely butch women are conversationally impaired. The condition is caused by an irrational fear of being perceived as "girly." Finally, 8% of lesbians are butch-femme fence sitters. All three of these conditions are forms of delusional thinking and distorted gender body image. Some earlier literature in the dyke archives suggested that a dyke cross-dresser syndrome might be a form of gender-related dykignosis, because of the incongruity of a butch lesbian in feminine attire, and the extreme discomfort of a femme in flannel. However, these cases of cross-dressing tend to be short-term, as in the butch lesbian who must dress up for a family wedding, or a femme who is experimenting with butch clothing. In both cases, they see the error of their ways quickly.

Treatment Considerations

Femme delusional disorders can typically be ignored, as they cause little harm, and even make for funny anecdotes to tell at lesbian brunches. If they cause relationship problems, the afflicted woman can be taught to chant affirmations such as "femme is fine." Butch conversational disorder can be a fairly serious problem that can profoundly affect relationship satisfaction. In some cases, falling in love can reduce the severity of the disorder. Lust hormones tend to loosen the tongue, an advantage for both conversation and sex. The butch who trusts her partner may open up in selected situations, such as after lovemaking. If the partner is satisfied with these ten minutes of intimate conversation once a week, the relationship may survive. Two conversationally impaired butches in a relationship together may learn to communicate by subtle gesture or twitch of eyebrow, and have no need to learn better verbal communication. Sometimes, however, the conversationally impaired butch needs to be paired with a Lesbian Emotionally Exhausting Processing (LEEP; see DDM 30) dyke for two or three hours, as a form of aversive therapy. This exposure to the process dyke helps her to appreciate her own partner and open up to her, but the therapist must be carefully not to overexpose the butch to lesbian processing or post-traumatic processing disorder may occur.

Those who have butch-femme fence-sitter disorder can often be treated through reality awareness training. Teaching her to really look at the diverse gender expressions of members of the lesbian communities around her can be eye-opening. When it comes to gender typing in contemporary lesbian society, resistance is futile and all dykes are encouraged to know their BF (butch-femme) number. There are currently several BF number rating scales and aptitude tests on the market to help afflicted and confused lesbians find themselves. Two such tools are included in the assessment section of this manual.

DDM 19. Chronic Lesbian Event Fatigue Syndrome

Overview

This condition is a subtype of chronic fatigue syndrome brought on by the lesbian event. Historically, before the internet and tweeting, lesbian events such as concerts, plays, talent shows, poetry readings, and other performances, were opportunities to share information, raise consciousness, impart the rules of the community, and help women connect with the lesbian community. However, in an effort to be inclusive and community building, even today when websites and listservs could be used for information dissemination, sometimes the announcements at the beginning of the event are longer than the event itself, and can become a source of stress, and even disorder, for participants.

Announcements generally include requests to avoid any scented products (too late since the audience is already there!) and to refrain from any comments or behaviors that might seem objectifying of women (e.g., no cat calls or whistling). Audience members are urged to boycott a dozen or so local businesses that were found to contribute to conservative causes, treat some local lesbian badly, whether she deserved it or not, or did not support the local dyke dog park. The organizers of the event take the stage to plead for support for local lesbian causes, such as the Dyke Urban Gardeners (DUG) association or the lesbian mystery writer's club. They attempt to solicit volunteers for political campaigns and take-back-the-night rallies, to help a lesbian whose dog needed surgery to pay for in-home doggy-nursing care, and to share the brunch, potluck, and softball schedules. The announcements often end with an impassioned recounting of the pain that lesbians have experienced from being excluded by society. The organizer then irrationally concludes that this event is all the more special because it is strictly for lesbians who are womyn-born-womyn, never sleep with men, are feminists, and does not allow male children over the age of ten to attend.

Next the speaker must acknowledge all the lesbians who helped to organize the event; the one who first mentioned to her partner, now ex, two years ago that the community should host this event, her current partner who supported her to manifest the idea, the dyke who designed the variation on the double women's symbol for the logo, the couple who donated a ream of paper to make flyers, the technologically advanced dyke who created the website, and the 40 members of the collective who planned the event, as well as their partners and pets who had to put up with their absence every Wednesday night for planning meetings.

A contributing factor to the lesbian event exhaustion syndrome is brought on by the anxieties of the lesbian sliding scale fee at the majority of events. Each impoverished lesbian enters the door in a cold sweat, trying to decide whether to pay full price or suffer the humiliation of having to say to the dyke at the door that she wishes to get some money back from her $20 bill. These transactions are conducted in hushed whispers and horrifying awkward moments.

Finally, because of the general lack of funds to support most lesbian events, the events are held in small, cheap, run-down locations. Poor ventilation combines with the exhortations against using scents and a general lesbian animosity toward deodorant, so the room can quickly reek of sweat, noxious animal odors clinging to the polyanimalry dykes (see DDM 1d), sage sticks carried in the purse of some dykes who never know when they might be in need of emergency aura cleansing or smudging, faint whiffs of patchouli from the old hippy dykes, and Brut cologne worn by working class butches in outright defiance of the prohibitions against scent. The lesbian smokers come in after one desperate puffing session in the alley, trying to get enough nicotine in their systems to hold them through the lengthy event. The stench from the tobacco that lingers in the hair and clothing of smokers may serve as a trigger for the dykes who have just quit smoking and enrages the even larger number of lesbians who are allergic or hypersensitive to tobacco smoke. The folding chairs, if there are any, are so rickety that audience members fear for their well-being if they breathe too deeply or change positions. The sound system borrowed from a local elementary school where one of the organizers works screeches and squeals at an eardrum piercing level. Finally, there is only one bathroom with two stalls, not nearly enough to accommodate the peri-menopausal crowd's overactive bladders. These physical conditions heighten the emotional exhaustion of the announcements and the event itself.

Case Example

Leanne lived in a small, close-knit lesbian community on the east coast. This community had ten lesbian collectives, a women's center, a lesbian bookstore, a dyke coffee house, and was home to several members of the 1970s women's music scene. The community had many events, averaging five per month, all of which were fundraisers for some cause, collective, or organization. Each event had a

148

"pay what you are able" policy. As a member of three of the collectives and co-owner of the bookstore, Leanne felt pressured to attend most of the events, but her meager salary as a social worker at the free medical clinic prohibited donations to every cause. One night in late June, after the tenth event that pride month, Leanne had a nervous breakdown at the door to the lesbian talent show competition to raise money for the feline leukemia fund. She saw the sign about the sliding scale, reached into her wallet to pull out some cash, but could not make a decision about how much to pay. She collapsed against the door whimpering about class privilege and the evils of money. The event organizers had to call the DDM hotline to send someone to talk her down and help her make this difficult decision. Luckily, the announcements before the show took 90 minutes, so Leanne was able to get a quick chiropractic adjustment, re-align her chakras, have a brief EMDR session, decide how much to contribute, and still have time to find a seat before the talent show began.

Prevalence and Etiology

Lesbians often feel isolated and need to take advantage of live community events to share as much information as possible. Unfortunately, this can lead to information overload and blow out brain circuits much like internet networks shut down when there is too much cyber traffic. Women who respond to the messages on these listservs rather than privately message the requests for information contribute to this information brown-out. For example, a request on one site for information about a cat hospice led to 247 replies in one day and led to the resignation of the volunteer moderator of the web-site.

Forty percent of local community lesbian events have excessively long announcements, and 20% of actual lesbian main events exceed the average dyke attention span and physical comfort zone. Individual lesbians at these events may suffer from tension headaches or have a tendency to daydream about some woman on whom they have a crush during long announcements, and consequently, do not hear/remember the announcements so they must be repeated at the next event, creating a vicious self-perpetuating cycle. Sliding scale payment systems are present in 82% of feminist events and 41% of non-feminist lesbian events, adding to the overall event stress level.

Treatment Considerations

Lesbian listservs and websites have done much to relieve this problem by providing more self-guided information options to share

149

lesbian social, recreational, and political activities, however, a newly emerging condition is the Lesbian Listserv Brown-out Syndrome. This condition is currently under study for the next edition of the DDM. For example, in March of 2014, one urban lesbian social listserv purportedly sent 26 lengthy posts per day for a week to the 19,674 dykes on the list, overloading the lesbian motherboard circuits in 46% of the computers.

Lesbians who suffer from event fatigue syndrome must simply reduce the number of events they attend each month, take a break from all events until they restore their mental health, or arrive 30 minutes late for the event, missing at least half of the announcements. For those with lesbian event addictions, the treatment is somewhat more complicated. They need extensive education about how to identify their limits and acquire strategies for not overindulging in lesbian events. When lesbians go to an event as a group, a designated driver can be selected, one who does not attend the event, but chaperones those who do and serves as a lay-therapist to reduce their anxiety or frustration symptoms after the event. Finally, event planners need to take into consideration their audience and attempt to find volunteer dyke physical therapists to help the older dykes get out of the uncomfortable chairs after three hours without causing serious injury to themselves and those around them.

DDM 20. Two-Stepping Twelve Steppers (2-12 Dykes)

Overview

A curious dual dykignosis among many lesbians is the concurrent addiction to 12-step meetings and two-step forms of dancing. Afflicted lesbians appear to be drawn to the counting aspects of these activities, and may or may not be in recovery from some substance or addictive behavior. The dykignosis of 2-12 is based on attending two or more 12-step groups per week plus at least one 2-step dance per week. Some two-stepping 12 steppers are therapy junkies who live in areas without a lesbian therapist, or who have burned out every lesbian therapist, bartender, hairdresser, potluck hostess, and softball team in a 100-mile radius. So, one-two (combined equals 12), the dance becomes another step. Lesbians with this affliction are likely to speak in an unusually truncated language that might be difficult for outsiders to understand. For example, if someone shares a difficult situation she is experiencing the 2-12 dyke may say, "one day at a time," "live and let live," or "easy does it." If a woman is chatting with another dyke at a brunch when the 2-12 dyke is trying to address the group, she may be accused of "cross-talking." In the United States, this is one of the most common co-occurring lesbian disorders. It remains to be seen whether a variation of this disorder might occur in countries without knowledge of 12 step programs, or whose dance customs do not include a two-step option.

Case Example

Nan is a 48 year-old lesbian from rural Texas. She attends at least one 12-step meeting every day, even though she does not drink or use drugs, and has never experienced shopping, gambling, food, sex, or Internet addictions. She writes religiously in her 12 step journals twice every day, and has worked her way entirely through the twelve steps three times in the past five years. She states that she likes the people who attend these meetings and resonates with the 12-step philosophy. She loves to read self-help books, especially the ones that lay out their programs in numbered steps or stages. Even though she has always been thin, she belongs to a weight loss program because she enjoys counting calories and attending support groups. When she introduces herself at 12-step meetings, she says, "Hi, I'm Nan and I'm a 12 step addict." Every Friday night, she goes to a Texas two-step dance, and on Saturdays, to a swing dance party. During the week, she has to travel 80 miles to another community for country line dancing on Wednesday nights. She calls her

AA sponsor twice every day to check in. Nan has had ten different sponsors in the past 18 months and is puzzled as to why she cannot seem to maintain a relationship with one consistent sponsor. Her solution to any life problem she encounters is "90 dances in 90 days."

Prevalence and Etiology

Two percent of lesbians have this combination of two-step and 12-step addiction, which appears to arise from a lack of meaning and structure in one's life creating an existential craving for even numbers and the comforting act of counting. 2-12 disorder is often prompted by some form of identity crisis, such as those that can arise from the traumas of coming out, graduating from college, breaking up from a long-term relationship, or losing a pet to death or ex-lover custody situation. The afflicted dyke feels adrift and does not know who she is.

Both two-step dancing and 12-step programs impose fairly rigid structures and rules for conducting one's life, on which these women appear to thrive. Some lesbians have an actual addiction problem, and for them, the right 12 step programs can be highly beneficial. However, they should be counseled to avoid dancing until their recovery is stable, as dancing can easily become a replacement addiction. Excessive dancing, even when not addictive, can have many negative consequences, including physical injury such as knee disorders and hip dislocations. It can also result in sexual problems such as the triggering of lust reactions with virtual strangers and the resultant aftermath of such couplings. Many older lesbians are suffering the consequences of excessive dancing episodes in their youth. For example, the number one cause of knee replacement surgeries in older lesbians is chronic exuberant dancing in their younger years.

Treatment Considerations

Many afflicted lesbians merely need a cause to give their lives meaning, so volunteering at the animal shelter or women's press collective may be sufficient to reduce her reliance on 12 step and two-step sessions. However, attendance at these other events must be closely monitored in case they become replacement addictions (see DDM 8 for information about the addictive quality of many lesbian events). Wiccan groups are contra-indicated for replacement therapies, because the requirement to have 13 women to constitute a coven is too disconcerting to the even-numbered 2-12 dykes. They are similarly disturbed by the idea of a threesome, and abhor softball because of the uneven number of

152

players on a team. A growing number of lesbian communities have initiated Dancers Anonymous, an 11 step meeting to help reduce the effects of excessive dancing on the health and wellbeing of lesbians, that will not have the addictive potential of a 12-step program.

DDM 21. Obsessive Cum-pulsive Disorder

Overview

Some lesbians who have had prior experience with selfish men, or who have Lesbian Mother Superior tendencies (see DDM 6), develop an obsessive need to strive for completely equal relationships. Each member of the duo (and it must be a relationship of 2, or at least even numbers) must pay exactly the same amount for household expenses, share equally in all the activities that constitute the household work, and participate in all decisions regarding the household at an equal level. If they go out to eat, they split the check exactly in half.

In terms of the relationship maintenance activities, each member of the relationship has to say, "I love you," exactly the same number of times each day and initiate hugs equally. When this disorder extends to sex, ideally the OC lesbian wants simultaneous orgasms. As lesbian sexnographic research has shown, this is difficult, and typically happens only in the movies. When thwarted in her attempt to stage simultaneous orgasm, the lesbian with this disorder must resort to the next best option—having the same number and intensity of orgasms in a sexual encounter. No matter how tired or distracted the partner, the afflicted member of the relationship strives for complete equality in amount of time devoted to lovemaking and quality and strength of orgasms. As noble a goal as this seems, in reality, it can be an exhausting and disappointing endeavor, and can destroy relationships.

Case Example

Billie is a 55-year-old lesbian separatist feminist who is exactly in the middle of the butch/femme continuum. She had been married to a man for 30 years before coming out, and is now in her first lesbian relationship with Tesa. They have been together for 11 months, and Tesa is threatening to break up with her. They come to therapy to see if the relationship can be saved. Billie reports that she finds Tesa's lapses into more feminine attire and behavior disturbing and wants her to be more androgynous so that they maintain an identical BF score. She is also concerned with Tesa's lack of interest in going to dog shows with Billie. Tesa believes that it is acceptable, and even desirable, to have separate interests and activities, but her concerns are mostly about their sexual life. She complains that Billie has a stopwatch and clipboard on the bedside stand and records the amount of time it takes for each to bring

154

the other to orgasm. Billie has also installed a seismograph in their mattress to record the intensity of the orgasm, and Tesa has begun to suffer from dyke sexual performance disorder (see DDM 11). Billie argues that not paying close attention to the details of their lovemaking feels too "hetero-normative." Tesa counters that Billie's obsession about equality in sex makes her long for her simpler heterosexual life when she could count on men being selfish and not caring about her pleasure. The therapist was unable to save the relationship, and Billie is still in search of the mythic equal relationship.

Prevalence and Etiology

Dykes suffering from the chronic form of this disorder are fairly rare (1.4%), however milder, temporary forms of orgasm bookkeeping occur in 24.2% of lesbians in at least one relationship in their lifetimes. Often the condition is found early in the feminist stages of the coming out process but typically dissipates naturally as the realities of relationships sets in. The cause is an idealizing of two premises of radical feminism. The first is a delusional belief that women are superior beings, and the second is an irrational assumption that total equality is possible in a relationship. Excessive reading of 1970s lesbian feminist texts is partly responsible for this condition.

Treatment Considerations

In extreme cases, like Billie's, reality therapy is aimed at showing that completely equal relationships are impossible. The afflicted dyke is banned from reading 1970s feminist texts exhorting the superiority of lesbian relationships or romance novels that perpetuate the myth of the simultaneous orgasm. Instead, those with the OC condition are assigned homework to study the relationship dynamics on seasons 3-4 of *The L Word*. However, all sex scenes must be deleted from these tapes to avoid reinforcing her unrealistic views of lesbian sex. She is absolutely prohibited from using a stopwatch or taking notes during sex. In some cases, it may be useful to limit the afflicted dyke to solo sexual activities with no sex toys, for a period of one month, with careful tracking of her orgasmic experiences. She may discover that if she cannot give herself consistently high quality orgasms, that partnered sex is also likely to be inconsistent and unpredictable.

DDM 22. Gay-Dar Deficiency Disorder

Overview

Although even the mainstream media is full of references to gay-dar, a unique ability of lesbians (and other queer folk) to intuitively identify each other, there are many dykes with very little of this precious commodity. Gay-dar is one of many forms of extragaysensory perception, and is almost as rare as ghost whispering. Theoretically, gay-dar is a genetdyk trait that controls a pathway in the brain. When the gaydar gene is not present, the individual lacks circuits in neural pathways to connect the auditory, olfactory, and visual cortices to the logical reasoning centers of the brain. That is, the gay-dar pathway facilitates the putting together of sensory cues from the lower brain regions, including visual cues such as how woman walks, auditory cues such as scent, and verbal cues such as lesbian code word recognition, with higher cortex reasoning centers, resulting in the "aha" moment of identification. Unfortunately, the reality of the situation is that gay-dar depends more highly on environment than biology, and stereotypes about how lesbians are supposed to look, sound, and smell, and what interests and activities she should engage matters more than the neurochemistry and neuroanatomy. If the object of the gay-dar focus is not stereotypically lesbian (and only a small number are) or does not have a t-shirt or button that declares her sexuality, even fully functioning gay-dar is riddled with error.

Case Example

Sally, a 38-year-old IT specialist, was at a work-related party when a woman joined the group where she was conversing with four other people from their large agency. She was introduced as Jamie, a woman of indeterminate age somewhere between 30 and 50; she was not wearing any make-up, had short spiky hair, wore sensible comfortable shoes, seemed confident and assured, and looked Sally directly in the eye when speaking to her. She smelled faintly of patchouli. In the course of the conversation, Sally discovered that she was an avid fan of a local university women's basketball team and played on a rugby team on the weekends. Gay-dar was setting off lesbian detector alarms in Sally's head, but then Jamie leaned on the arm of a good-looking male coworker and started flirting outrageously. Was she or wasn't she? Sally called the DDM hotline because she was attracted to Jamie, and was concerned that her gay-dar was malfunctioning.

156

Prevalence and Etiology

Gay-dar deficiency disorder affects 75.8% of lesbians in the U.S. Unlike many of the disorders in this manual that are created by glitches in education or socialization, gay-dar deficiency stems from a gene-environment interaction. Fewer than 5% of women have a double dose of the gay-dar gene. Those fortunate women are nearly 100% accurate in identifying other lesbians, no matter how closeted. Women with only one allele for the gay-dar gene, or with partial expression (10.2% of the population), are accurate about 60% of the time. The majority of dykes lack the gene, and have to rely on endogenous stereotype detector proteins in the brain to identify other lesbians. No matter how much training they have, they are no better than chance at identifying another lesbian unless she displays at least three lesbian stereotypes or directly announces her sexuality. Even then, some lesbians do not believe that she is really a dyke. The most negative consequence of gay-dar deficiency disorder is that many afflicted lesbians will waste precious weeks and even months pursuing a straight woman who fits one or more lesbian stereotypes, but completely miss the signals of a very real lesbian who does not fit stereotypes. Femme women in particular suffer from this lack of gay-dar in other women. One research participant in a DDM study reported that her lesbian gynecologist (a semi-butch woman) had such poor gay-dar, that the patient had to come out to her as a dyke on every single annual visit for 14 consecutive years. Even though her identity as a lesbian was written in the file, this gay-dar deficit doctor could not see her as a dyke.

Treatment Considerations

Gene therapy has not yet been successful at remedying this condition. Researchers are in the process of perfecting an invisible ink that can be used to label lesbians with a large lavender L on their foreheads for easy identification, negating the need for gay-dar entirely. Each dyke upon coming out would be supplied with special contact lenses or glasses to be able to read the lavender L. In addition, Congress is on the verge of approving a new government agency, the Lesbian Recruiting Office where dykes can register. Since the repeal of Don't ask, Don't tell, Lesbian Recruiting Offices will be located within military recruiting centers, as well as in post offices across the country. These important bureaucratic centers will administer dyke fitness tests, train women to act unambiguously like dykes, and apply the lavender L tattoo, so that they do not confuse potential lovers and friends. In the future, GPS navigation units may be equipped with lesbian sensory detectors, so that dykes can find each other as easily as they can find an ATM. With a little technological finesse, perhaps the GPS can give directions to her heart as well as identify DDM dykignoses.

DDM 23. The Barn OWL

Overview

In many rural lesbian communities, mature, mostly White lesbians, or OWLS (older, wiser lesbians) do much of their socializing on "women's land." These properties are typically old farm houses with a few out buildings that are owned or rented by lesbian feminists, wiccans, neopagans, spiritualists, and/or those suffering from a concurrent polyanimalry disorder (see DDM 1d). If there is a shed large enough for more than three lesbians to congregate, it is designated a "barn." Many activities may occur in the barn, including country line dances, drumming rituals, crone inductions, meetings of lesbian collectives, smudging, steam room rituals, basket weaving classes, goddess rites, coven meetings, exorcisms, feminist therapy sessions, consciousness raising groups, and a variety of appropriations of other cultural rituals and practices. Although some lesbians become Barn OWLS to get away from society, a subset are committed to the betterment of lesbian society in general by offering "back to nature" experiences at their land. For example, if they have an extra bedroom, they may bill the place as a "bed and breakfast" for lesbians and teach sheep cheese-making techniques as a bonus. Other Barn Owls grow their own produce and bake all organic vegan goods to sell at local dyke farmer's markets. Barn OWLS are to be distinguished from the larger social organization of "land-dyke" or lesbians who own rural properties because they can no longer afford to live in the city, but without demonstrating Barn OWL tendencies.

Case Example

Sharon and Lucy lived on a small parcel of land with a two bedroom house, ramshackle shed, and drafty old dairy barn on the edge of a small city in the Midwest, located one block from the super Wal-Mart. Sharon, at 63 years of age, was an "earth mother" type who wore Birkenstocks year round, fringed peasant skirts and shawls, and had her red hair in a long braid down her back. Lucy, who was 59, favored a lesbian-goth look, dressing in black billowing skirts and she dyed her hair a pitch black that was disconcerting against her pale white skin and blue eyes. Phyl, who was Lucy's ex thrice removed, occasionally lived with them when she was between relationships (she suffered from Lesbian MSM, see DDM 27, so that was often), and was their "handi-dyke." She was skilled with the weed whacker and tended to dress in coveralls and flannel. In their first year on the land, they turned the shed

159

into a sweat lodge and installed a "sacred pool," a used hot tub that they designated for lesbian goddess rituals. These goddess induction ceremonies were actually an excuse for Sharon and Lucy, who suffered from Lesbian Bed Death (see DDM 12b), to look at other women's naked bodies. They had frequent community events on their property, which other dykes in the community referred to as "THE LAND," in a hushed sacred whisper. The national anthem at THE LAND was the Indigo Girls, *Closer to Fine*. This triad also suffered from lesbian polyanimalry, and had a herd of llama along with eight cats, four dogs, ten chickens, three geese, a heard of sheep, and five pygmy goats. The llamas were all female, and were used in some of the goddess rites as symbols of female sexuality because lesbian llamas are particularly sexually active creatures.

Prevalence and Etiology

Most studies of Barn OWLs have been conducted in rural areas of the United States, because the OWLS appear to suffer in overcrowded urban areas where they are forced to interact with too many men and straight women, and they typically have to flee back to the country. Approximately 5% of the lesbian population over the age of 50 suffers from the Barn OWL affliction, which stems from an irrational glorification of the primitive past and refusal to keep up with new lesbian trends in theory, music, politics, and leisure activities. Barn OWLs can remain mired in 1970s separatist lesbian culture by isolating themselves in these remote locations, blocks from the nearest Target superstore in homes without high-speed internet access. One member of the expert panel noted that there may be an urban counterpart for the Barn OWL that has many of the same features without the land component—they may seek houses with basement rumpus rooms that can be converted into sacred pagan caves or hermetically sealed womyn-only spaces. This urban variation of Barn OWL may isolate socially rather than geographically. This subtype has yet to be thoroughly explored.

Treatment Consideration

Barn OWLs are largely harmless, although some land dykes have a tendency toward Lesbian Mother Superior disorder (see DDM 6). Most of them have never seen *Queer as Folk*, *The L Word*, or *Orange is the New Black*, so viewing of the pilot episodes of any of these series may open their eyes to contemporary varieties of lesbian culture and the broader queer community or frighten them back to the sacred pond.

Dykes with strong affiliations with that wider queer community rarely interact socially with Barn OWLs, and make highly inappropriate partners. In future revisions of the DDM, the Barn OWL may be shifted to a personality type of lesbian rather than a disorder per se. They are more of a curious anachronism than a disorder, and may actually serve a useful purpose as collectors of lesbian history and rituals.

DDM 24. Lesbian Erect-tile Dysfunction

Overview
This condition reflects the tendency of do-it-yourself inclined lesbians to begin construction projects but never finish them. There appears to be substantially more DIYs per capita in the lesbian community than among heterosexual women, with some reported data estimating that nearly 40% of lesbians have some degree of DIY tendencies compared to 17% of heterosexual women. The afflicted lesbian may lay two square feet of new tile in the kitchen, but a year later, has not finished the other 50 square feet. In addition to tiling completion deficits, this dyke suffers from lack of completion of plumbing, carpentry, painting, and electrical tasks, as well as difficulty washing the dishes and folding clothes. Occasionally, the disorder extends to sex as well, and this afflicted lesbian stops in the middle of sex to start a load of laundry or stir some paint, and fails to return to bed. The clothes begin to mold in the washer because she forgets to move them to the dryer in a timely fashion, and the paint dries into rubbery goo. Even worse, her partner may develop a dependence on sex toys to satisfy her unfulfilled desires when the ED dyke wanders off during sex.

Historically, there was another condition with a similar label of lesbian erectile dysfunction that referred to an inability to wear one's hair in short spikes. However, it was noted that lesbian hairstyles fluctuate too much to have a stable diagnostic category for lesbian hair, and the term is now reserved strictly for project completion disorders.

Case Example
Lee is a 24-year-old student and file clerk who had a secret desire to be a general contractor. Lee is a 2.8 on a butch-femme scale of 0 to 10 where 0 = extremely butch. She lives with Maya, her partner of ten months, in the older home that Maya inherited from her grandmother. Initially, Maya was thrilled to have a DIY girlfriend, as she herself was not skilled with power tools. Thus far, Lee has removed the kitchen cabinet doors to be sanded and re-stained (they are stacked in the garage), and pulled up carpeting from the living room to reveal unsalvageable warped wood floors beneath (the old carpet is mildewing in the garage, where it has been blocking access to the lawnmower for three weeks). She has removed the toilet from the guest bathroom in preparation to lay new tile floors (the toilet now sits in the middle of the hallway), and prepped the bedroom for painting with blue painter's tape,

162

but has not selected the paint color yet. She is vacillating between lavender and purple. Lee's tools are strewn throughout the house, and Maya has stubbed her toe twice on the sledgehammer parked in the bathroom. Lee also has a tendency to drop her clothes on the floor when she undresses, and none of her clothing is on hangers or folded in dresser drawers. Maya has given Lee an ultimatum; complete at least one project in one month, or she will end the relationship.

Prevalence and Etiology

Lesbian erect-tile dysfunction is present in 26% of lesbians with a DIY tendency and may co-exist with an HGTV addiction, but manifests differently along various points of the butch-femme continuum. Butch lesbians are most likely to fail to complete home re-modeling projects after the initial demolition; femme lesbians often fail to complete sewing or home decorating projects; and lesbians in the center of the continuum may start hobbies such as stained glass projects, and leave the shards of glass on the dining room table for six months. Some lesbians have superficial symptoms of this disorder, but they are only pretending to be DIY dykes so that they can wear the tool belt. In this case, task non-completion is inevitable, so the treatment is the same for DIY pretenders and actual lesbian erect-tile dysfunction disorder. In both cases, the DIY dyke and the Erect-tile Dysfunction dyke should be considered as SIY (start-it-yourself) rather than DIY. Finally, some lesbians develop erect-tile dysfunction because of an underlying addiction to the demolition process, a much more stimulating and easy process than construction. This attraction to demolition may be an unconscious defense mechanism related to societal homophobia. It is not socially acceptable for the stigmatized dyke to act out aggressively toward homophobic bosses, churches, vice presidents, or IRS agents, thus they take out their violent impulses on kitchen cabinets. Another theory is that demolition is favored because it requires absolutely no skill, whereas construction requires considerable practice and acquiring of abilities to measure, calculate, and commit to hard work.

Treatment

For lesbian hobby non-completers with plenty of living space, a room or workshop can be designated for projects, so that the un-afflicted partner does not have to live in the mess. Non-completion of construction projects is more challenging to treat. One method involves drawing up a contract with a timeline for completion and a signed commitment that the affected dyke will have to pay for a professional to complete the job if she violates the contract. This works particularly well with butch dykes, who feel considerable shame if they have to hire a professional plumber or carpenter, and thus, are highly motivated to complete the task herself. If a concomitant HGTV addiction is involved, giving up cable TV is strongly advised. If both partners of a relationship are affected with Erect-tile dysfunction, the relationship might work, but their home is doomed. They will never meet qualifications for hosting lesbian potlucks because of the disarray of their home. Erect-tile dysfunction during sex is inexcusable and grounds for immediate relationship breakup. In fact, a concurrent dykignosis of Erectile Dysfunction in both members of a relationship may constitute a new home décor personality type, with the house in the middle stages of a "flip" for long periods of time.

DDM 25. Late-Onset Lesbians (LOL)

Overview

One piece of lesbian folklore advice in the U.S. is "do not get involved with a newly-out woman." This wisdom stems in part from the experiences some dykes have had with a subset of women who come out later in life. These LOL lesbians do not come out until after decades of heterosexual marriage, and therefore, heterosexual brainwashing. Most women who come out later in life successfully make the transition to dyke social, emotional, and cognitive processing, and do so rather quickly. However, small subsets of women who come out later in life are not able to shed their heterosexual conditioning, and have this LOL disorder. Because of their many years of heterosexual gendered socialization, they often have expectations and behavioral repertoires that are offensive to dykes who have been out for years. For example, some LOLs merely expect to replace their male husbands with a female version, targeting only dykes with good jobs who they consider to be adequate "breadwinners" (i.e., sugar mamas). On the other hand, they may have false expectations about lesbians. For example, they may want a female partner who will sexually satisfy them, but not be concerned with reciprocity. They are often sorely disappointed to find out that stone butch lesbians are extraordinarily rare. They may not want to look like a lesbian couple in public, so they avoid being friends or lovers with butch, androgynous, or "too political" dykes who wear their sexual identities openly, such as in t-shirts, buttons, or "dykey" outfits and hairstyles.

LOLs may also find the more egalitarian household sharing activities of dykes to be confusing and overwhelmingly complex, because every activity must be negotiated, often repeatedly. Finally, some LOLs find that trading an emotionally bankrupt, communication-impaired male husband for a process-oriented, emotionally oversensitive dyke to be too large a culture shock. They typically revert back to heterosexuality or seek refuge in a convent, where they can have sex with other women but pretend not to be lesbians. Sex may also present a challenge to LOLs, who may be highly skilled at faking orgasms with men, but who do not know that many dykes are orgasm detector specialists and cannot be fooled. Lesbians generally expect much more from sex than did their husbands.

Lesbians who have been out for longer periods of time (more than two years) often try to avoid women newly out of heterosexual relationships because of these potentially difficult assumptions about

165

relationships. As a result, the LOL women may be challenged in finding available partners in their critical early months of lesbianhood.

Members of the expert panel familiar with dyke cultures outside of the United States have informed the author that these late bloomers, who are often avoided or viewed with considerable suspicion in U.S. lesbian communities, are actually preferred partners in other cultures. This is because they are perceived to be more experienced at long-term relationships than lesbians who came out early, before they were developmentally mature. This perception of the LOL as more experienced with relationships does not take into account that she is completely new to lesbian relationships and may have a long learning curve to learn the nuances of dyke communication and relationship patterns.

Case Example

Deborah was married to a man for 26 years, has four children, and two of them, ages 13 and 16, are still living with her. Her husband left her a year ago for a younger woman, and Deborah, after much soul-searching, decided to seek a woman for a partner this time. She recalls having a few mild crushes on gym teachers in her youth and loved Annette Funicello movies. Thus, she deduced that she is innately a lesbian. Deborah lives in a red state without a lesbian community center to guide her. As she started scouring the lesbian online dating sites, she put in her preferences: "seeking women age 45-50, professionals with stable job only, willing and able to financially and emotionally support me and co-parent two sullen teenagers, and is handy around the house. Please, only feminine, non-gay acting women need apply. Me: mid 40s, sexy, full of feminine wiles, able to keep your household in good working order. Photos are optional, but please send notarized copy of last year's tax return." After six months, she is puzzled because she has not had a single response to her dating profile. She was shocked to find out that her profile on craigslist was flagged as offensive to lesbians. Deborah has not yet found a lesbian hairdresser to point her in the direction of accurate lesbian re-education, so she remains single and perplexed.

Prevalence and Etiology

LOL is caused by a lack of lesbian socialization and education during the adolescent and early adult years, combined with particularly potent heterosexual and sexist brainwashing. About 7% of women come

166

out as lesbians after the age of 40, and the majority of them quickly adjust. Only 12.2% of them fail to shed all of their heterosexual assumptions by the first year, and thus, meet criteria for a dykignosis of LOL. Most LOLs eventually learn that lesbians are not the same as heterosexual men and women, and come to reject gender stereotypes about relationships, so the condition resolves spontaneously. A small subset, however, who only want to replace a male husband with a female version of the same traditional family model, may find a Desperately Seeking Susan (DDM 10) or a U-Haul lesbian (DDM 7) with the caretaking qualities that they are seeking. This subset of LOLs must be distinguished from the more deliberately opportunistic heterosexual POWs (pussies on welfare) who seek out lesbians to support them, knowing that many lesbians are easy to "hook" into emotional dependency. LOLs really want women as partners, although they are seeking women who function in the place of men in the relationship, whereas POWs prey on lesbians for purely financial reasons. Unfortunately, most POWs have not been informed of the impoverished status of most lesbians, and they are often disappointed to find that they have entered a relationship with a dyke in debt.

The cause of the LOL condition is entrenched gender and heterosexist socialization patterns from excessive reading of women's fashion magazines such as Cosmopolitan and Vogue. The condition is exacerbated by the undue influence of anti-feminist conservative women such as Michele Bachman, Kellyanne Conway, and all the blond women who appear on Fox news programs. In most cases, the condition resolves spontaneously after a year of failure in lesbian dating and socializing. Another potential cause of the LOL is the lesbian-enabler--heterosexual men whose behavior is so disgusting that they turn their girlfriends or wives into lesbian wannabes.

Treatment

Obviously, education in the form of lesbian consciousness-raising is the treatment of choice, and this condition could be prevented entirely with better relationship education in secondary schools. For women who have not been exposed to lesbian relationship education in their youth, attendance at lesbian potlucks, concerts, and feminist book readings can fill in the gaps of her education. DVDs of lesbian comics talking about relationships (e.g. Suzanne Westenhoefer, Karen Williams, Lizzy the Lezzy, Marga Gomez, Wanda Sykes) are also an effective way to learn about dykes. In addition, lesbian Big Sister programs in larger communities can be helpful tools for re-socializing baby dykes who come out at any age, but are particularly useful for LOLs. The big sister acts as a mentor and escorts the LOL to lesbian events, serving as her interpreter of lesbian culture and dynamics. Lesbian lending libraries are also a good resource for LOLs. All LOLs should be required to read all volumes of *Dykes to Watch Out For* (by Alison Bechdel), and have to pass a quiz at the end about lesbian behavioral characteristics and personality types prior to being allowed to date.

LOLs who do not respond to this initial educational approach should be committed to a three-month stay at lesbian boot camp to detox from heterosexism and sexism and develop a feminist recovery sensibility. One expert suggested that a radical form of primary prevention might be to train men to be better at relationships so that basically heterosexual women would be satisfied in their male-female relationships and leave lesbians alone. Others in the lesbian feminist or queer studies research world vehemently oppose this idea that women could be biologically or essentially heterosexual, and they locate all women on the lesbian continuum. Finally, there are some dykes who reject the lesbian continuum, stating that women such as Margaret Thatcher, Sarah Palin, and Ann Coulter should never be placed anywhere near dykes in any classification scheme.

DDM 26. De-Dyking Anxiety Disorder (DAD)

Overview
A common form of anxiety among closeted and semi-closeted lesbians occurs when preparing for visits from family members, bosses, coworkers, or neighbors who have not been informed of the woman's dykehood. As societal changes have allowed women more freedom to come out and live openly as lesbians, there has been a steady decline in DAD, but even today, there are circumstances under which lesbians must remain closeted. There are two variations of this condition, depending on whether the afflicted lesbian is single or living with a partner. The need for de-dyking strategies among those closeted lesbians has accelerated in the past ten years because of the growing capitalist marketing research that identifies lesbians as prime buyers of dyke specific gear of all kinds, and the explosion of websites and retail outlets designed to sell these products. On average, dyke households today contain three times as many lesbian-specific or queer-related items as households of twenty years ago.

DDM 26a. Single DAD
A single closeted lesbian facing a visit from folks who do not know of her dyke membership must scrutinize every aspect of her home for telltale signs of her sexuality. These signs are insidious, especially for lesbians who have been out to themselves for extended periods because over time dyke specific items such as coffee mugs, books, CDs, DVDs, wall hangings, clothing items of all types, fashion accessories, sex toys, dishes, toilet seat covers, automobile license plates and bumper stickers, candles, magazines and newspapers, and even dyke-specific paint colors and stencils creep into the home. The anxiety of identifying and covering up all these items can be great, and the anxiety is compounded by intense fear of missing a critical item and being detected, creating an awkward moment over dinner or cocktails.

Case Example
Rose is 24 years old and has been out as a lesbian for only eight months, but lives in a community with many lesbian and LGBT novelty item shops, and her house reflects that fact. She has been working up to telling her parents, who are conservative Christians, but is not yet ready on this particular visit for her sister's wedding. Roses' parents are spending the weekend in her small apartment. She has a giant rainbow

painted on one wall of the living room and a large *Dykes to Watch Out For* poster on the opposite wall. Rose can explain the rainbow, because as a child she was obsessed with the Muppets and Kermit the Frog's song, *Rainbow Connection*, but the poster has to go. The book shelves hold all six seasons of the DVDs of *The L Word*, and four seasons of *Queer as Folk*, as well as three shelves of lesbian romance novels and erotica short story collections. In her only bedroom, a footlocker at the end of the bed holds an impressive variety of sex toys, and her dresser drawers contain 18 t-shirts with lesbian or queer slogans, five pairs of edible dyke underwear, and an Olivia cruise sweatshirt. There are pink triangles on her socks. Rose spent three days feverishly de-dyking the home, hoping that her parents would buy her story about going minimalist. She had to rent a storage locker to hold the contraband. Finally, she was ready for their arrival, but to her horror, as the doorbell rang and she opened the door to greet her parents, the mailman was handing her mother the mail, including a Wolfe Video catalog with a bold title "Lesbian Sex Issue" and Curve magazine, declaring "The Dyke Drama Issue." Rose was forced into premature disclosure, adding further drama to the family wedding saga. Her sister remained angry for two years for Rose taking away attention from her wedding, that was supposed to be a happy occasion, but turned into a coming out brawling session after too much champagne had been imbibed.

DDM 26b. DAD Doubled
When a couple lives together, the de-dyking anxiety intensifies because of the need to de-dyke one's partner as well as the house. If the partner is in the middle to butch side of the gender continuum or is a lesbian activist of any BF number, this can present a challenge for the afflicted dyke to explain her as a mere roommate. This perceived need to alter the partner prior to family visits can create intense dyke drama within the household, such as arguments about why the afflicted dyke is not out to her family and it can raise insecurities about whether the partner really loves her as she is or wishes she looked or acted more feminine. When both partners are closeted or semi-closeted, there is more empathy and understanding of the need to de-dyke, but double the potential for family visits and thus double the level of de-dyking anxiety. Closeted couples whose families live close enough to drop by unannounced live under a constant level of vigilance, stress, and anxiety.

Case Example

Mai is a 46 year-old corporate lawyer who has been partners with Charlie, a contractor specializing in bathroom remodels, for 16 years. Mai is out to her parents and siblings, but over the years, they have all urged her not to come out to her grandparents because, "It would just kill them." No dyke wants to be responsible for the premature death of elderly family members, so this tactic to keep them closeted generally works. Now the grandparents are coming for an overnight visit and Mai must de-dyke the house and decide what to do about the very butch Charlie whose language is a bit colorful. Her grandparents know that she makes a very good living as a lawyer, so it is difficult to explain her away as a need for a roommate, so Mai has decided to send Charlie on an Olivia Cruise for a week so that she can de-dyke the house and not have to answer questions about a roommate. She had five days to completely erase Charlie's presence from their home. The visit went off with only one slight glitch, when Mai's grandmother reached into the sofa cushions and pulled out a purple rabbit vibrator. Luckily, Mai's quick thinking saved the day. She snatched the item from Grammy's hand before she could look at it too closely, and said that it belonged to a neighbor's child. A coming out scene was successfully averted, but at what cost?

Incidence and Etiology

Approximately 22% of lesbians are not out to their parents, 34% are not out to grandparents or aunts and uncles, and 16% are not out to coworkers, setting up the conditions for de-dyking anxiety disorder. DAD symptoms typically begin at the very moment of the announcement of the visit, and intensify for the three days prior to the visit. During the visit, the afflicted dyke must remain highly vigilant—she may have removed the physical items from her home, but she still has to monitor her own language and the content of the conversation, and hope that a particularly dykey friend does not drop by. De-dyking anxiety can become a chronic condition when family members live close by and visit often. The fear of an unannounced drop-by visit of family members is the source of most cases of ulcers among DAD afflicted lesbians. DAD is caused by being closeted, a sometimes necessary condition of lack of full disclosure of one's sexual identity and/or relationship status. Ironically, often the fear of disclosure turns out to be unfounded, as the relatives and coworkers knew or suspected the afflicted lesbians dykehood all along.

An assessment tool for rating the degree of de-dying anxiety can be found in a later section of this manual.

Treatment Considerations

Closeted lesbians are encouraged to keep, and frequently update, an inventory of the dyke-specific or queer items that enter their homes and develop a checklist for ease of de-dyking. Without an updated inventory, telling items may escape detection during the de-dyking process and result in full blown coming out traumas. In some urban communities, one can employ De-Dyking Home Services that are combined with house cleaning and interior design consultations that supply tasteful non-queer household accessories for rent during family visits. These accessories can be tailored to family preferences, such as French country, early protestant modesty, or urban chic, depending on visitor's inclinations. These companies are less successful at dealing with partners, however, and sometimes must resort to kidnapping. The best treatment for de-dyking anxiety disorder is to come out to everyone, obviating the need for any de-dyking.

AXIS II DYKE CATEGORIES

Axis II catalogues dyke personality differences; dysfunctions that stem from deep-seated personality factors, evolutionary forces, genetdyk aberrations, emotional dyke-reactivity, and long-established habits that affect one's relationships and ability to cope in the world. As was true of Axis I disorders, lesbians are susceptible to many of the same Axis II disorders as are other segments of the population, such as antisocial personality or narcissism. Some conditions, however, are unique to lesbians or manifest in different ways in dykes than in heterosexuals. Narcissism, for example, is common in both heterosexual and dyke communities, and may be focused on physical appearance, perceived importance in the world, or an illogical belief in the superiority of a specific community. Among lesbians, narcissism may manifest as preoccupation with how she looks in the softball uniform or spending hours gazing in the mirror at her double women's symbol tattoos. A group form of narcissism exists in some lesbian communities whereby these dykes feel superior to heterosexuals or to other subsets of the lesbian community who are considered less politically or spiritually evolved. Axis II disorders may also include problems with impulse control. In lesbians, for example, sexual addictions may be found at about the same rate as in the general population, but sometimes manifest as a severe chronically repeating serial monogamy pattern (see DDM 27) or can be sublimated into a polyanimalry condition (see DDM 1d). The eight disorders described in this section must be considered as only an initial compiling of the potentially long list of dyke personality traits that will no doubt be uncovered with further research.

DDM 27. Lesbian MSM (Multiple Serial Monogamy)

Overview

Not to be confused with the male version of MSM (men who have sex with men), Lesbian MSM is a very common, chronic, and resistant-to-change personality trait of many dykes. The condition involves delusional thinking that the afflicted lesbian is committed to monogamy, and manifests as four repeating phases: (1) crush; (2) soul mate; (3) cohabitating; and (4) break up. During the initial crush phase (days 1-30), lesbians with MSM are exclusively attracted to only the crush object, and suffer from a damaging delusion that the relationship will last forever. Not only do they focus entirely on the one crush object for romantic/sexual purposes, they typically ignore their friends and family while in the first month of those intense relationships. They are also prone to calling in sick to work, and may not leave their home/apartment (or bedroom) for days at time.

The crush phase is followed by the soul-mate phase (days 31-90), and often results in a solemn verbal commitment to live together forever. Those who commit to a relationship while in the crush or soul mate phases do so because of an inability to distinguish between lust and love (see DDM 7, U-Haul Syndrome for more about this). Unusually high levels of lesbian lust hormones released by the crush centers of the brain impair judgment. Concerned friends may stage interventions, but this does not deter the lesbian MSM from believing that this woman is THE ONE.

Phase 3 is the period of time that they actually live together. Cohabitation for the lesbian MSM typically lasts six months to three years. During this time, reality sets in and the high of the crush wears off. Fortunate lesbians who purely by accident fell for compatible women may be able to sustain the relationship through true affection and shared values, and their relationship may last. For the majority of couples, however, most know by the seventh month of cohabitation that the relationship is not working because the lust hormones drop and they can more clearly see the behaviors and personality of THE ONE. This eye-opening realization changes THE ONE to THAT ONE, or "How did I ever get taken in by THAT ONE."

For many dykes, the loss of intense physical attraction ushers in Phase 4, the breakup phase, also lasting six months to three years. Lesbian breakups typically take the same amount of time as the relationship lasted. After the breakup is complete, or as complete as any

174

dyke relationship ending can be (see DDM 3, Lesbian Fusion Disorders), afflicted lesbians begin the cycle again with a new crush object, seeking to recreate that rush of lust hormones. Each time, they approach a first date with the delusional belief that this woman will be the true soul mate.

Signs and symptoms of Lesbian MSM include: absolute certainty within one week that this new woman is the love of her life, based on incomplete and/or inaccurate information; cognitive distortions bordering on delusions about the potential compatibility of the couple; and inability to see the other as a flawed human being until well into the relationship. In fact, serious flaws may be rationalized away as minor "quirks" and even can be declared as "cute" by afflicted dykes under the influence of lust hormones. Some have described this affected dyke as seeing the relationships through "lavender-colored glasses." For example, in the first two weeks of an infatuation, if the lust object can only eat a tuna sandwich that has been cut on the diagonal, the MSM labels this behavior "cute." The same behavior seven months later is labeled as "annoying" or "crazy."

Lesbians with this affliction often label even very short dating experiences (less than six months) as "relationships." They are completely devastated by each break-up and desperately seek out their next soul mate, often within a few weeks of the end of the last affair and long before they have emotionally processed the relationship and identified their MSM pattern. Rather than process what went wrong so that they could identify and avoid these patterns in the future, these dykes would prefer to repress their feelings and find a replacement source of lust or emotional connection. Surprisingly, many lesbians appear to prefer a new lusty crush to spending months of serious self-examination with a therapist or other sage.

Case Example

Tami is a 43-year-old dyke from a small city in the western U.S., and is a very accomplished civil rights lawyer. She is a highly intelligent woman in every way except for relationships. She has suffered from lesbian MSM her entire dyke life. She came out at age 22 in college and had a two-year relationship with her college roommate. They broke up over ideological issues in their law school pursuits: Tami wanted to help people and Monica wanted to make money. Since that time, Tami has had 15 "relationships" lasting from three months to three years. Each time, after only two or three dates, Tami announced to all of her friends that she had "found the one I've been waiting for all my life!" In fact,

Tami has never had a date that did not lead to what she defined as a relationship. The average time from first date to proclamation of "soul mate" is 19.6 days across Tami's 15 "relationships." Even though friends have tried not to enable her MSM, and have even initiated interventions to stop her from rushing into relationship, Tami persists in this delusional thinking for several months, until some major reality shock event occurs. In one instance, once she came home early to find her soul mate of five months in bed with the FedEx driver; another time her lover was stealing from her and turned out to be a POW. Unlike lesbians with fusion and ex-lover fusion disorders (see DDM 3), once she has broken-up with a woman, Tami never wants to see her again. Ironically, this clean break means that Tami is ready for another crush in record time. Tami has been in lesbianalysis for eight years, but this personality trait is a chronic, relapse-prone condition. Her therapist expects the treatment to continue for at least another five years and six relationships before Tami is able to break this pattern.

Prevalence and Etiology

Lesbian MSM arises from an interaction of biology and environment. On the biology side, evolutionary processes favored those dykes who were resilient and able to form new relationships quickly when their current partner could not stand the stress of being a lesbian and married a man or entered the convent. Thus, the MSM gene was naturally selected for centuries. A biological co-factor is overactive lesbian lust hormones, making some lesbians particularly susceptible to impulsive coupling. Some scientists have speculated that the lesbian lust hormones are a variation of the substance oxytocin, the so-called bonding hormone. In lesbians, a special type of this hormone, called dyksetocin, accelerates the transition from crush to soul mate phase. The elevated hormones must also be paired with strong levels of socialization into couple-hood, idealized romantic notions of relationships, and a strong belief in the concepts of "love at first sight" and soul-mates. Dykes who have elevated lesbian lust hormones without the concomitant socialization about couple-hood are more likely to manifest the Gay Male Lesbian Disorder (see DDM 14).

Lesbian MSM might also be characterized as Rapid Repeat U-Haul Syndrome. Some women learn their lesson from one episode of U-Haul Syndrome and it becomes an isolated, acutely painful event in their lives. Sadly, others with this MSM personality tendency relapse and repeat the same U-Haul behavior over and over. About 27% of dykes suffer from this deeply ingrained personality trait that leads to the chronic behavioral pattern of lesbian MSM. The 27% of lesbians with MSM disorder have an average of 14.3 partners in their lifetimes, compared to the 3.2 partners of non-afflicted lesbians, partly because MSM dykes are more likely to label short-term dating situations as relationships than are non-afflicted lesbians.

Treatment Issues for Lesbian MSM

For some lesbians, the condition resolves eventually, if by chance they connect with a compatible partner and the relationship lasts. In this case, the condition should be treated as an acute but successful U-Haul episode, and requires no treatment. For others who continue the pattern, and repeat U-Haul-like behaviors three or more times, a dykignosis of MSM is appropriate, and more drastic means are needed to change the personality patterns. Lesbian therapists specifically trained in management of Lesbian MSM have had great success using the following strategies:

1. Institute intensive cognitive re-training to establish the differences between lust and love, and between dating and relationship. In one U-Haul delay tactic, afflicted women are trained to meditate to the mantra "it takes two years to know a dyke" and they are prohibited from using the term "relationship" until after at least one year of dating;

2. Establish dating contracts with afflicted lesbians, that specify:

   - The first six dates with a new woman must be chaperoned by a lay therapist or dyke relationship coach who administers a mild electric shock if the MSM dyke moves too quickly. This strategy is counterproductive with an S&M MSM, and other means of delaying sex must be considered.
   - If lust symptoms escalate to a dangerous point, chastity belts are prescribed or the couple is restricted to Skype dating until some sanity is restored. The Skype calls must be monitored, as some lesbians have been known to initiate sex across the airwaves. Treatment for lesbian blue balls may be needed at this point.
   - No texting, especially of the sexting variety, is allowed for three months.

- Like a driver's license, the afflicted lesbian begins with a probationary dating permit that can be revoked by the therapist if the dyke drives too fast, swerves out of her lane, or violates other aspects of the dating contract. Serious violators may be sentenced to three months of solitary confinement with only Fox news channel to watch, forcing her into self-analysis to maintain her sanity. This intense shock treatment must be reserved for only the most intractable cases, because the lust hormones can be so overwhelming that an affected dyke might end up attracted to Megyn Kelly or another Fox News blond with potentially devastating effects on the self-esteem of the lesbian.

DDM 28. Multiple Dyke Personality Disorder (MDPD)

Overview

This personality trait stems from the desperate need to have a particular girlfriend, no matter how ill-suited this woman is as a potential partner. This creates a situation where the afflicted dyke fixates on this one desired love object and resorts to desperate attempts to become the woman that the object of her affection (or sometimes, obsession) wants in a relationship, regardless of the afflicted lesbian's true nature. Sometimes this takes the form of gender vacillations, with the afflicted dyke switching between positions on the lesbian gender continuum from extremely butch to extremely femme, to please a potential girlfriend. These vacillations can be in physical appearance, interests, preferred activities, or some combination of these factors. Other times, the disorder affects non-gender-related personality traits and activities, such as cooking, gardening, sexual proclivities, dancing prowess, interest in game playing, nurturance abilities, or athletic prowess. Some women have attempted to change from extroverts to introverts or vice versa. In lay terms, this condition might be called the false dyke syndrome. It must be distinguished, however, from passing as straight in lesbians who must hide their sexuality to keep a job or children.

Case Example

Joy is a 34-year-old lesbian librarian who has been single for two years. She grew up in a family where her parents had different expectations for her, so she was constantly shifting her personality to suit her father (who wanted her to be an analytical lawyer) and her mother (who wanted her to be a social worker and be emotionally expressive). She came out at 29 and fell madly in love with Mai, a butch woman who wanted a femme girlfriend. Joy let her hair grow out, took make-up lessons at the nearby department store, fastidiously studied fashion magazines, and spent nearly $3000 on a new wardrobe. Eventually, Mai broke up with her, saying that she looked like a drag queen that walked like a jock. Joy was devastated until she fell in love again four months later. Her second girlfriend was a lesbian separatist jock, Cheri, who was addicted to women's sports. Joy studied rulebooks for soccer, basketball, and softball, and joined a gym to try to become more athletic. She enrolled in a lesbian Dojo and a dyke golf league. She took all of her femme clothes from the experience with Mai to a consignment shop, and retooled her wardrobe from REI. When Cheri dumped her, Joy developed an attraction to a woman who had "Daddy" issues. Joy attempted to butch herself up again, and tried to act like the authoritarian, strict patriarch that this woman wanted. She signed up for BDSM lessons at the local lesbian sex club, but failed the course. When that relationship failed, Joy was in total identity crisis and did not know whether to go shopping or demolish her bathroom cabinets to feel better.

Prevalence and Etiology

About 15% of lesbians suffer from this disorder at some point in their lesbian lifecycle. In many cases, the disorder resolves without treatment after three or four unfulfilling relationship experiences, but 4.8% of lesbians have a chronic case of MDPD. The disorder stems from lack of a strong dyke self-image and a mythological idealization of the soul mate, the idea that there is one and only one perfect mate for each dyke. This belief results in a desperate attempt to hold on to the one perceived to be the soul mate by any means at her disposal, including submerging her own identity entirely to become the fantasy woman of her love object's dreams. Dykes who have this behavior pattern in relationships may also manifest symptoms to some degree in lesbian organizations or social groups. For example, an afflicted dyke might give up meat to become a granola dyke after one consciousness-raising group, or become Wiccan because of attraction to the head witch rather than any real philosophical commitment. Women with multiple dyke personality disorder are particularly susceptible to the manipulations of a Lesbian Mother Superior (see DDM 6). Sometimes a lesbian mother superior may even seek out a multiple dyke personality disordered woman as a partner/lover, thinking that she can mold this woman into exactly the kind of partner she wants.

Treatment Issues

As a preventative measure, all lesbians need at least two years of dyke identity development classes prior to dating to establish their essential BF (butch-femme) number, core values, likes/dislikes, and personality type. For women who have a long history of this disorder, lesbian identity boot camp is recommended (this is also helpful for lesbians in recovery from fusion disorders: see DDM 3). Recovery from the multiple dyke personality disorder involves intensive personal work including gender-typing, lesbian personality tests, such as the

Multiphasic Dyke Personality Inventory, and the lesbian version of the Rorschach inkblot test. The later consists of Georgia O'Keefe flower prints and is used to identify dyke sexual behavior preferences and skill sets. Soul-mate education classes are provided so that afflicted dykes come to understand that a true soul mate loves her partner EXACTLY AS SHE IS and does not ask a partner to change. Finally, courses on lesbian relationships will have skill building sessions on how to craft an online dating profile that accurately depicts one's true nature, and advice about how to stay within one's authentic dyke self on dates. One piece of advice in the dating arena to explore extensively in self-analysis is to "be yourself and you only get hurt once."

DDM 29. Lesbian Co-Dependent Disorders

Overview

In the general population, co-dependency refers to a passive personality style that leads to meeting another person's (or animal's) needs ahead of one's own, an indirect style of communication, conflict avoidance, having loose or absent personal boundaries, passively allowing bad behavior in other beings, and/or rationalizing abusive behavior away. In dykes, co-dependency can manifest in relationships in similar ways that it does in heterosexual women, but there are also three uniquely dyke forms of the disorder.

DDM 29a. Co(ed)-dependent disorder

This condition refers to the tendency of lesbians to fall in love with their college roommates. These attractions can sometimes be mutual and turn into relationships, and in that case, do not qualify as a disorder. For LUGS or LUTS (see glossary), graduation resolves the crush or relationship, and they return to heterosexuality, so likewise, do not have a chronic disorder. For other women, the attraction is un-requited and causes tremendous pain and suffering. This afflicted dyke dotes on the roommate and pines over her for years, often never revealing her attraction. The pattern of repressed feelings may be repeated over and over again in the future, keeping this dyke from having an actual relationship. In extreme cases, it prevents the woman from coming out at all. If she does come out and get into a relationship, the cloud of the unrequited feelings for the roommate may hover over the new relationship, preventing her from totally committing to the new partner. Sometimes the roommate situation is prolonged beyond college, resulting in stunted emotional growth in the afflicted dyke, and ultimately leads to the debilitating Laverne and Shirley syndrome.

Case Example

LaShay is a 26-year-old lesbian who came out to herself at 20 in college, after she fell in love with her sophomore year roommate, Caroline, a conservative Christian. She never shared her feelings with Caroline, who was president of the Campus Christian Coalition, secretary of the Family Values League, and a regular protestor at the local abortion clinic. Caroline often crawled into bed with LaShay to "cuddle," and laid her head in LaShay's lap when they watched TV, causing agonizing physical and emotional symptoms in LaShay. They played on the Lacrosse team together, and Caroline often offered to soap LaShay's back in the shower. In fact, LaShay suffered from an extreme case of the lesbian blue balls and is infertile as a result of the damaging effect of the repressed sexual feelings. Now six years later, LaShay has not been able to find a real girlfriend, because she is still pining over Caroline. When she has been a little interested in another woman, she acts aloof because of her conflicted feelings, and the other woman gives up on the relationship within a few dates. Caroline went on to run for congress and is a prominent member of the greater Virginia Tea Party.

DDM 29b. Co(pet)-dependent disorder

Some dykes, particularly those afflicted with cat or dog fetishes (see DDM 1), allow the pets to rule their lives. They have a tendency to enable bad behavior in those pets, such as letting them sleep in their bed, while the human sleeps on the floor, or not punishing the pet for peeing on her partner's shoes in jealous fits. Dyke dog park fetishists with a co-occurring co(pet)-dependent disorder let their dogs jump on unsuspecting lesbian passers-by or slobber on their girlfriend's pant legs. They think it is cute when their Saint Bernard humps the leg of the dyke at the coffee shop. Co(pet) dependent lesbians lack boundaries with their pets, are unable to sever even very bad pet relationships, and may stay in a relationship with an abusive pet for years. Friends often attempt interventions to get the afflicted dyke to see how pathological the relationship is, but typically, the afflicted lesbian chooses the pet over the friend and the abusive cycle continues.

Case Example

Luce is a 38-year-old dyke with five cats in a three-bedroom house, of which 90% of the useable space belongs to the cats and their paraphernalia and 10% is for Luce. The living room has a six-by-six foot cat-climbing tower, a floor to ceiling scratching post, and is littered with cat toys. The dining room has no table, because the place where the table should be is the sunniest spot in the house, therefore taken over for cat napping in the sunny south window. The main floor bathroom has five cat litter boxes, because none of the cats will share. Luce uses the half bath in the basement for her toiletries. Her garden in the tiny backyard is totally devoted to the growing of catnip. Luce often comes to work covered with scratches and bite marks inflicted when the cats disapprove of her behavior (occurring multiple times each day). Friends and coworkers have tried to convince her to leave the cats and go to the domestic pet violence shelter, but she claims that the cats are merely showing their love for her, and are trying to make her a better person. She truly believes that she deserves their abuse and contempt and desperately tries to please her cat masters.

DDM 29c. Co(ex)-dependent disorder

Another common lesbian manifestation of codependency is the extreme reliance on ex-lovers that manifests in a significant minority of lesbians. This condition may underlie the ex-lover forms of fusion disorder (see DDM 3 for more detail), and expresses as an inability to function independently in the world without constant input from an ex. The afflicted dyke maintains an unhealthy dependence on the ex-lover and desperately seeks her approval. Most co(ex) dependent dykes did not forge any boundaries after their supposed break up. Thus for all intents and purposes, they are still in the same intimate relationship, just not having sex.

Case Example

Kathleen is a 55-year-old lesbian with two ex-lovers, Jan and Larissa. She suffered from lesbian fusion disorder with both of them, and was the passive partner in these relationships. In both relationships, her partners had affairs with other women and left her (the technical term for this is being "dumped"). Kathleen was not able to break her emotional dependence on either ex, five years after Jan left her and eight years after Larissa. Kathleen spends at least two hours of each day talking to one or both of them in person or on the phone. She returns to Jan's house once a week to do Jan's laundry, and she serves as a chauffeur to Larissa who travels for her job and frequently needs rides to the airport. Jan crafted her online dating profile, and Larissa monitors her correspondence with potential dates to screen out inappropriate women. Kathleen feels completely immobilized when she needs to make a decision and Jan and Larissa are not immediately available. For example, once on a second date with a woman that she thought she might like, Kathleen experienced a major crisis. Her date walked her to her car after dinner, and then leaned in to kiss her. Kathleen backed away, excused herself and ran to the alley to call Larissa to get permission to kiss the woman. When she returned after the 30-minute phone call to process how she felt about her date and the potential kiss, she was dazed to find out that the woman was gone.

Prevalence and Etiology

Co-(ed)dependent dyke disorder occurs in 15.6% of lesbians overall, and is elevated to 31.6% if summer camp bunkmates are counted. Of those with a cat or dog fetish disorder (see DDM 1), the rates of co(pet)-dependent disorders are alarmingly high, afflicting 27%. Curiously, co(pet) dependent disorder is rarely found in those without a concomitant DDM 1 dykignosis. Co(ex) dependent disorder occurs in 18% of lesbians. The cause of the disorder is an excessive need to be loved coupled with low lesbian self-worth that results in viewing the pet, ex, or unavailable lover as morally superior to the lowly human dyke and an irrational belief that unrequited love is the highest form of human sacrifice. There is often an element of martyrdom in the co-dependent of any variety.

Treatment Considerations

Like co-dependents in the general population, dykes with this disorder need therapy to help them love themselves and stop enabling bad behavior or hanging on to impossible crushes. Co(ed) dependents need work on letting go of old crushes and unrequited love for roommates. This therapy can take years, as dykes are notoriously resistant to giving up on even impossible relationships. Co(pet) dependents need to develop pet-free zones in their homes, and develop a weekly schedule that includes a minimum of two hours per day of pet-free human activities. Pets with bad behavior need to see a pet discipline expert for human companion empathy and compassion training, and if that is not successful, they should be sent to pet batterer education classes. As a last resort, pet military school may be needed for drastic re-socialization. When the disorder progresses to Lesbian-Pet Fusion Disorder, desperate measures are needed, such as surgical separation of the human and pet, a procedure known as petecomy.

Finally, co(ex) dependents have the most challenging disorder from the treatment standpoint, and the best solution is complete isolation from the exes for a period of at least one year, coupled with lesbian self-identity and assertiveness training. For prevention, lesbian boundary training starting in middle school is needed to reduce the possibility of enmeshed relationships in adulthood. When boundary training is provided in lesbian therapy and orientation sessions, it too often neglects pets. All lesbian therapists need to be trained to perform petecomies.

DDM 30. Lesbian Emotionally Exhausting Processing (LEEP)

Overview

LEEP may be the most serious and debilitating of all the dyke disorders, and is the source of considerable dyke drama in relationships and laggles. As women, lesbians have been socialized to be emotionally expressive, insecure about relationships, responsible for taking care of other people's (or pets) emotional needs, and to crave detailed conversations about feelings. They are compelled to process each disagreement, however small, until all parties come to mutual understanding and consensus. In fact, disagreement over an issue is considered to be a potentially disastrous event, to be avoided at all costs. Some dykes have taken this socially conditioned tendency to the extreme, and it has become a main source of lesbian relationship break-up. In fact, there is extraordinarily high demand in most communities for lesbian therapists, because many dykes refuse to process endlessly with their afflicted partners, dooming them to years of intensive work with their therapists. This disorder is best treated by a highly trained professional who has back up. Lay therapists such as hairdressers, often experience considerable harm from attempting to treat LEEP without special training and supervision. The repeated presence of even one LEEPer in her waiting area can drive away other customers and run her out of business.

To make an accurate dykignosis, the therapist must distinguish between good communication and LEEP communication patterns. Good communicating involves immediately addressing a conflict between two or more people, and finding a solution or a compromise within a thirty-minute discussion. LEEPers typically wait until three or more days after the conflict occurred, and then want to talk about it for another three days with no solutions offered or accepted. Good communicators check in immediately if their partner or coworker says or does something that they do not understand; LEEPers draw wild conclusions that the behaviors or words have catastrophic meanings without checking the veracity of these conclusions. Good communicators talk about their frustrations or disappointments with the other person, and then move on, but LEEPers use the silent treatment initially, hold resentments for months, and continue to process the same issues repeatedly. Good communicators say what they are thinking and feeling, but LEEPers drop subtle hints or clues and expect that their partners will be able to correctly interpret them.

Introverts and conflict avoidant LEEPers may manifest symptoms in a different way than in-your-face extroverts. Introverts often wait until their girlfriend goes to work, and then writes a 2000-word email outlining all their fears and concerns. Alternatively, they may leave lengthy voice mail messages at times when they know the girlfriend will not answer the phone. If they use a brief communication technology such as a text or tweet, instead of saying "I need to talk to you about..." they choose a cryptic and dramatic message such as "suicidal" or "URGENT. Need tok 2 U." The partner must then decide whether the issue is a potentially serious one that warrants leaving work or taking a break to call home. An extroverted LEEPer is a girlfriend's nightmare. She may show up at work or the middle of a dyke collective meeting and begin processing loudly in public.

LEEP is a disorder of the individual, but when it occurs in one or more members of a couple, triad, or laggle, it has escalating effects on the relationships of all involved. LEEPers can also be the death of lesbian collectives, and are a major cause of friend burnout. There are two types of LEEP disorders in lesbian relationships.

DDM 30a. Disconcordant LEEP

In this case, only one member of a couple is afflicted with the disorder. That afflicted member vacillates between the silent treatment and following her partner around the house, pleading to talk. She may awaken her partner in the middle of the night to explain something she said at the lesbian potluck two weeks ago. Unless the partner is extremely LEEP tolerant, or has developed LEEP coping skills, this relationship will wear out the non-afflicted partner within six months. Lust hormones often mask LEEP affected dyke's symptoms during the initial few months of a new relationship. These hormones temporarily reduce the afflicted dykes need to process, and they inhibit the non-afflicted partner from recognizing early warning signs. LEEP symptoms will typically begin to manifest at about month four, and full blown LEEP disorder takes hold by months six or seven.

Case Example

Shelly is a 57 year-old lesbian with a long family history of over-involvement in each other's lives and excessive processing combined with lack of ability to resolve any issue. Shelly is riddled with doubts, second-guesses everything she says and does, and questions her partner's motives constantly. If Mo is five minutes late coming home from work, Shelly is convinced that Mo doesn't love her anymore and is probably having an affair, but she waits until the next week to express her fears. Once Shelly suggested that they go to an Indian restaurant, and Mo said she didn't like Indian food. Shelly interpreted this to mean that Mo did not love her anymore. Mo, who has some co-dependent tendencies, entered the relationship with the erroneous belief that she could be a stable force in Shelly's life and calm her fears. Consequently, she spent the first year reassuring Shelly that she would not abandon her. She let herself get sucked into lengthy processing conversations in the first year, and because of her failure to create any process boundaries, now they are the primary feature of the relationship. Mid-way into the second year, she is emotionally exhausted and desperately wants out, but feels that she has trapped herself. She wants to take a flying LEEP out of the relationship, but is afraid of what will become of Shelly, who might actually LEEP out of a window for attention if Mo suggested they consider a breakup.

DDM 30b. Concordant Lesbian Processing

When both members of a relationship are excessive processors, this is a truly painful dynamic to observe. There are two scenarios possible for the concordant LEEP pair. In the first scenario, they become completely fused into one being with no social life outside of their own internal relationship processing, much like pathologically close twin behavior. They must be financially independent, because processing will take up the majority of their waking hours, precluding time for anything but part-time work. Alternatively, in the second scenario, their relationship may end in extreme drama, because each one is processing their own issues without listening to the other. Concordant LEEP couples are rarely invited to lesbian potlucks or parties because their conversations are too painful to be witnessed by the many lesbians who are survivors of a LEEP relationship. Their behavior may trigger symptoms of post-traumatic LEEP disorder in others in the community, for many have suffered from having a LEEP lover or friend at some point in the dyke-cycle.

Case Example

Janice and Rachelle are both in their late 20s and met at a lesbian astrology discussion group, where they found that they had a lot in common. They were both born on the 18th day of their respective birth months, and they both read their horoscopes every morning and planned their days accordingly. They attended different 12-step group for co-dependents, and they were both cat lovers. They fell in love as soon as they compared their charts (on the first date) and found that the stars sanctioned their relationship. In the first three weeks, they talked constantly and processed every step of their budding relationship. For example, their 45-minute coffee date prompted a three-hour phone call to process how they each thought it went. At first, these processing sessions were heady and optimistic conversations. However, the conflicts began when Janice brought up the U-Haul issue at their one-month anniversary dinner, and suggested that they move in together. Although both LEEP-afflicted lesbians, Janice's underlying pathology was fear of abandonment, thus she wanted Rachelle in her sight 24 hours a day, but Rachelle's pathology was a fear of entrapment. She wanted to talk endlessly with Janice on the phone and see her almost every day, but had a phobic reaction to moving in together. Although they discovered this serious incompatibility in the fourth week of their relationship and decided to break-up, the dissolution actually took another eight months of daily processing in couple's therapy, and weekly individual sessions with their respective therapists.

Prevalence and Etiology

On the individual level, 32.6% of lesbians have a mild form of LEEP, and 13.5% have severe cases. This means that a substantial portion of lesbian couples will have one or two afflicted members. LEEP is much more common among lesbians on the feminine side of the gender scale, although the few afflicted lesbians on the butch end of the scale have often mastered the silent treatment (see DDM 18b). Although butch lesbians may not be excessive verbal processers, they express their symptoms through body language such as clenched teeth, tight shoulders, morose, accusatory eyes, and constipation.

Underlying causes of LEEP are the combination of exposure to dysfunctional family communication patterns during the formative years, and female gender role socialization. For example, girls who played with Barbie and Ken dolls as children are five times more likely than tomboys who climbed trees to develop LEEP as adults. Interestingly, girls who secretly paired Barbie and Midge dolls instead of Barbie and Ken, rarely have LEEP. Girls who experienced a combination of a LEEP mother and who played house at least weekly as children are twelve times more likely to develop LEEP than girls without LEEP mothers who did not play house excessively. This research finding has led some child psychologists to recommend banning the game "house" for all young girls, as it's toxic influences appear to extend well into adulthood.

Treatment Considerations

LEEP is extraordinarily difficult to treat, and LEEPers represent an ethical therapist's idea of the nightmare patient, and the unethical therapist's gold mine. LEEP patients are the primary cause of lesbian therapist burnout, and lesbian lay therapist nervous breakdown. Years of lesbianalysis are needed to bolster the self-confidence and teach the afflicted dyke to manage her underlying fears. Sometimes early in therapy, one should consider strategic pairing of roommates and lovers. For example, a deaf partner or one who does not speak English is an ideal roommate for a LEEP afflicted woman undergoing treatment. This is effective at least until she learns to process in sign language or learns enough words of the partner's native language, thus putting her partner at risk for emotional trauma. Some therapists help LEEP afflicted lesbians to limit their processing time to 30 minutes per day Monday through Friday, with a bonus 45 minutes on the weekends, by using a kitchen timer and a set schedule for the couples processing time. Partners of LEEPers need to maintain clear boundaries to protect their own sanity. Many non-afflicted partners need 6-12 months of therapy following a breakup with a LEEP-impaired girlfriend, because the LEEPer so undermined her self-confidence. Some larger communities have support groups for ex partners of LEEP relationships called Ex Lesbian Agonized Chicks Kollectives (EXLACKS) to purge themselves of the toxic relationship byproducts.

DDM 31. Dykolepsy

Overview

Dykolepsy is a condition characterized by sporadic fits of lesbian outrage. Rita Mae Brown, in Radicalesbians, defined a lesbian as "the rage of all women condensed to the point of explosion." Dykolepsy is the release of those pent-up reactions to the lesbophobic society in which lesbians are forced to live. The symptoms include expressions of verbal and emotional frustration, anger, disappointment, and feminist ranting at in-opportune moments. Of course, many dykes rant and rave in the privacy of their own homes or vent with friends, and this must not be construed as disorder. Dykolepsy, on the other hand, is expressing ones' lesbian outrage at the wrong time and/or place. Dykolepsy is highly influenced by current political events. The 2016 election sparked a 478% increase in dykolepsy in the United States, and Brexit prompted a similar spike among lesbians in the U.K.

Case Example

Janet is a 43-year-old lesbian who worked in a large chain bookstore where her coworkers thought of themselves as "tolerant" of her as an out Black lesbian in their midst. She was able to "tolerate" their misguided liberal White guilt most of the time by coming home and venting to her partner, or discussing stress-management strategies in her weekly dyke process support group. One day Janet had a full-blown attack of dykolepsy at work. It started when one coworker said, "One of your people was in today and bought Glen Beck's book. I thought you people hated him." She repressed her gut-level reaction to that, and calmly said that she assumed he meant gay people by "you people," and that there were a wide variety of political beliefs among the gay population. Next, she noticed a flyer announcing a conservative author coming to the store the following week to give a talk about the threats of the gay community to traditional family values, and she wondered who had invited this idiot. Then she overhead two other employees, who were stocking a shelf with a new bestseller on same-sex marriage talking about how they wished that Janet would not be so blatant about her sexuality. One coworker said, "I don't know why she has to have a picture of her partner on her locker." By this time, her rage was definitely condensed to the point of explosion and she could not stand it anymore. She went to the store loudspeaker and shouted, "Yes, I'm queer. I'm here. Get used to it. I'm blatant and I'm going to flaunt it when I can get married and you can all just take your homophobia and stuff it where the sun don't shine." The bookstore was so quiet you could have heard a pin drop in the reference section. Luckily, Janet's boss was a middle class White heterosexual woman who was so afraid of being perceived as racist or homophobic that she did not fire or reprimand Janet for this inappropriate, although understandable, behavior.

Prevalence and Etiology

Nearly 100% (99.1%) of out lesbians have had acute dykoleptic attacks, sometimes in public places like the mall, classrooms or boardrooms. They occur even more often at family holiday events when parents, siblings or other relatives say outrageously lesbophobic things, particularly after a few cups of eggnog or communion wine. A small number (17%) of dykes suffer from chronic dykolepsy, contributing to the stereotype about the "angry dyke." Sometimes these dykoleptic attacks have significant negative consequences such as loss of a job or ejection from a family, but other times they result in a sense of relief, reduction in blood pressure, and elimination of the lesbophobic comments in the environment. Coworkers or family may still be homophobic but they have learned their lesson about airing their opinions to the volatile dyke in their midst. The cause of dykolepsy is justifiable anger, but the anger is not channeled appropriately into a socially acceptable outlet, thus causes potential harm to the one expressing herself.

Treatment

Some out lesbians have the luxury of expressing their rage or outrage to the parties that exhibit the lesbophobic behavior. The majority of closeted lesbians, those with young children who could lose custody if they are perceived as "angry feminists," and those who do not have financial or job security, may have to remain silent to avoid severe consequences. These lesbians need coping strategies to relieve the tension, lest they actually implode. Rita Mae Brown was wrong about the explosion part; a consequence of pent-up fury is typically implosion rather than explosion. Therapists often use scream therapies or beating on blow-up dolls that resemble Rush Limbaugh as a safety valve. In a more controversial treatment approach, afflicted women are assigned readings from *Hothead Paisan, Homicidal Lesbian* (by Diane diMassa: this cartoon character is the ultimate dykoleptic), or required to watch films such as *Basic Instinct* or *Kill Bill*, to vicariously act out their furies.

193

Another option is to purchase a Donald Trump piñata and beat it with a stick.

Some outlet must be provided for the rage, or internalized dykophobia can develop and heighten the risk for stroke or heart attack. Prevention of dykolepsy is a major public health priority. One form of prevention involves banning a vulnerable dyke from reading newspapers or watching television, as these media outlets contain multiple Dykolepsy triggers. Ultimately, though, the whole world can be a trigger, so learning coping strategies for calmly and rationally addressing lesbo-phobic events in public must be taught at dyke orientation sessions. She must learn to delay her outburst until a time and place that is safe for all parties.

DDM 32. Dyke Event Antisocial Disorder (DEAD)

Overview

Some dykes eschew lesbian events in favor of other activities, and in fact, may even exhibit a dislike or phobic anxiety about specific types of lesbian events. Instead of softball, lesbian game nights, or potlucks, they may prefer going to the ballet (not the all lesbian one) or watching NFL football. They seem to have little or no interest in lesbian music, theater, or politics, although they may be avid jazz or blues fans and active in the local green party. Instead of lesbian mystery stories, they read Pulitzer or Man Booker Prize winning books by heterosexuals. They may enjoy going on cruises with straight people rather than book an Olivia cruise, or vacation at the Dinah Shore weekend. Some choose to have brunch with their biological siblings rather than other lesbians, and many even have heterosexual best friends. These tendencies may lead the rest of the lesbian community to consider this afflicted dyke as DEAD to the community.

Case Example

Ling is a 55-year-old lesbian who came out at 42. She is a competent and accomplished professional in the world of high finance, and a connoisseur of the arts. As a youth, she played cello in the high school and college symphonies. She also loves art museums, documentary film, and fly-casting. She is new to a dyke community in the upper Midwest, and joined a lesbian meet-up group to start checking out potential girlfriends. After attending a barn dance, dyke bingo night, and a mixer at a dive bar, she has developed a reputation as a snob for suggesting that some lesbian events could be held in well-lighted, clean venues with a little more "culture." Some local community lesbians banned her from the meet up website because after attending a premiere of a lesbian-made romance film, she commented that the dialogue was "clichéd." She quickly became DEAD to the other dykes who belong to the meet-up group, and she is feeling like she may never find a girlfriend. Ling wonders if something is wrong with the lesbian centers in her brain. Her first girlfriend, now ex-lover best friend suggests that Ling came out late, thus missing the formative lesbian socialization years when the baby dyke enjoys bars, potlucks, and softball games. Ling is not so sure; she thinks that she would not have been interested in these events even if she had come out at 18.

Prevalence and Etiology

Since professing a dislike of lesbian events is so stigmatizing, there are no reliable data available on the prevalence of DEADs in lesbian communities. There is much anecdotal evidence of their presence, and most lesbians have had at least one encounter with a living DEAD. If there are several DEADS in a dyke community, they may form secretive societies amongst themselves and go to the opera undetected. Affluent and/or highly educated lesbians with professional careers are more likely to suffer this affliction than lower socioeconomic class dykes. DEADs must be distinguished from Dyke Deadheads (Grateful Dead fans), as the treatment is quite different. Dyke Deadheads may collect dancing bear stuffed animals and lapse into teddy lezzie disorder (see DDM 1).

Treatment

There is no cure for being DEAD. Rather, lesbian communities need to develop tolerance for these afflicted souls who often suffer greatly from lack of access to other lesbians. Occasionally, lesbian events could include non-lesbian-oriented cultural events, or dyke organizations could hold some lesbian events in more upscale bars and restaurants to accommodate these women. Some non-afflicted dykes may even find that they enjoy a holiday from the usual lesbian community events every now and then. Lesbian diversity training is recommended on an annual basis to remind dykes everywhere of the differences that enrich their communities, and to promote tolerance and acceptance of lesbians who are outside of the local community lesbian norms.

DDM 33. Mommy Dykes

Overview

Not to be confused with dyke daddies, a form of sexual preference among a subset of dykes, Mommy dykes are women who have put all of their time and energy into their motherhood role. This preoccupation with the motherhood role extends to their adult relationships and friendships, and manifests regardless of whether or not they actually have children. The Mommy Dyke has become so immersed in parenting behaviors that she has forgotten how to talk and behave in adult-to-adult interactions. Whereas some lesbians may initially think that they want to be mothered, it quickly becomes annoying when a date or partner constantly says things such as, "Clean up your plate," "Sit up straight," and "Finish your housework before you turn on the TV." The Mommy Dyke often spits on a hankie to clean her partner's face at a restaurant, and sets a curfew for her roommates.

If she actually has children, she carries hundreds of photos of the children on her iPhone, including pictures of the donor sperm (and sometimes the sperm donor), the turkey baster used for insemination, the dyke midwife who supervised the home birth, the tee-pee or birthing tub in which she or her partner gave birth, the co-mothers, the ex-co-mothers, the gay godparents, the pet siblings, and all the ancillary aunties. If the child was adopted, there may be photos of the trip to China or Central America to pick up the baby, and pictures of the ceremony they held to honor their initiation into motherhood (often hosted by a Barn OWL at a women's land setting). When a Mommy Dyke holds a leadership position in a lesbian organization or social group, she may mother an entire gaggle of dykes. Her employees may become totally dependent on her to tell them what to do, when to eat lunch, and when to go home. If she is part of an extended ex-lover laggle, she is the matriarch of the group, and everyone goes to her for nurturing or advice. She becomes the hub around which all the spokes of the laggle revolve.

Sometimes a relationship dynamic develops that is one form of a lesbian fusion couple, but in this case, they have a mother-child dynamic. The Mommy Dyke tells the child partner what to eat, what to wear, how to behave, and punishes her for all indiscretions. The child partner in this dynamic tends to pout, throw tantrums, and rebel, but ultimately, submit to the will of the Mommy. Unlike the Dyke Daddy who spanks and sternly disciplines, the Mommy Dyke controls via guilt-trips.

Case Example

Emily is a 38-year-old lesbian who always dreamed of being a mother. She played with dolls until she was old enough to babysit, and chose early childhood education as her major in college. Now she runs a day care center. She is in a relationship with Lea, a 42-year old multiple serial monogamist co-dependent, who loved Emily's nurturing behavior the first 18 months of their relationship, but is now starting to rebel and assert her independence. Their therapist explained that the relationship is entering into the "terrible twos" where Lea wants to individuate, but Emily was resisting and smothering her. For example, when they went shopping for clothes, Lea complained, "I just want to do it myself," and Emily tried to ground her for a week from watching Glee. Lea is demanding that Emily allow her a later bedtime and stop ordering for her in restaurants. Emily's defense is that she does these things for Lea's own good because she is too immature to make good choices.

Prevalence and Etiology

Women are socialized to be nurturers in general, and mothers in particular, but some have received more intense conditioning by their own mothers or sisters who enlisted them in excessive doll play or playing house as children. Lesbians who as impressionable children played with dolls that pee and poop are particularly susceptible to becoming Mommy Dykes. This premature exposure to body fluids is traumatizing to susceptible dykes and activates a mothering script in the developing brain. These dolls, like playing house, are traumatic childhood experiences that seriously impair adult adjustment in a significant number of dykes. Nearly 3% of lesbians without children show the symptoms of Mommy Dyke, and 14.2% of dykes with children generalize their parenting behaviors to the adults in their lives. An extreme manifestation of the Mommy Dyke is the Mommy Dearest Syndrome, a deeply pathological, but rare condition. Lesbians who encounter a Mommy Dearest must be warned to stay out of the closet, or they might trigger the "WIRE HANGER" wrath of the Mommy.

Treatment Considerations

Mommy dykes are treated first by verbal re-training, whereby they are prohibited from using baby talk and words like "time-out" and "grounded" when communicating with their partners. They are prohibited from reading juvenile literature to their partners and they receive training in adult communication styles and topics of conversation. For example, they may be given a homework assignment to watch *The Rachel Maddow Show* and have a 15-minute conversation about it. Spit rags are strictly prohibited. Repeated watching of the TV series, *Jon and Kate Plus 8,* may deter some lesbians from pursuing mothering behaviors.

In the case of the mother-child lesbian fusion subtype, the child partner needs therapy or coaching to grow up and act like an adult to avoid triggering her partner's maternal reactions. She is encouraged to donate her stuffed animals and video games to a local charity and start assuming more responsibility in the household. The Mommy partner needs detachment therapy and supportive counseling through the "empty nest" period when the child partner achieves maturity and leaves the emotional relationship. At this point, they are ready to relate on an adult level. Those in relationships with Mommy Dearest partners must be immediately removed from the home for their own safety and placed in dyke foster care for healing.

DDM 34. Lesbian Marriage Resisters

Overview

Media coverage of the same-sex marriage debates in the United States seems to imply that all lesbians are pro marriage and desire to pursue the "American Dream" of lifelong wedded bliss in the house with the white picket fence. In fact, a subset of dykes, both historically and currently, are strongly anti-marriage, some of them so much so that it affects their health and wellbeing in the lesbian and larger LGBTQ communities. These afflicted dykes are either defiantly outspoken, risking social ostracism, or desperately hide their anti-marriage feelings and lie in public to avoid social rejection and suspicion. One differential dykignosis for lesbian marriage resistance is marriage phobia, a condition related to commitment phobia, not political antipathy for marriage. The marriage phobic may be a Party Dyke (see DDM 9). Another condition that might be confused with marriage resistance is marriage reality syndrome. In this case, the lesbian partners have carefully studied the laws and policies of their particular state of residence and concluded that they cannot afford to get married because of the higher rate of taxes or because of the high likelihood of divorce, given their MSM tendencies (see DDM 27). A true LMR is politically and philosophically opposed to the institution of marriage, but not necessarily to committed relationships.

Case Example

Lisa and Winn have been together for six years. Lisa has a long history of open relationships and frequent changes in primary partners, whereas Winn has been a serial monogamist with three four-year long relationships in the past fifteen years. They are both politically opposed to marriage and are unhappy that their friends and family have been pressuring them to get married ever since same-sex marriage was legalized in the U.S. To stop this harassment once and for all, they made a YouTube video of a non-commitment ceremony and posted it on Facebook. In the video, Lisa said, "I, Lisa, do solemnly swear that I do NOT take thee Winn as my legally wed spouse, now or ever, under any circumstances. I vow to stay with you for as long as we both want and no longer." Winn replied in return, "Without the need for any ring, I thee do not wed. Let our ringless fingers be a symbol of our life together, be it short or long, 'til death do us part or until tomorrow." At the end, in unison, they chanted, "May our friends and family witness and respect our declaration that we shall never enter into unholy matrimony." They have received considerable hate mail from this video, and the low ratio of "likes" to negative comments on Facebook has shown them just how controversial the topic is. In fact, one Facebook friend started a petition to ban anti-same-sex marriage comments on FB entirely, and thus far, 286,395 people have signed it.

Prevalence and Etiology

Because of the stigma associated with anti-marriage views in the early twenty-first century, it is impossible to determine how many lesbians hold these attitudes. In the 1970s, many dykes were openly critical of marriage, but they were forced underground with the new wave of lesbian conservatism and gay-by boom in the 1980s and by the mid 1990s were ostracized because of their anti-military views as well. Prior to 1985, nearly 40% of lesbians were anti-marriage. Some speculate that the increase in over zealous same-sex wedding planners and the wave of consumer capitalist marketing of dyke weddings and wedding cake toppers depicting two women has created the current climate of marriage glorification. In addition, party dykes see the wedding as another excuse for a big party, and angry dykes just want to see their relatives squirm while they say their non-traditional vows. Some just want the presents.

There is growing evidence that this condition is not an actual disorder. Rather, their own lesbian or broader LGBT society ostracizes afflicted lesbians. A form of mass hysteria around supporting same-sex marriage appears to have gripped the United States. Since no one is harmed by the view of lesbian marriage resisters, there is growing pressure to remove the dykignosis from the DDM. A few vocal minority voices are advocating that the irrational glorification of marriage by some zealous dykes might approach the level of disorder. The diagnostic category of Marriage Zealot is being explored for consideration in the next revision of the DDM.

Treatment

If some lesbians are oppressed by societal views about marriage, then the onus should be on changing society and educating lesbian and broader queer communities, as well as heterosexuals about the pros and cons of marriage. If the facts were more widely known, and the stigma lifted, there would likely be a higher rate of lesbian marriage resisters in any given dyke community. Like the removal of homosexuality from the

DSM in the 1970s, the authors of this manual predict that Lesbian Marriage Resisters will be omitted from the next revision of the DDM. No treatment is required for Lesbian Marriage Resistance. In the meantime, a growing political movement of pro-choice wedding activists are spreading a message of tolerance and allowing individual couples to choose whether to marry or not without pressure from the outside.

NOTES ON EMERGING DISORDERS

There are many conditions, clusters of symptoms, and emerging disorders that simply lacked enough research to include them as definitive diagnostic categories in this version of the DDM. An expert panel is already being assembled for the DDM-V, and this section outlines some conditions that may make their way into the next version of the manual.

Geographic Categories

Place matters in relationship to health and wellbeing. For example, there is recent research on the influence of place or geography on lesbian diagnostic categories and behavior patterns. In particular cities, lesbians may even be subtyped by the neighborhoods in which they live. In San Francisco, lesbians who live in the Valencia corridor seem to have very different qualities than those living in the geographically adjacent Bernal Heights. Local lesbian census data in the year 2010 showed a ratio of one baby carriage to every seven dykes in Bernal compared to one in eighteen in Valencia; and 2.3 tattoos per dyke in Valencia compared to 0.8 in Bernal. Another dyke community survey identified a disproportionate number of lesbian priestesses in Marin County, California compared to San Francisco, with an average of 2.8 drums per lesbian household in the North Bay compared to 0.6 in San Francisco. Distinctions between Berkeley dykes and San Francisco lesbians are well known.

Other geographic regions outside of cities may also have unique configurations. For example, Barn OWLs typically live on the edge of town or in the country, whereas party dykes are mostly located within five miles of a gay bar. Whether factors in the neighborhood cause the differences, or lesbians with different characteristics are drawn to certain neighborhoods is unclear as of yet. This line of research may add to our knowledge and expand a geographically based theme for the DDM, of which the Barn OWL may be only one subtype.

In addition, there is growing evidence of a Multi-Culti Dyke Syndrome. This disorder may manifest as the lesbian who adopts an identity as a global citizen with only a superficial understanding of the cultures that she is exploiting. This lesbian may adopt one baby from China and another from an oppressed community of color in the U.S, dreadlock her straight blond hair, belong to a Buddhist sangha as well as take Torah classes, and decorate her home from every ethnic section of

Pier One. Instead of promoting racial, ethnic, religious, or national origin unity, the Multi-Culti Dyke may actually contribute to increased tensions and divisions and be seen as a co-opter of other people's cultures. This false sense of enlightenment may increase the overall levels of dyke drama in local lesbian communities and contribute to the fractioning into sub-communities. This condition may stem from the inexplicable delusion that experiencing one kind of oppression automatically makes one knowledgeable about all other types of oppression.

Similarly, there is an inexplicable phenomenon among some dykes to exclude bisexual women from their communities and/or personal lives. The symptoms include delusional beliefs that being left for a man is worse than being left for another woman, and that bisexual women carry male privilege around with them like second hand smoke, thus tainting "lesbian-only" space. A related condition involves similar delusions about transgender people.

Post-(post)Modern Categories

In academic circles, particularly among dyke graduate students and scholars of feminist or queer theory, there is a rare, but potentially debilitating condition that results from over-identification with post(post)post/modern theories and the idea of the cyborg. Sometimes the condition is related to an infatuation with the authors of such theory, rather than to the tenets of the theory itself, but the effects are virtually the same. The afflicted LezBorg has a blue tooth device permanently installed in one ear, metal studs in the eyebrow and nose (and typically in the nether regions as well), and has an iPhone activated vibrator that allows her to stimulate her girlfriend without any messy flesh-to-flesh contact. They communicate mostly via Skype or Facetime, tweets, and texts and often have bi-coastal lives at different academic institutions, because rarely can one university sustain two radical dyke queer theorist LezBorgs on faculty. They write constantly about sex, but rarely engage in it. As hybrid dyke-machines, they have little use for actual physical lesbian communities, but thrive in cyberspace in blogs, websites, Facebook, and email. A common physical health problem of the LezBorg is texting thumb, a chronic inflammation of the thumb joints caused by rapid repetitive texting.

Another emerging condition is the Dyke UFO Hunter (DUH), a condition whereby a lesbian claims a UFO encounter, alien abduction, or membership in any genre of the undead, such as vampires, werewolves, or zombies. Spirit channelers, psychics, and levitators may make up special subsets of this disorder. The presence of these conditions in lesbian communities is suggested by the disproportionate number of lesbian short stories and blogs centering on these issues, as well as from conversations overheard in lesbian coffee houses.

Lesbian To and Froing

Another category under investigation for the next version of the DDM is the Lesbian To-ing and Fro-ing Syndrome. Dykes appear to require a minimum of 7 phone calls or 14 emails to schedule any meeting because they are socialized to be sensitive to the other's needs, but have an underlying selfish streak. The first five messages are to establish the day and time for the meeting or gathering. The initiating dyke uses carefully crafted indirect language to try to determine whether the other has a preference and avoids stating her own preferences too strongly. Her aim is to try to find a time that will not inconvenience the other but will meet her own desires. Once the time and day are established, the next five emails are designed to decide upon a place. Typically, this place is one that is equi-distant between the two (or more parties) so that neither must commute excessively. If food is involved, there needs to be another six exchanges to establish any dietary preferences, allergies, or issues with the political beliefs of the restaurant owner. The final 3-4 emails are to confirm the time and place. This is when only two lesbians are involved. If triads or larger groups of lesbians must be assembled for any reason, they need a clear leader to tell them when and where to show up, or they may correspond for three months without making any significant progress in finding a meeting place or time.

Driving Under Insanity (DUI Lesbians)

The author has also observed a common phenomenon among some femme lesbians, tentatively called Driving Under Insanity (DUI). This lesbian gets lost going across the street, and seeks much guidance to find her way. She typically ignores her GPS and the instructions from friends because of the lesbian tendency toward rebellion, but then she calls a friend or lover on her cell phone when she is lost. Even if that person gives her accurate directions, she continues to defy the instructions and take a different route. Although heterosexuals can also have DUI, the afflicted dyke needs a somewhat different treatment, as it is contra-indicated to tell her to "Go straight." In addition, dyke rebelliousness prohibits her from trusting her GPS and she will typically do the opposite of what GPS (or her friend) tells her to do. A DUI dyke often has a concomitant parallel parking disorder and circles the block for hours searching for an angle parking spot for her Subaru.

Dyke Drama Diva (3-D)

In addition, the expert panel is considering adding the Dyke Drama Diva (3D) to Axis II. The 3D causes approximately three times the amount of dyke drama in a community as the average lesbian and is characterized by two prominent traits. First, she holds strong political viewpoints that are outside the mainstream of her dyke community, such as an S&M dyke in a mostly vanilla laggle or a republican activist in a progressive community. Second, she has a certain assertive, in-your-face argumentative personality style and tries constantly to convert others to her way of thinking. She has absolute certainty about the veracity of her position, and never recognizes that she is the cause of the drama. "Let it go" is not part of her vocabulary. If a 3D also has symptoms of dykolepsy, she can create chaos in both heterosexual and lesbian community events. If two 3D women with competing ideologies show up at the same event, there will be fireworks and occasionally a four-alarm fire. 3Ds have difficulty finding partners, and are often flagged in online dating sites as problematic.

Additions to Lesbian Pet Fetishes

A recent development, identified in the lesbian listserv archives, is the growing lesbian bunny fetish. This may represent another subtype of the lesbian fetish (DDM 1) along with cats and dogs. A 2011 posting from a dyke on an urban listserv illustrates the potential parameters of this little-known disorder.

Do you love CREPUSCULAR LAGOMORPHS? I'd love to meet other Houston rabbit owners for "bunny play dates." My girl bunny Ashley and I have been together for six years. Ashley has 3 cat and one small dog siblings to play with when I am at work. I am seeking other bunny-dykes to get together in a safe, pesticide-free, grassy area to allow our "kids" to play together on warm weekend afternoons in areas free of dogs and other critters that might eat them. No boy bunnies please as Ashley is a dyke bunny. I have a 30" high by 5 foot diameter round pen we can set up anywhere shady and grassy to babysit them while they play. Ashley is my baby and she is very intelligent, responsive and enjoys being given attention when she wants it. Does this describe your bun too? If you'd like to connect with other bunny dykes of the lavender persuasion, hop on over to my place to arrange a play date.

In other countries, lesbians with pet fetishes may differ from the U.S. where preferences for cats, dogs, and bunnies are by far the most common. For example, the author has been introduced to an Australian dyke with six wallabies, and an Egyptian dyke who loves her camel above all others.

Orange is the New Black Fanatics

The original research for the DDM was started during the run of *The L Word*, and thus it permeated lesbian culture at the time. As the younger generation is being socialized to OITNB, there may be major differences in diagnostic categories that stem from the differences in the characters and the setting. While it is true that lesbians are incarcerated at higher rates than straight women, unrealistic depictions of women in prison on OITNB may have adverse effects on the next generation of lesbians. Alex, the ex-heroin dealing lesbian convict has seemingly replaced the drug-using, anorexic, commitment phobic Shane as the sweetheart of the younger lesbian community. Piper, the blonde bisexual, has removed Alice from the spotlight. It remains to be seen whether this change in lesbian icons is any improvement.

LezHeimers Disease

This condition is related to loss of memory for one's lesbian past. As we age, we sometimes forget events in our lesbian lifecycle, sometimes to the peril of repeating old mistakes. This condition should not be confused with Lesbian Past Reconstruction, where dykes deliberately change details of their past to make their behavior seem more acceptable, or women in the dyke witness protection program who must create a new past for themselves for survival sake. We need to exercise the lesbian memory centers of the brain on a regular basis to keep those memories alive, via techniques such as reciting lyrics from lesbian musicians and re-reading old journals to not forget why we left that ex-lover. Loss of memory of U-Haul experiences or ex-lover fusion episodes may increase the risk of relapse for the afflicted woman. In addition, the average lesbian couple celebrates so many different anniversaries that Lezheimers disease in one of the partners can cause much relationship discord. Strategies suggested for older heterosexual women, like Sudoku, are not as effective as lesbian-specific games, such as "name that ex," and reciting one's celebrity crushes in order of occurrence.

The Lesbian Caste System

Observational studies of lesbian communities have revealed a common social phenomenon that is accentuated in lesbian communities compared to heterosexual populations. Asking a U.S. dyke about her income leads to an awkward silence, followed by a near panic fight-or-flight reaction. Income level and finances are taboo topics in most U.S. subgroups, not just within lesbian communities, but preliminary investigations suggest that there are at least four unique and distinct social classes among dykes that create a great deal of the conflict and dysfunction at the local community and larger lesbian societal institutional levels. Socioeconomic status is the lavender elephant in the room in lesbian communities. Because discussion of income levels is so taboo and there are very few verifiable statistics about income levels in dyke communities, there is little actual knowledge about the nuances of dyke socioeconomic class. The few pilot studies, done in secret, have revealed the existence of at least the following four castes:

> *Money and Privilege* (MP) Lesbians. These are women from wealthy or upper middle class families, who had the advantage of attending good colleges and getting high-paying jobs. Some do not have to work at all, but can choose a career as a hobby. Think of Helena from *The L Word*. They rarely use the term "dyke" to refer to themselves, as supported by a common lesbian joke: "What is the difference between a lesbian and a dyke?" The answer is "about $40,000." MP lesbians often create separate social and professional networks from the other classes of dykes, although some have processed their privilege and cross class lines for political and social reasons. Their wealth, however, cannot protect them from developing many of the conditions described in this manual, but they can afford years of lesbianalysis with an actual trained professional to work on their problems. Their symptoms may manifest in subtly different ways that have yet to be elucidated. For example, an impoverished dyke with a dog park cruising dykignosis, may get her dog from the animal shelter, whereas the MP lesbian has a purebred, registered show dog. MP lesbians are predominantly women of

208

no color and log cabin lesbians are disproportionately found in this caste. Fewer than 5% of lesbians are MPs, but 92% of log cabin republican lesbians are MP. The remaining 95% of lesbians are more or less equally distributed among the following three castes.

Downwardly Mobile Dykes (DMD). These are mostly women from middle class and higher socioeconomic status families who began with some degree of privilege or had opportunities to live a life of greater privilege. They made conscious decisions to seek lower paying social service, political, and social justice jobs. They are the most likely of any of the lesbian caste system categories to be out in public, and the most likely to publicly identify as feminists. Many, but not all of them, have processed issues of classism, racism, sexism, and other isms (often in lesbian collective and/or feminist discussion groups), own their privilege to some extent, and try to reach out to the classes of lesbians above and below them on the economic ladder. They are the creators of the lesbian sliding scale fee. DMDs are the ones who run lesbian communities through their extensive involvement in lesbian collectives, political organizations, and as hostesses of lesbian potlucks, speed dating, wine tasting parties, and other events. They are also the most likely to become lesbian therapists. In other words, power and control in lesbian communities are held by the DMD even as they deny and challenge hierarchies and societal power structures.

Stuck in the Middle Dykes (SITM). Some women from lower middle and middle class families received some lucky breaks or encouragement as children to excel, received scholarships to school, and realized at a very early age that they would have to be financially independent and take care of themselves. They selected jobs/careers that ensured some job stability and financial security, and therefore, may not be free to be out at work, thus are less likely to be active in local lesbian politics and events. SITM often have higher incomes than DMD, but are listed lower on the social scale because they are so often closeted and less likely to be actively involved in lesbian communities, out of necessity, not choice.

Down from the Get-Go (DFTGG) Dykes. These are lesbians from working class and impoverished families who struggle to survive and are acutely aware of their lack of privilege. Many DFTGG dykes have experienced multiple forms of oppression such as varying combinations of racism, classism, sexism, and ableism. They often resent the attempts of DMD dykes to include them on committees and collectives…they want to be involved, but often do not have the time or resources. In fact, they are the most likely to suffer from Lesbian Class Consciousness-Raising Burnout Syndrome. It is embarrassing and emotionally exhausting to have to point out other dykes' privileges all the time. However, DFTGG and DMD groups are the most likely of the four caste positions to interact with each on a regular basis.

Most intimate relationships are class-segregated, and even social arrangements are largely based on class distinctions. An MP lesbian is rarely seen with a DFTGG dyke, although they may occasionally "slum" with SITM dykes who might work in middle management positions at the same jobsites. Inter-class partnering and social affiliation among DFTGG, SITM, and DMD dykes are relatively common. In fact, the DMD dykes are the most likely to cross all social lines in their positions as community organizers, activists, and brunch hostesses. These class distinctions often underlie other differences in lesbian communities based on interests (softball versus golf, classical versus country music, ballroom versus hip-hop dancing, champagne brunches versus homemade food potlucks), politics (radical, liberal, conservative, queer, or a deliberate rejection of any involvement in politics), religion (yes, no, or create your own), fashion trends, geography, and other factors that lead to splintering of communities into even smaller factions.

One example of how these economically based communities occasionally converge is the lesbian cruise. MP lesbians can do the cruises regularly and get accommodations on the upper deck with full view windows. They attend wine tastings and socialize with each other. Stuck in the Middle and Downwardly Mobile Dykes save up for a cruise for months or years. They may go on a cruise once every 5-10 years, and select more modest accommodations on the inside or a lower deck. The DFTGG dykes may get to go on a cruise once in their lifetimes and are relegated to the inside rooms on the lowest deck, in the locations with the most engine noise and/or motion. Whereas the different classes of lesbians may see each other coming and going to events, they do not have much interaction across classes. Think of the movie *Titanic*...an Olivia cruise may be as class segregated as any heterosexual cruise boat.

Other points of intersection of all the castes include events like gay pride celebrations, dyke marches, and film festivals. MP and DFTGG lesbians may encounter each other in the same geographic or physical location, but they typically have no social contact. On the other hand, MP lesbians may have to interact with DMD dykes as therapists, CPAs, and LGBT event organizers, and cross-caste conversations may actually occur.

It is not yet clear how these caste distinctions impact DDM diagnoses, but it is likely that they do so in potent ways, as socioeconomic class is a powerful factor in all of human life. For example, it is highly likely that the majority of Lesbian Mother Superiors (see DDM 6) come from the Downwardly Mobile Dyke category. Down-from-the-get-go dykes are highly unlikely to have Helena Peabody impersonation problems (see DDM 2) and MP lesbians are virtually never Serious Softball dykes (see DDM 16). Other conditions, such as lesbian fetishes (DDM 1) and Multiple Serial Monogamy (DDM 27) appear to cut across all castes and class distinctions. Further research is needed to tease out the subtleties of class distinction among lesbians, but this research will be treacherous and the brave ones to broach these topics may be ostracized from the community. The DDM Expert Panel will have to process this issue for months in their Collective meetings before deciding whether to include a class-based diagnostic category in Version V of the DDM.

Lesbian Extermination Anxiety

In the past ten years, blogs and articles in academic journals, the HuffPost, and even the New York Times have announced the impending death of the lesbian. Some of these posts focus on butch lesbians becoming transmen, others on the shrinking number of women who embrace the label lesbian, and others are concerned with assimilation into heterosexual society. It is not clear yet whether these fears are widespread in the general dyke population, and the position of the DDM Academy at this point, is that there will always be dykes, whether the term lesbian disappears or not. We are, however, closely monitoring the situation.

LESBIAN BED DEATH: New Research Findings

The DDM IV contains a dykignostic category for lesbian bed death (DDM 12), but one of the DDM Academy interns has conducted research that adds to our knowledge of this condition. Her dykertation on the paper is excerpted below:

The term lesbian bed death is often attributed to a heterosexual sociologist, Pepper Schwartz, who did a study in the late 1970s and early 80s about American couples, including straight, gay male, and lesbian couples. She suggested that long-term lesbian couples had less sex than the other types of couples, and had less variety in their sex lives. This assertion that lesbians have less sex than straight couples or gay male couples has been repeated in the academic literature many times. But since when did dykes ever accept something someone outside of the community said about them? The fact that the term entered the lesbian lexicon and is still there suggests that there might be some truth to the concept. So this study takes a serious look at what we know about this phenomenon, and speculates on what factors have been proposed to cause it, if it truly exists.

First we have to address a complicated question. What is normal lesbian sex? To determine if couples are not having the right amount of sex, we have to figure out how much is the right amount. How often? How long? How much variety is necessary? What if one member of the couple is satisfied with their sex life, but the other is not? Do both have to be dissatisfied with their frequency of sex to call it lesbian bed death? None of these questions are easy to answer. For example, what if we try to measure how many times per month a lesbian couple has sex. What do we mean by sex? For example, Joan and Deirdre who are on their third date, get into bed at 9 pm, do various things that result in three orgasms for Joan and two for Deirdre, take three pee breaks and one snack break around 1 am, and finally fall asleep at 4 am. Was that one sexual encounter or several?

This is hard to compare to the heterosexual couples in that earlier study who had sex twice a week, but the average duration of a sexual encounter was eight minutes. Have you ever heard of an eight-minute sexual episode among lesbians? The DDM's preliminary research on this indicates that average duration of a lesbian sexual encounter is closer to an hour. What if Babs and Quince have been fighting a lot lately, but are trying to repair their relationship. Babs is holding to on to some resentment, and Quince has been trying for an hour to bring her off with no luck. Do we count that as sex? So far, no lesbian sex expert has suggested a magic number of times or duration for normal lesbian sex. For the sake of argument, let's say that the optimal sex frequency for a lesbian couple is twice a week, with a duration of one hour per sexual encounter, with both partners having an orgasm or feeling satisfied at the end. Schwartz' research suggested that 47% of long-term lesbian couples had sex once a month or less, clearly not optimal according to our definition, so something must be going on. Let's turn our attention to why nearly half of lesbians showed a significant decline in their frequency of sex. Here are some of the prevailing theories to explain lesbian bed death.

Possible Causes of Lesbian Bed Death

One influential lesbian sex expert of the 1970s, Joanne Loulan, proposed long ago that the tendency of lesbians to fuse or merge might be the culprit in lesbian bed death. She suggested that lesbians spend so much time cuddling and cooing at each other, and get so emotionally enmeshed that this kills the sex. This theory never made any sense to our experts at the DDM Academy. How can too much love and affection ruin sex? In fact, it seems like fused lesbian couples might be able to get by with half as much sex, as each one probably experiences the other's orgasms. Perhaps that accounts for shorter duration of sex as a relationship progress. In general, though, the DDM Academy dismisses this theory as illogical and improbable.

Leslie Lange, author of Dyke Drama, proposed that what we call lesbian bed death is actually just the second stage of a lesbian relationship. The first phase, the romance stage, involves sex marathons, adrenalin surges, long and tortuous phone conversations with painful physical longing when separated, and serious lack of sleep. The body eventually cannot keep up the pace, and forces the couple into phase two, which Lange calls "lesbian sexual rejuvenation phase." The tragedy is that most women do not recognize this physical need to recover, and break up before they can advance to phase three, which would entail a more moderate sex life. This explanation seems quite plausible, and worthy of greater study.

Another well-known lesbian pathology is the U-Haul Syndrome. Two women who mistake lust for love get into a relationship way too quickly, and soon discover major incompatibilities. Disillusioned with each other, they grow apart and are no longer attracted to each other. Sometimes they actually become repulsed by each other, making sex

213

unlikely. Far too many lesbians suffer from U-Haul Syndrome, so this theory is also a possible explanation for lesbian bed death. The cause of the loss of sex life in this case is unacknowledged or basic incompatibilities masked by an initial physical attraction and romantic fantasy.

Another possibility is laziness. It takes work to stay actively involved in a relationship, initiate sex, try new sexual positions or activities, and romance one's partner. It's easier to develop a new crush and let that hor-mone enhanced sex drive predominate for a few months, and then start over. Crushes can be addictive, so dykes sometimes chase the high of the lust phase of relationships, relapsing every time the high starts to wear off. In addition, many long-term couples fall into habits and routines, and anything done the same way too many times can get boring. This factor, of course, is not unique to lesbians.

In some relationships, the members of the couple are highly involved in community events, child care, planning brunches and potlucks, organizing the book club, or running the volunteer dog rescue league. They have no time or energy left for sex. In fact, the more dyke drama that happens in a community and gets manifest in lesbian events, the more energy is drained from couples, and this affects relationships. In this case, the desire is not gone, just the energy to satisfy it. This is something entirely different than lesbian bed death and constitutes a differential dykignosis.

Some lesbians become emotionally over-involved with their pets, particularly cats and dogs, and transfer all of their affection to the animals, leaving none for their partner. The partner may get groomed occasionally and taken for a walk, but there is no sex. A disproportionate number of lesbians are emotionally fused with their pets, and their partners generally suffer from neglect, particularly when their bed is overrun with animals. By the time the pet-fused lesbian has said goodnight to the eight cats in the bed, her partner has fallen asleep unsatisfied. Pet-induced lesbian bed death may very well be a fact.

Finally, there is the lesbian process disorder theory. Our lives are so full and busy during the day that the only time we have to process the details of our relationship is in bed. This processing can take hours, starting with a comment such as "I wish you wouldn't interrupt me when I'm talking on the phone to Joey (her ex)." This leads to the partner pointing out that she talks to Joey for three hours every evening, and that the partner feels neglected and jealous. Joey has now been brought into the bedroom along with the jealous and hurtful feelings, factors that are

214

not good for sexual arousal. Lesbian couples spend more time processing their relationship than any other segment of the population. In fact, they spend more time talking about their relationship to each other than heterosexual women spend talking to their therapists or gay best friends about relationships. Some processing is necessary and healthy for a relationship, but excessive or ill-timed processing can lead to lesbian bed death.

After careful consideration of these theories, the DDM Academy concludes that a decline in sexual activity can occur in long-term lesbian couples (any who have been together for a year or more), although it is probably no more prevalent in dykes than in heterosexual couples. The causes can be multi-faceted, but the biggest contributors are 1) U-Haul Syndrome; and 2) Lesbian Processing in bed. U-Haul Syndrome is a complex phenomenon that requires careful study and intervention, but the solution to the processing disorder is simple: NO PROCESSING IN THE BEDROOM, EVER, EVER!

Leslie Lange may be right about encouraging dykes to refuse to label declines in sex as lesbian bed death, and consider the loss of sex as a sign of something else. We can deal with the something else, and our relationships thrive. So the best solution to the problem might be, just say no to lesbian bed death.

LIMITATIONS OF DDM AXIS I & II

This edition of the Dyke Dykignostic Manual has expanded the preliminary work on lesbian pathologies from the first through third editions into a more substantial science with dykignostic criteria and treatment suggestions. However, it is doubtful that the DDM is now complete. The expert panel and the author were biased in terms of age (in chronological as well as lesbian years), amount and type of lesbian-specific education, Butch-Femme number, geographic locations, ethnicity, and social class. There are likely to be time or place-specific expressions of these conditions, and unique disorders among other subsets of the lesbian population. For example, in the near future, no doubt we will have a manual divided into sections by lesbian gender. There is growing evidence that the disorders of butch lesbians tend to be different than the conditions of the femme, and those who eschew butch and femme identities altogether are yet entirely different. For example, DDM 1a, Femi-Feline Fetish may have different expression: Butch lesbians are less likely to dress their cats in tutus or dye their fur pink than femmes. There may also be a need for different classifications for MP lesbians as compared to DFTGG dykes, for urban versus rural dykes, for lesbians of color versus White dykes, and for younger versus older lesbians. Finally, this manual has not addressed the differences between lesbians with children and those without, the differences between dyke right and left-handers, or how disorders are distributed across astrological signs.

This manual has not attempted to scratch the surface of our broader queer community, although acquaintances in the gay male, bisexual, transgender, and nonbinary communities have demonstrated some clear-cut pathologies that are sometimes similar and sometimes quite distinct from the lesbian conditions. Experts in those communities must draft their own versions of the manual. These classification systems will likely help to smooth rifts between these communities that stem from cultural misunderstandings. Now that the individual level disorders have been fully explored, the next three sections of the manual introduce the broader sociocultural contexts in which dyke disorders develop. This knowledge is critical to identifying community-level interventions to prevent the long-lasting effects of dyke drama. The last section of the book also introduces some assessment tools that can be used for early identification of dyke drama and disorder.

AXIS III:CO-OCCURING BRAIN AND PHYSICAL DISORDERS

Axis III of the corresponding DSM addresses the conditions or disorders of the brain that affect human behavioral expression as well as the physical health conditions that can affect one's everyday functioning. Many of these conditions affect lesbians in similar ways that they affect heterosexuals. For example, having a serious chronic illness can result in depression for people from any social identities or communities. However, there is growing research on the conditions that are unique to lesbians, and these are the subjects of this section of the DDM. Neurodycology is a newly emerging subspecialty of brain research and is devoted to the study of the lesbian brain. There are some promising trends that may lead to the identification of lesbian centers, pathways, and nuclei in primitive brain structures that control sex, love, personality, gay-dar, and emotional reactivity.

NEURODYKOLOGY

There is considerable research that attempts to identify brain differences related to sexual orientation, although the majority of this body of work has focused on men. There is very little study of the lesbian brain, although the categories in this book, as well as research from other academic disciplines strongly suggests that lesbian brains are different from heterosexual women's brains. Dyke brains are quite distinct from the brains of men of any sexual orientation or identity. Some preliminary work has identified a few nuclei or pathways in the brain that seem to be unique to lesbians, and some areas that are shared in common with gay, bisexual, and transgender individuals, such as the gaydar nuclei. The figure below shows some of these pathways or nuclei that may (or may not) be related to development of any of the DDM diagnoses.

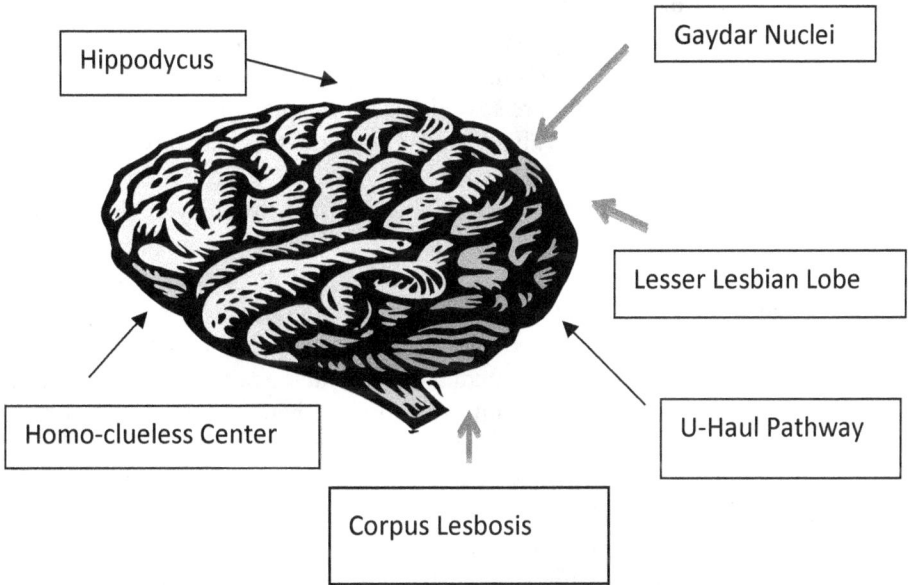

Some DDM disorders have already been linked to the brain, such as the gay-dar deficiency and U-Haul syndromes. The Homo-clueless center may be the biological underpinning for the late-onset lesbian (LOL, DDM 25) or the DEAD disorder (DDM 32) that lead to the individual person lacking the pathways to connect to the broader lesbian community. The lesser lesbian lobe and hippodycus cells have recently been identified, but their functions are elusive. The hippodycus is a cell cluster within the hippocampus, the center of the brain related to memory and spatial navigation. Some butch lesbians have a larger hippodycus than average, and this may be related to their tendency to back into parking places. The impairments in driving and directions among some femme lesbians may be caused by a shrinkage of the hippodycus. The Lesser Lesbian Lobe may be the site of more primitive behaviors, such as lesbian event addictions (DDM 8) and Dykolepsy (DDM 31). Finally, the Corpus Lesbosis may be responsible for some lesbians' lack of fashion sense and style, and may contribute to unappealing hairstyles.

Other Physical Health Influences

Studies of the effects of hormones on dyke behaviors and disorder have shown that sex hormones such as estrogen and progesterone can be subdivided into two types of chemical substance: hor-mones and her-mones. Hor-mones are the secretions that are related to lust and underlie conditions such as the U-Haul syndrome (DDM 7) and other early, or premature sexual coupling behaviors. Dykes with high levels of hor-mones may have indiscriminate sex and those with low levels may suffer from the Hypoactive Sexual Desire (DDM 12). Her-mones, on the other hand, are related to menstrual cycle issues and menopause, nesting syndromes, and the drive for emotional closeness and fusion. High levels of her-mones appear to double the risk for Lesbian PMS (DDM 15) and Fusion Disorders (DDM 3). More accurate assays of these two types of hormones are needed to determine their relative influence on dyke mental and dental health. Some scientists propose that having a community with higher than average levels of both hor-mones and her-mones can increase the ambient levels of dyke drama significantly. Other researchers hypothesize that lesbians' tendencies to synchronize menstrual cycles may reflect an underlying sensitivity to both the hor-mones and her-mones of other women. The synchronizing of hor-mones might be responsible for the indiscriminate sex and frenzied dancing seen at some lesbian nightclubs and party weekends.

As noted in an earlier section of the manual, dyksetocin is related to rapid and intense emotional bonding. It may interact with other hormones in the dyke minstrel cycle. This is not to be confused with the menstrual cycle that is linked with her-mones. The minstrel cycle is akin to the medieval travelers who shared songs and poetry for the entertainment of others. The dyke minstrel travels to talent shows, open mike forums, brunches, and private parties to inflict her love poems about the bonded partner or unrequited crushes upon unwilling listeners. For reasons as yet unknown, good lesbian love poetry is an extraordinarily rare commodity.

There is also a limited, but growing body of research on physical health disorders that can adversely affect dyke mental health, and cause or contribute to DDM diagnoses. Some of these that are currently under study include Lesbian Blue Balls; a physical condition related to the unrequited crush, that if prolonged, causes considerable dyke drama and pathology. Lesbian Blue Balls can be a boon to lesbian sex shops, as the main treatment is to purchase a new device that offers quick relief of unexpressed sexual tensions. Lesbianitis, a condition related to extreme preoccupation with everything related to lesbians and dyke life, can lead to a form of narcissism that others in the community find tedious or even offensive. The author suffered from an acute case of this while working on the manual, and was banned from one lesbian brunch group for talking too much about the DDM. There are also a variety of athletic injuries, such as softball shoulder tendinitis, that can severely impact lesbian self-esteem and cause significant distress to Softball dykes (DDM 16), as well as contributes to sexual performance problems. In addition, conditions such as carpal tunnel syndrome can totally incapacitate a LezBorg's ability to text or email, forcing her into painful personal interactions.

Many women afflicted with a DDM disorder can be identified merely by examining their teeth. Poor lesbian dental health results from the tooth grinding and tightened jaw that is a secondary consequence of dyke drama and dysfunction. Dyke drama has a visceral, immediate physical effect on the body that manifests primarily as jaw clenching. Over time, this can result in excessively high dental bills, pain, and impairments in conversation. Lesbians have approximately three times the number of annual dentist visits as straight women, even when we account for factors such as the high prevalence of cute dyke dentists.

Dyke drama infarctions can stem from internalized physiological consequences of dykolepsy, and are prevalent when the rage cannot be expressed outwardly. Dyke infarcts are a lesbian-specific form of stroke caused by the anger turned inward and can damage some of the other lesbian centers of the brain, such as the gaydar nucleus and the hippodycus. Butch lesbians who suffer petit-mal dyke infarctions lose the ability to parallel park. This inability to park can deflate the butch self-esteem and lead to considerable suffering and BF self-doubts.

Obviously, there remains much work to be done on mapping the lesbian brain, hormones, and physical functioning. The National Center for Lesbian Wellness is currently seeking psychoneurodyke-endocrinologists to study the effects of hor-mones and her-mones on the dyke centers of the brain. Lesbian scientists from all disciplines are needed to explore the impact of bodily impairments on lesbian well-being. Finally, there is growing evidence of genetdyk traits that underlie some of the conditions described in this manual. A few of the genes currently under study at the DDM Academy include the genes that control the gaydar pathways, lust and love detector genes, dominant and recessive genes related to gender expression and BF numbers, and stereotype detector proteins. Someday soon, there may be simple gene therapies to cure some of the biologically based dyke disorders. Another curious genetdyk phenomenon that merits study is that of the lesbian aunt. It appears that the majority of the population reports having a lesbian aunt, at rates triple that of gay uncles and far exceeding bisexual grandparents or cousins. Those who have a lesbian aunt experience less bullying in school and generally have happier and healthier lives.

The Aging Lesbian

Although lesbians tend to have more positive attitudes about aging than heterosexual women, many still find the physical, mental, and emotional changes that occur with aging to be challenging. One of the major challenges is maintaining an active sexual life as the body changes, but the libido does not. The DDM collective has assembled a list of sex tips for the elder lesbian. These have yet to be tested empirically, but the Collective is currently seeking participants for a community-based clinical trials research study at the OM (Orgasm Meditation) center in Greater Pittsburgh.

The lesbian sex books and videos are geared to a much younger audience and may result in advice that can lead to serious physical injury and emotional damage to the ego of the older dyke. We include below eight empirically derived tips for navigating lesbian sex with an ever changing, aging body. Keep in mind that "elder" is a relative term. Some lesbians in their 80s may be able to perform acrobatic sexual maneuvers, so they must judge for themselves whether they fit the category of old. If an elder dyke can do the downward facing dog, she may disregard these suggestions. To account for changes in short-term memory, this list has only eight sex tips rather than the typical ten.

Number 8. Simplify the sex toys.

As women get older, they may need to replace complicated technology with simpler devices. A trip to the local woman-centered sex toy shop will demonstrate how complex and high tech some vibrators have become. One best-selling model has a 6 by 6-inch control panel at its base that resembles the instrument panel of a jet plane. It has 16 buttons, three dials, a complicated on/off switch, and four separate motors, each with 21 settings. This is definitely a young dyke's toy, and even then, is not made for the easily distracted or anyone who loses focus during critical moments of sexual encounters. Older lesbians should seek out models with foolproof, large buttons to avoid an accidental frenetic pulsing when what they want is a gentle buzz. Manufacturers of vibrators can use the telephones designed and marketed to older adults as a model; the ones with large lighted numbers, amplified speakers, and that only make phone calls and do not surf the net, shoot motion pictures, or sext girlfriends. Likewise, older dykes should avoid harnesses with 17-page instruction manuals, and vibrators that simultaneously stimulate four different body parts. Perhaps one sensation at a time is enough for aging hearts.

Number 7. Buy fortified lube.

As women age, lube becomes an essential item for a successful sexual encounter. Older dykes should demand that the local sex toy stores supply palatable products that do not dry in ugly streaks on their cheeks or stain their favorite satin sheets. Dark chocolate flavored lube could serve many health functions for the aging lesbian body and soul, not to mention its benefits for lesbians with hypoglycemia who need a little sugar to make it through a lengthy love-making session. Those who have to take a break and go to the kitchen for a snack may forget what they were doing and leave their partner hanging (see DDM 24, Erect-tile Dysfunction). Along with a pleasing taste, elder lube should provide nutrients to sustain women through strenuous activities. With age, energy levels flag a bit, so nutritional lube would be very useful. Along with protein-fortified, vitamin-rich, dark chocolate flavored lube, older lesbians should keep a large bottle of water on the bedside stand, granola bars under the bed, and Red Bull in the refrigerator in case of a sexual emergency.

Number 6. Practice the Kama Sutra Arthritica.

Many older lesbians need instruction for appropriate positions to accommodate bad backs, creaky knees, and arthritic fingers. The young person's version of the Kama Sutra with 64 sexual positions just won't do for older lesbians, particularly those with memory problems like Lezheimers disease, who can realistically remember only six sex moves. Positions in the Kama Sutra Arthritica manual include the GIRD maneuver, the post knee- replacement kneel, and the vertigo avoidance move. Lesbian sex-ercise classes are useful venues for learning these maneuvers. Pelvic floor activities are particularly helpful, as they serve double-duty for strengthening the vaginal muscles and preventing incontinence, thus saving partners from an unwanted golden shower if one sneezes. Sex-ercise classes can also teach chair sex. This is much like chair yoga and is useful for older adults who have difficulty getting off the floor, for those with disabilities, and for dykes who are just plain lazy.

Number 5. Use only approved old lesbian dating services.

For the older lesbian, speed dating is absolutely prohibited, as the dash for a date is too hard on the knees, and remembering what a dozen other women said during the three-minute rotating discussions is nearly impossible. Instead of the typical online dating service matching procedures, such as focusing on shared interests in music, athletic activities, or desire for children, elder lesbian dating services could provide matching on the basis of medical profiles and need for accommodations during sex. First meetings of potential partners ideally take place at a buffet, where the pair can share their food incompatibilities.

Number 4. Watch only age appropriate sex videos.

Most lesbian sex videos are geared to the younger, more athletic dyke, or worse, they are pure fabrications created by advanced digital technologies. These activities should not be attempted without clearance from a lesbian sex advisor. Sex videos geared for younger lesbians will only set up expectations that cannot be realized or may lead to serious injury. *The L Word* DVD case should contain a warning: "Closed course with professional sex actors...do not attempt these moves at home." The lesbian-themed videos of the 1970s that only implied sex are considered safer sex for older lesbians, because they can improvise the scenes of moaning in the dark with age-appropriate accommodations.

Number 3. Seek accommodations for visual and hearing impairments.

As vision fails, older dykes may need to make accommodations. One useful product would be stick-on target arrows in florescent colors to mark critical areas. Another useful product would be a transparent magnifying dental dam. As hearing begins to decline, some lesbians may not accurately interpret their lover's instructions. Amplification may be needed to catch requests such as "Faster," and "A little to the left." Alternatively, Braille stick-ons can provide specific suggestions to the hard of hearing; "this is the spot," for example.

Number 2. Make accommodations for memory lapses.

As lesbians get older, they tend to wander through the house, starting activities but forgetting what they were doing mid-job and never completing anything. When this happens during sex, partners understandably often get testy. A technological device worn on the wrist is currently under production. It keeps track of what the woman was doing, and then gives instructions on what to do next. One setting is a Lesbian Sex GPS. A sexy Catherine Deneuve voice instructs the lesbian during sex, with suggestions such as "make a right turn at her thigh and proceed for five minutes," "veer slightly left and do not change lanes," "wrong turn!" and/or "you have reached your destination." Like navigational GPS, it provides an estimated time of arrival so the elder dyke can pace herself.

Number 1. Keep at It

The older women get, the greater chance that they will experience lesbian bed death. The best course of action to avoid both actual and sexual lesbian bed death is to develop a daily practice. The DDM Collective recommends that older dykes pace themselves, monitor their health and that of their partner, but keep at it. The body may be changing, but sex is 99% in the brain, so if women heed these tips, they can keep their lezbido alive.

AXIS IV: SOCIAL DETERMINANTS OF DYKE DRAMA

Axis IV of the DSM shows the powerful influence of social and environmental factors on human mental and dental health. As even a cursory review of the DDM categories in this manual will reveal, most dyke disorders are related to those social and environmental factors rather than individual proclivities, tendencies, hor-mones, her-mones, genetdyk, or brain factors. The study of social determinants is potentially the most fruitful arena for research on prevention of DDM conditions. All human beings live in social communities and physical environments that impact their health and wellbeing. Lesbians, as shown throughout this document, have unique social formations that differ from those of heterosexuals. In addition, some adopt lifestyles that may create different physical conditions in terms of air, soil, and water quality, type of housing, and potentially other aspects of the environment. For example, femi-feline disorders lesbians may have considerably higher levels of pet dander in their homes than the average U.S. house, putting them at risk for environmental health concerns. DIY dykes may inhale more sawdust and paint fumes than the population at large, putting them at risk for lung diseases. Those who live in areas with a high density of tea party members are exposed to a particularly toxic smog that can smother and sicken entire lesbian communities. These lesbian-related environmental hazards have yet to be studied, so this section focuses on social determinants of dyke drama.

Social Determinants of Dyke Drama

The figure below shows some of the promising leads in the field of research on social conditions that are risk or protective factors for dyke drama. In the future, entire lesbian communities can be assessed for their toxicity and the risk for development of DDM diagnoses of dykes who live in those communities can be calculated.

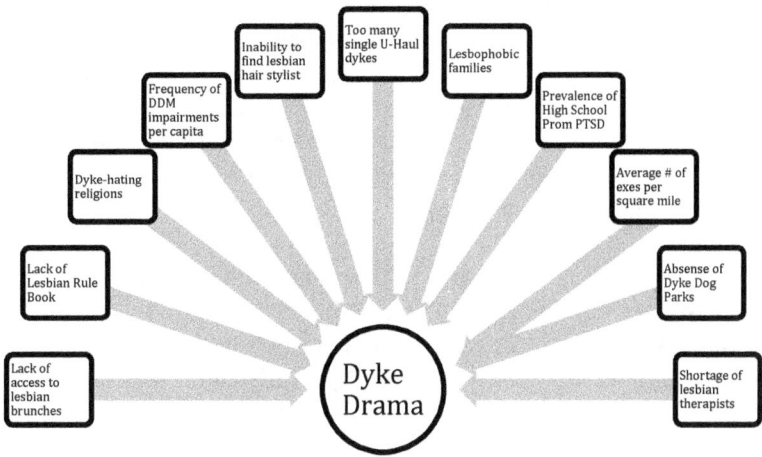

The diagram shows "Dyke Drama" at the center with arrows pointing to it from the following boxes:

- Lack of access to lesbian brunches
- Lack of Lesbian Rule Book
- Dyke-hating religions
- Frequency of DDM impairments per capita
- Inability to find lesbian hair stylist
- Too many single U-Haul dykes
- Lesbophobic families
- Prevalence of High School Prom PTSD
- Average # of exes per square mile
- Absense of Dyke Dog Parks
- Shortage of lesbian therapists

Some dyke community scholars have reflected on the relationship between lesbian fusion disorders (see DDM 3) and dyke drama. Fusion disorder was first described as the human behavioral counterpart to nuclear fusion, the process by which two or more atomic nuclei merge or "fuse," to form a single heavier nucleus. This process usually results in the release of large quantities of energy, hence the development of nuclear power plants. Large-scale thermonuclear fusion processes, involving many nuclei fusing at once, occur in situations with very high densities and temperatures. In the simplest case of hydrogen fusion, two protons must be brought close enough together for the weak nuclear force to convert the solitary protons into a neutron, thus forming the hydrogen isotope deuterium.

In lesbian communities, mass fusion can occur when there is a high concentration of single lesbians (the protons) with U-Haul tendencies (the nuclear force) at a lesbian event such as lesbian music festivals, dances, pride festivals, or large brunch gatherings (the high density and temperature conditions). Under these fertile conditions, they may begin almost immediately to merge. The fusion of two or more lesbian protons into one neutron, or in this case, dyktron, release considerable amounts of energy into the local lesbian community in the form of dyketerium. Consequently, this mass fusion contributes to higher levels of ambient dyke drama via the cloud of dyketerium that settles in lesbian households, softball diamonds, potlucks, and pride festivals. When dyketerium is released at a lesbian event, such as a collective meeting, it may affect all the members present, and they may bring particles of dyketerium home on their clothing. The second hand dyketerium may then infect their partners and pets, increasing the risk for dyke drama. If this energy could be captured and transformed for the good, it could fuel lesbian political projects far into the future. If not contained, however, there is always the risk of dyke community meltdown.

Other research has shown that a lack of lesbian-specific hair stylists in a community can also create near crisis conditions, particularly for dykes in the middle to butch ends of the gender continuum. Androgynous and butch lesbians typically have less tolerance for gay male stylists who fuss over them, thus are in greater need of hairstylists who specialize in lesbian hair and can achieve the critical degree of dykiness in hair style that creates the minimal level of fuss and bother. Femme lesbians appear better able to adapt to mainstream hairstyles and systems of hair management, and they often even enjoy the three-hour gossip sessions that accompany the hairstyling at these locales. Shane Impersonators in rural communities must often drive hundreds of miles to a city to find a stylist who can accomplish that particular look.

Communities with dyke dog parks tend to contain more stable couple relationships than communities without a dog park. It appears that couples who meet each other at dog parks are more successful than couples who meet each other at lesbian dances, brunches, or other venues, presumably because dog aficionados tend to have high qualities of loyalty and fidelity (or fido-lity). Dog parks with adjacent bars do not have this protective effect.

Communities suffering from a shortage of lesbian therapists are also at high risk for DDM disorders. Some areas, in desperation, have established scholarship funds to train local community members with aptitude for working with dykes to become therapists. Unfortunately, at this juncture, merely having a lesbian who is trained as a therapist is no guarantee that she will be skilled in identifying or treating DDM diagnoses. Thus far, psychology/counseling programs teach only the DSM, and none as of yet require that students read the DDM. The Dycology Academy will begin a certificate program for DDM specialization in the near future, rectifying this serious omission in higher education. The Academy recommends that lesbian communities contain a minimum of one therapist to every 25 dykes to deal with the epidemic levels of some of the conditions outlined in this manual. There also needs to be one lesbian collective counselor per every ten lesbian collectives or political groups in a community. Some particularly stressed communities also need brunch mediators and step-pet trainers.

Access to lesbian positive media in a community is another factors. Lesbians without access to cable or internet dyke content tend to suffer poorer dental health than those with access. Lesbian humor, in particular, seems to relieve symptoms of many of the dykignoses in this manual, and at least weekly viewing of Lizzie the Lezzie or random lesbian YouTube videos can reduce dental bills substantially. Over-identification with drama-laden media dykes, like Piper on *Orange is the New Black*, however, may increase dyke drama quotients.

A recent unpublished community assessment of three lesbian gaggles points to the need to do wider community level assessments rather than only focus on individual pathologies. After all, lesbians are relational in nature and only a larger systems approach can begin to unravel lesbian community dynamics. This groundbreaking study found that locations with a higher concentration of DDM diagnoses had higher overall levels of dyke drama. For example, in the community with the highest rate of DDM diagnoses (over 60% of lesbians reporting at least one current dykignosis), the level of dyke drama was at code red, compared to communities with lower rates of DDM diagnoses per capita, with threat level yellow. In fact, U-Haul corporate data geeks have used dyke drama tracking procedures to determine where to locate their rental offices, recognizing that lesbian communities with high rates of U-Haul Syndrome are gold mines. Similarly, pet food outlets are concentrated in lesbian communities for the same reason. Although lesbians are known to be particularly thrifty in most ways, they do not scrimp on their pets and they are loyal customers of U-Haul. More research is needed to extend our knowledge beyond the lesbian couple, to create a body of knowledge about triads and laggles in community settings, as these have only rarely been studied.

One encouraging line of research is in the attempt to create a device to measure dyke drama in the air of lesbian communities. This apparatus that works on the same principles as a Geiger counter can detect potentially hazardous levels of dyketerium in specific locations so that warning signs can be posted and text messages sent out to the community to avoid these areas until the levels decline to a safer reading. There is also a dyke non-profit collective dedicated to the development of a lesbian household dyke drama detector that would operate much like radon testing in basements of older houses. The collection apparatus would be opened in the couple's bedroom and set to collect dyketerium particles in the air over a period of one week, then sent to the lab to generate a report on the dyke drama level of the household. Finally, a vaccine is in the initial stages of testing to inoculate lesbians against dyke drama. Side effects may include a conversion to heterosexuality, so the vaccine is not yet approved for widespread use.

It is useful for the local department of lesbian health to have knowledge of the frequency of DDM dykignoses in the general population, so that they can plan community prevention activities. The figure below shows the lifetime and current prevalence of some of the more common dyke drama generators from data from May, 2017. These data show that the rates of current dykolepsy jumped from 4% in May of 2017 to the current level of 15%. DDM researchers speculate that the election is responsible for this spike.

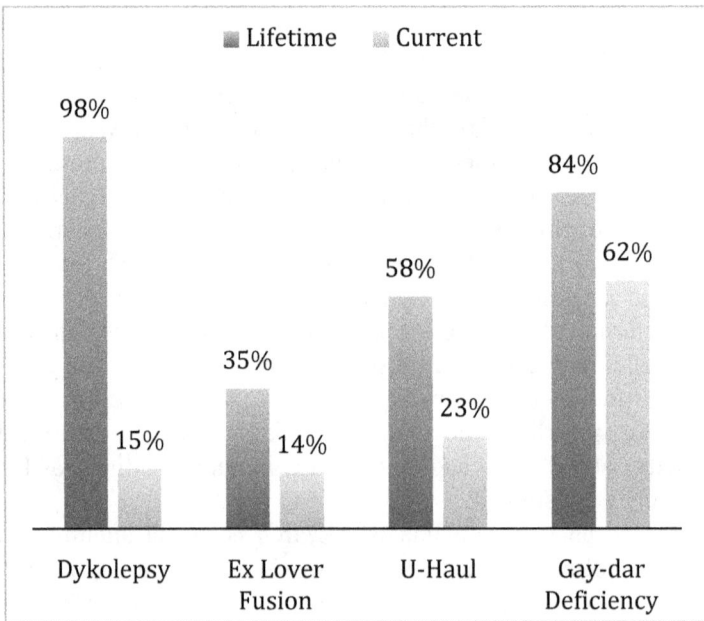

AXIS V: DYKE FUNCTIONAL ASSESSMENT TOOLS

There is a pressing need for tools for evaluating the risks of developing a DDM dykignosis, or experiencing the inordinate stress and dyke drama that can be precursors to dyke dysfunctions. This section explores several new instruments for measuring dyke drama and dysfunction, and these questionnaires can be used as screening tools at the Lesbian Recruiting Office, by dyke therapists evaluating new clients, and/or as a criterion for being admitted to a lesbian collective. Alternatively, they can be administered on a second date to determine eligibility to become a girlfriend. Careful screening at the beginning of a dating relationship may save considerable drama later. All single lesbians are encouraged to schedule second dates at quiet coffee shops or libraries where administration of compatibility and sanity screening tests can be completed. This section offers a few newly developed instruments, but more are in product development at this time and will be launched in the next revision of the DDM.

High rates of dyke drama are responsible for the near epidemic frequency of dykolepsy (see DDM 31) in some communities, and dyke drama underlies much of the pathology in lesbian communities. Thus, meticulous assessments of dyke drama levels are critical. The first instrument assesses the types and amount of dyke drama in a woman's life. The second scale is related to a unique lesbian anxiety disorder stemming from the stress of not being out to family or coworkers. This closeting phenomenon leads to a ritualistic lesbian behavior called "de-dyking the house" (see DDM 26). The third assessment tool is a first date warning signs checklist, used to prevent premature and ill-advised couplings. The next scale measures the degree to which a woman meets lesbian stereotypes, therefore is easily identifiable as a lesbian. Finally, the DDM Academy Collective offers two tools for identifying one's BF number. In the future, this number may be required on online dating profiles and on application forms at the lesbian recruiting office.

Dyke Drama Scale

Instructions: On the scale below, rate how much drama comes from each potential source of stress in your life. Check N/A if it is not applicable to your life.

Drama Quotients	N/A	Low Drama	Some Drama	Lots of Drama	Over-the-top
Within the Dyke Community					
My girlfriend(s)/partner(s)					
My lack of a girlfriend					
My first ex					
My second ex (Add additional columns for each ex who is still in your life)					
My first animal companion (Add additional columns for each pet)					
My team/collective/lesbian potluck/support, etc group					
Pressure from others in lesbian community to conform to rules (e.g. exposure to a mother superior)					
Lack of appropriate brunch location in the community					
Outside the Dyke Community					
My family of origin					
My coworkers					
Lesbophobic neighbors					
The Dept of Motor Vehicles					
Exposure to anti-gay churches or religious leaders					
In the Broader Society					
Anti-lesbian politicians and news commentators					
Absence of good lesbian films					
Sexist, lesbo-phobic media					
Other List:					
***Total Score*:** _____					

Scoring. Now add up the score, assigning a 0 to N/A and "low drama" responses, a 1 to "some drama," 2 to "lots of drama," and a 3 to "over – the-top" responses. Scores of 25 or higher are indicative of dangerous levels of stress and require immediate intervention lest the affected dyke explode (dykolepsy) or implode (dyke drama infarctions). Scores of 18 to 24 indicate a moderate risk for development of dykolepsy and other stress-related dyke diagnoses.

Knowing your DDQ is akin to knowing your blood pressure. It is an indicator of your overall health and wellbeing and predicts your vulnerability to dykolepsy (see DDM 31) and dyke drama infarctions, the lesbian equivalent of a stroke. The higher the DDQ, the more tightly you clench your teeth. Very high levels are associated with lock jaw. This scale is designed to pinpoint the sources of drama in your life, so that you can take action to change the circumstances that produce drama. Dykes with very low DDQs can easily be recognized because they exude a lesbi-buddha state of calm, centeredness, and they are sought out for their wisdom. You, too, can become a lesbi-buddha by carefully following the instructions in this book. There is a linear relationship between the DDQ score and various states of lesbian being, as illustrated below. Scores of 10 and above indicate risk for stress, and scores of 20 and higher, with lesbian drama disorders.

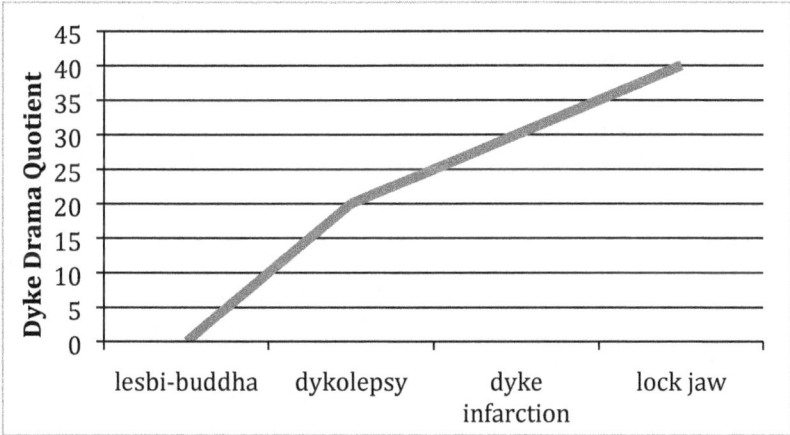

Strategies for Reducing Dyke Drama

Now review the following list of options for reducing dyke drama and select the one most suitable for the person or situation that causes you the most stress. Do this for each source of stress on the list. The options are listed in order from the most to least effective.

1. *Move away*. How far you move depends on the extent and intensity of the drama in your life. If conditions are mostly unfavorable in your local community, you may only need to leave the county to find more amenable lesbian community and acceptance. If you have a particularly toxic ex with more than 2 DDM dykignoses, you may need to leave the country without a trace. A potentially evil stalker ex-girlfriend may warrant seeking the help of the dyke witness protection program.

2. *Exorcism.* If the toxic person in your life is straight, a standard exorcism may be sufficient to correct the problem. However, if the toxic person is a lesbian, a dykxorcism is recommended. Find a lesbian high priestess, dyke anthropologist (but not an archeologist as their excavation techniques may be too intrusive to the average dyke), or in a pinch, a vet, to help you oversee the potentially dangerous rituals of dykxorcism to rid yourself of the influence of the toxic lesbian in your life. The specifics of the ritual cannot be described in this manual because of security clearance issues.

3. *Expulsion.* If the source of drama is a person, remove every trace of the person from your life. Delete email addresses, cell phone numbers, texts, emails, facebook posts (and make sure to un-friend her), tweets, letters, post-it notes, her toothbrush, clothing, sex toys, gifts to you, and anything else that may remind you of this person. Do not forget to delete all emails from both your inbox and the sent box. If you are a typical lesbian, this activity alone may take days. If the toxic being is a pet, remove all the toys, beds, food and treats, and hire a cleaning service to thoroughly vacuum every bit of pet hair from every inch of the house. Do not forget to remove any remains from the backyard as well, or you may step in a pile and suffer a post-traumatic memory.

4. *Shunning/Hiding*. If you are too daunted by the effort required by the first three options, try shunning. That is, do not answer the person's phone calls, texts, emails, posts on your wall, pokes, tweets, or other attempts to engage you in conversation. Avoid places where you might see this person, and hide in your house or apartment with the drapes tightly closed until which time you

feel a decrease in stress-related symptoms. If this person has a particular hold on you, you might choose to hide out at a lesbian therapist's office for the month or two that it takes to acquire skills for extricating yourself from this person, or from having a painful encounter when you do finally meet again (and you will).

5. ***Grin and bear it***. The final suggestion is to get a mouth piece to wear at night to avoid grinding your teeth into nubs, and practice jaw relaxation exercises twice daily. Along with this, get lesbianalysis and chiropractic adjustments weekly or more if you can afford it, until you have learned to cope with the person or situation or gained the motivation to take action.

De-Dyking Anxiety Scale

The next instrument is designed to help closeted lesbians identify sources of stress from family visits and aid in their de-dying activities.

Instructions: Do you have to de-dyke your house before family members or coworkers visit? Please check off how many of the following activities in which you must engage to successfully de-dyke your house.

Check if applicable	Activity
	Turn dyke books around on the shelf so that the titles do not show (scores double if you have more than 25 of such books and triple if you have 50 plus).
	Remove photos, posters, and wall hangings with a rainbow flag, labryris, pink triangle, double women's symbol, or anything with the words lesbian, dyke, gay, queer, or pride (scores double if you have more than 10 such items).
	Re-furnish the guest bedroom so it appears your girlfriend/partner is your roommate.
	Hide your automobile because of the LGBT bumper stickers
	Re-locate the sex toy box under the bed to a remote corner of the attic
	Remove the feminist or lesbian-themed earrings and other jewelry hanging in the bathroom or bedroom.
	Remove the rainbow flag from the front yard and the Dyke March flag from the backyard.
	Hide your girlfriend or partner because she looks too dykey (triple the score if she is distressed by this)
	Other (specify:

Scoring: Count up the number of activities you must do to de-dyke your house or apartment, and multiply it by the number of family or clueless coworker visits per year. Stress levels increase by four-fold if family members live close enough to drop by unannounced. Scores of 10 and higher indicate the potential for a debilitating de-dyking anxiety disorder.

Strategies to reduce DAD

1. Come out. Now your house can become a dyke shrine and sanctuary.

2. Do not invite anyone to your house (become a hermit). You can make excuses for not hosting events at your home, such as "My cat is people-phobic and freaks out when I have guests." "My house has dangerous levels of radon," and "I'm in the middle of a renovation." The renovation ploy can keep you safe for at least 18 months, giving you time to make a plan to come out. You can meet family and friends at restaurants or parks instead of your home, but do be sure to monitor your clothing choices so that you do not inadvertently wear a *Dykes to Watch Out For* t-shirt to the Olive Garden. In addition, make sure that your car has no tell-tale bumper stickers or decals (e.g. Michigan Women's Musical Festival Parking Pass or Rainbow stickers). HRC equal signs are typically safe choices, as long as you have a ready explanation for what it means if your grandfather asks.

3. Make your living space a "lesbian-free zone." This option requires constant vigilance on your part. Do not name your cat Sappho. Make sure that you do not purchase items at pride festivals or lesbian music weekends that may be left lying around the house. Even if you do not purchase such items, if you have dyke friends over, they may inadvertently leave objects that give away your sexuality. For example, your aunt Peggy may find a double-women's symbol earring between the arm and cushion of the sofa, or toddler nephew Bobby may find the Lesbian Avenger button that lodged between the refrigerator and counter.

4. Join a convent. You will have an 8 by 8-foot cell and no personal belongings, so you will finally be safe from detection...except from other lesbian nuns with functioning gay-dar.

First Date Early Warning System Checklist

This tool may be helpful to dykes with U-Haul Syndrome (see DDM 7) or chronic Lesbian Fusion Disorders (see DDM 3) to delay getting emotionally involved with a woman prematurely. The Dycology Academy Collective recommends carrying a copy of this instrument on first dates and filling it out when the date goes to the bathroom during dinner. At the latest, complete it immediately after the date and BEFORE having sex.

Instructions: After a first date with a new woman, evaluate her conversation and behavioral patterns and indicate if she:

- ☐ Mentioned being abducted by an alien
- ☐ Said she loved you at the end of the date
- ☐ Still lives with her ex
- ☐ Spent more time talking about how awful her last relationship was than getting to know you
- ☐ Ordered the chicken Caesar salad without the chicken, with balsamic vinaigrette instead of Caesar dressing, and no croutons (a sure sign of high maintenance tendencies)
- ☐ Exuded signs of desperation, for example, wanting you to commit to a specific time for a second date before you were halfway through your meal on the first date.
- ☐ Owns shares in U-Haul
- ☐ Talked about her cat or dog more than any other topic
- ☐ Talked about *The L Word* characters as if they were real people
- ☐ Wanted to process the date for an hour after the two hour date
- ☐ At happy hour, ordered 2 drinks at a time (for herself)
- ☐ Spent an hour of the date telling you what you needed to change about yourself
- ☐ Talked for 3 hours about herself, then said, "what about you?" while looking at her watch
- ☐ Said or did anything that gave you a creepy feeling in the pit of your stomach

Scoring: If you checked two or more of these items, do not schedule a second date. If you checked four or more, change your name or move to another city; you have a potential stalker on your hands.

To be absolutely safe, complete the checklist a second time, this time rating your own behavior on the date. It may be possible that you yourself have some of these characteristics that will introduce risk into your relationship. If you find you have two or more of these warning signs, consider taking a break from dating and seek help from a certified DDM therapist as soon as possible.

Warning: This instrument may not be sensitive enough for use at lesbian speed dating, where the time limits make it impossible to cover all the items on the scale at the first very brief meeting. The DDM Academy advises all women to avoid lesbian speed dating because of the potential hazards. You will be inclined to select women purely on the basis of their physical appearance or pheromones, unless you have an eidetic memory. If you do choose to attend a speed dating event at your own risk please refer from drinking or use of any mood altering substance that may impair your judgment, and stay vigilant for warning signs. If you meet a woman at speed dating that you decide to see again, you must not, under any circumstances, consider the speed date as a first date.

BOD (Big Ole Dyke) Scale

This measurement tool assesses how likely it is that you will be publicly identified as a lesbian. It measures the number and strength of lesbian stereotypes that you fit into.

Instructions: Indicate how true each statement is of you.

Statement	Gasp! Never! (0)	Maybe (1)	Absolutely (2)
I have owned a motorcycle (scooters do not count)			
I have short hair (no hair reaches the collar)			
I know what WNBA stands for			
I do not wear makeup (chapstick does not count as makeup)			
My closet is full of shit-kicker boots			
I own a wallet, not a purse			
I get called "sir"			
Young men have yelled "dyke" at me out car windows			
I walk like a jock			
I have owned a truck			
I have played on a softball, field hockey, or rugby team			
My closet is full of flannel and button-down collar shirts			
I prefer beer to wine (or did before I got sober)			

Scoring. Add up the scores and check the chart below for your BOD classification.

     9-12   Congratulations, You are a big ole dyke
     5-10   You are an aspiring or pseudo-BOD. Try a little harder.
     0-4   Sorry, you are way too girly to even be a BOD

Becoming a Big Ole Dyke

Some of you may want to improve on your score so that you do not need to constantly come out to others. This is simple. Do the things on the list. On the other hand, if you wish that people would not consider you a big ole dyke, you will need to target and change at least half of the items on the scale. More importantly, you need to evaluate why it bothers you to be labeled as a big ole dyke. Could it be a bit of internalized lesbo-phobia? Embrace the inner dyke.

Finding Your BF (Butch-Femme) Number: The quick version

Many lesbians rely only on physical cues to rate others along a gender continuum, but butch-femme coding is actually much more sophisticated than a quick glance at haircut, clothing, and walk. On this scale, rate your degree of femininity, masculinity, or androgyny on four dimensions. This scale is compatible with societal norms about masculinity and femininity, thus, is based on stereotypes. For queer theorists and lesbian academics, this scale will not be satisfactory, but it will be sufficient for an initial assessment of butch/femme continuum placement. Those who desire a more academic critique of butch/femme scales are referred to the next instrument in this manual.

1)   the physical body and mannerisms (curvy figure, full hips, swishy walk versus narrow hips, broad shoulders, jock walk),

2)   gender expression (frilly, lacey clothing, shoe, and accessory choices, hairstyles, makeup versus functional comfort clothes and shoes, few accessories, a haircut and no makeup),

3)   communication styles (flirtatious, indirect, emotive, chatty versus direct, rational, person of few words), and

4)   preferences for leisure activities, hobbies, and careers (shopping, girly hobbies, dressing up versus sports, construction versus childcare).

Circle the score that best corresponds to the gender stereotypes for the culture in which you live.

Descriptor	The Body	Gender Expression	Communication	Preferences
Extremely Feminine	10	10	10	10
	9	9	9	9
	8	8	8	8
	7	7	7	7
	6	6	6	6
Androgynous	5	5	5	5
	4	4	4	4
	3	3	3	3
	2	2	2	2
	1	1	1	1
Extremely Masculine	0	0	0	0

Now add up the scores and divide by four. This will give you your BF number. Commit this number to memory like your social security number.

My BF: ____

This number will do in a pinch, but if you want a more nuanced and complex assessment of your gender for use in online dating profiles, use the next scale.

What planet are dykes from? The lesbian gender conundrum

Nearly all lesbians are aware of the book, *Men are from Mars, Women are from Venus*. The totally clueless and sexist author, John Gray, was, and still is, all over the media with books, videos, workshops, and talk show appearances. While the DDM Academy totally disagrees with almost everything Mr. Gray says, it is undeniably true that men and women inhabit different worlds. So if heterosexual men are from Mars and heterosexual women are from Venus, where do butches and femmes and all the other lesbians hail from? There are clearly differences among lesbians, and some of them very loosely resemble the differences between heterosexual women and men. As biological women, though, gender differences among lesbians are not separated by planetary distance, but more by neighborhood. Perhaps it is closer to truth to say that butches are from Home Depot and Femmes are from Victoria's Secret. But even that statement is merely stereotype and too based on heterosexual models. We really need a more nuanced classification of gender for lesbians. Thankfully, the DDM Academy has been working on studies of lesbian gender for more than 30 years.

Once at a research conference on human sexuality in the 1980s, a heterosexual male speaker proposed that lesbians were intermediate between heterosexual women and men, and he showed a slide with a gender continuum that looked like this:

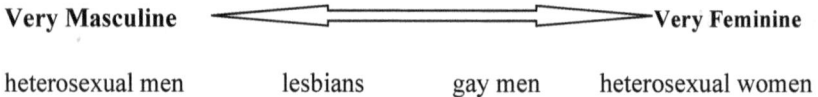

Very Masculine ⟵━━━━━━━━━⟶ Very Feminine

heterosexual men   lesbians   gay men   heterosexual women

This heterosexist and sexist scholar clearly did not understand that some femme lesbians are far more feminine than their heterosexual sisters, and some butch lesbians throw like girls. One gender size does not fit all—this system was far too simplistic to address lesbian gender. The DDM Academy, in its fledgling years, made a first attempt to construct a scale that might work better. Lesbian feminist tomes of the times demanded that there was no need to put heterosexual women or men of any sexuality on the scale at all; that it would be fine to focus just on dyke gender, so the following scale was created in 2008.

Very Masculine

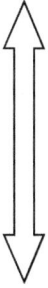

FTM/Transmasculine
Butch (bulldagger, stud, gender queer, diesel dyke)
Soft butch (baby dyke, mild butch, sissy butch)
Chapstick lesbian (kiki, androgynous, flannel dyke)
Butchy-femme (a service butch)
Femmy-butch (plumber femme, etc)
Tomboyish girl (grrrls)
Lipstick lesbian
HIGH femme (as in "your highness" the princess-lesbian)

Very Feminine

Although the scale was an improvement over the straight white male scholar's ideas of the gender continuum, focus groups with lesbians revealed the flaws in the system. Even the DDM Academy in all its wisdom was unable to escape a heterosexist binary gendered model with terms that linked masculinity to men and femininity to women. It took another ten years of research to develop a better system. It turns out that lesbian gender is much more nuanced and complicated than we ever imagined. There were no universal terms for lesbian gender variations in the academic literature, so the DDM Academy decided to break out of heteronormativity by using the terms "butch-aline" and "femme-nine" for these broad concepts of lesbian gender. They decided that there are at least four components of gender and sexuality to consider before one can come close to understanding lesbian gender differences. After years of deep thinking and ethnographic study of their fellow lesbians, the DDM Academy came up with this preliminary guide to lesbian gender. The following section distills this research and is written for a lay lesbian audience to help you to navigate the world of lesbian gender and find your place within the system, or at least make you think more deeply about the relationships between sexuality and gender. First, we need to explore the concepts of butch-aline and femme-ninr, whether you use these terms to describe yourself or not. Even if you vehemently disagree with these concepts, someone else is likely to rate you along a butch-femme continuum, even if you think you are exempt.

Butch-Femme for Dummies

The four components that make up lesbian sexuality and gender are:

> ➢ the biological body that Mother Nature gives us (got a pear
> shape? Thank Mother Nature not just the Krispy Kremes);
> ➢ gender expression or what we do with that biological body
> and the ways we can accessorize, accentuate, hide, or alter it;
> ➢ gender expression attraction patterns (what kind of woman
> we are attracted to); and
> ➢ personality/behavioral factors (the wild card).

The archetypal symbol of lesbian culture is the triangle. Therefore,
lesbian gender is more like the triangle below than a simple line or
continuum. Imagine that the triangle is lavender and that all the factors
inside the triangle overlap. There are no real clear-cut boundaries as there
are in diagrams.

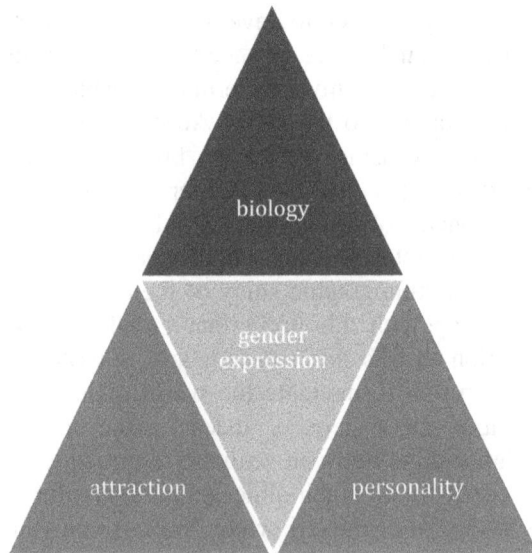

Biological Sex
Let's start with the biological body, because it is the simplest.
Which statement below best describes your physical body when you look

at yourself naked in the mirror? Imagine that you just stepped out of the shower and have not applied any product to your body.

Do you have:

_____   a. broad shoulders, narrow hips, small breasts, a squarish face, and walk with a swagger?

_____   b. mostly like a, but walks more like a jock than a pirate

_____   c. somewhere in the middle between a and e

_____   d. mostly like e, but not completely

_____   e. wide hips, medium to large breasts (real or enhanced), a triangular face, and walk with a swish?

If you checked a, b, or c, you may have had children ask you, "Are you a boy or a girl?" This is the body that Mother Nature gives us. However, in the scheme of lesbian gender, this matters very little. It's only the raw material. The only way that it matters at all is that if you feel yourself to be high femme, but you have a more butch-aline body type, you have to work harder at the presentation. If you have the femme-nine body and feel yourself to be very butch, you have more alterations to make, like lots of practice walking with attitude. So let's move on to the components of lesbian gender that do matter in our daily lives.

Lesbian Gender Expression

This is the part where you get to find yourself on the butch-femme appearance scale. That is, how do other people (mostly other lesbians—heterosexuals and gay men are notoriously bad at identifying the nuances of lesbian gender) classify you? This part consists of a test. Answer each question to the best of your ability—be brutally honest! Circle the answer that best fits you.

1. *Imagine you are going to dinner with good friend; no one you need to impress. How long does it take you to shower, dress, and get out of the house?*
   a. Less than 10 minutes
   b. 10-15 minutes
   c. 15-30 minutes
   d. 30-60 minutes
   e. More than an hour

2. *How many different hair products can be found in your bathroom? If you have 6 bottles of the same shampoo bought on sale at Costco, they count as one product!*
   a. 1
   b. 2
   c. 3
   d. 4
   e. 5
   f. 6 or more

3. *Are you wearing:*
   a. A shirt
   b. A blouse

4. *Do you carry your driver's license, credit card, cash, etc in a:*
   a. Wallet in your back pocket
   b. Fanny pack (or belly pack if you are a little geeky and wear it in front)
   c. Back pack
   d. Purse
   e. A wheeled bag because a purse just isn't big enough to carry your essentials
   f. I don't carry those things myself: my partner carries them for me

5. *When the urge to shop strikes you, you head to:*
   a. Home Depot
   b. REI or other type of sporting goods store
   c. Office Depot
   d. Macy's
   e. Victoria's Secret

6. *What is a camisole? (Note: the author had to look up the spelling, giving tell tale clues about her gender expression)*
   a. Huh? I have no idea.
   b. I know what it is, but do not have one
   c. My girlfriend gave me one once, but I have never worn it
   d. I have several in various pastel colors

7. *Which famous lesbian would be most likely to play you in the movie of your queer life?*
   a. Lea Delaria
   b. Rosie O'Donnell
   c. K.d. Lang
   d. Rachel Maddow (as seen on TV with make-up, not in real life)
   e. Ellen Degeneres
   f. Portia de Rossi

8. *If you were in the woodworking shop, would you know what to do with a router?*
   a. Absolutely
   b. I think so
   c. Maybe
   d. Not a clue

9. *If you were home sick with the flu, and could watch only one reality show, would it be:*
   a. Survivor
   b. Flip that House
   c. Dancing with the Stars
   d. Project Runway
   e. America's Next Top Model

10. *What lighting fixture would you choose for your living room?*
   a. None, the overhead light is just fine
   b. A simple and practical floor lamp that can be easily adjusted for reading
   c. An antique table lamp with character
   d. An ornate fixture that resembles an artistic sculpture
   e. A frilly, beaded, lacey thing, whether it gives off any light or not

11. *On laundry day, how many piles do you have?*
   a. 1—everything is washed together
   b. 2—hot and cold
   c. 3—hot, cold, and warm
   d. 4—hot, cold, warm, and delicates

e. 5—(I'm at a loss to explain, but some of you know the other possibilities)

12. **Which item is most likely to be found in your pocket, purse, or other carrying device?**
    a. Chapstick
    b. Lipstick
    c. Lipstick, gloss, and lip liner

13. **Of the hats in your closet or hat rack, how many of them have a bill?**
    a. All of them
    b. Most of them
    c. A few of them
    d. None of them—I wouldn't be caught dead in a baseball hat

14. **Is your living room furniture supposed to match?**
    a. Yes
    b. Don't know
    c. No

15. **Do you go brazilian?**
    a. What's that?
    b. Never
    c. Did it once and never again
    d. Usually
    e. Always

Scoring the Test:
Now add up your scores, using the following scale:

All "a" answers are scored as 0
All "b" answers as 1
All "c" answers as 2
All "d" answers as 3
All "e" answers as 4
All "f "answers as 5
My Score: _____

What do these numbers mean? Well the scientific interpretation of the scores, based on statistical analysis of years of data from thousands of lesbians around the globe, is explained below. The lowest possible score would be a zero, which means you are FTM or extremely transmasculine, without a hint of femme-ninety in your gender expression. A score of 45 or higher means you are extremely femme.

0 to 5	Very butch-aline. To the undiscerning eye, you are male.
6 to 15	Mostly butch, but you lapse now and then into androgynous or even girly territory
16 to 30	Safely in the androgynous middle
31 to 44	Somewhat femme, with an occasional butch slip-up
45 or higher	Very femme-nine. Look out world, the princess is in the house!

Lesbian Gender Expression Attraction Patterns

Now that we have determined where you are on the gender expression scale, we need to determine the type of person you are attracted to. Some of us are into butch-femme relationships, others into butch-butch or femme-femme, both right in the middle of the continuum, and some are lesbi-flexible, being attracted to things other than the partner's gender expression. To get at this issue, let's explore some of the items on the butch-femme scale, but this time applied to what turns you on.

1. *Which famous lesbian would play your ideal partner in the movie of your queer life?*
   a. Lea Delaria
   b. Rosie O'Donnell
   c. K.d. Lang
   d. Rachel Maddow (as seen on TV with make-up, not in real life)
   e. Ellen Degeneres
   f. Portia de Rossi
   g. None of the above
   h. All of the above at different periods of my life

2. *Are you generally attracted to women who are:*
   a. FTM/ transmasculine
   b. Butch

c. Somewhere in the middle
d. Femme
e. High Femme
f. None of the above
g. All of the above at different periods of my life

If you did not choose the "all of the above" option and your answers on these two questions are fairly similar, that means you fit somewhere along the butch-femme continuum and are erotically driven by gender expression. If you answered "all of the above" to both questions, you are lesbi-flexible, and probably attracted to something other than the gender cues. If you said "none of the above," I'm sorry, but you aren't a lesbian. Put this book down now.

For those who are drawn to particular gender expressions, now you can map out your attraction patterns on the grid below. Indicate where you are on the butch-femme quiz, and indicate what your ideal partner would look like on the right hand column. Now you can laminate this chart and use it on first dates to determine compatibility. Show your date your personal BF score and your ideal partner BF category and compare them. BF incompatibility is a major cause of lesbian break-up, so take heed of the numbers.

Place on the Continuum	I am	My ideal partner is
Very butch (0-5)		
Somewhat butch (6-15)		
Somewhere in the middle (16-30)		
Somewhat femme (31-46)		
Very Femme (47-52)		

You dykes now have it made. Go forth and administer the other assessments in this book until you find the woman of your dreams, your ideal gender match. You can easily determine if you want a butch-butch, butch-femme, femme-femme, or andro-andro kind of relationship.

Now, let's deal with the lesbians who are not drawn to the gender cues. You may need to do some deep soul-searching, or some extensive personal research or psychoanalysis to identify what attracts you to some women but not others. Could it be that you are drawn to certain body parts? Are you drawn to eyes, the window of the soul? To breasts? Perhaps you are an elbow kind of gal. Are you drawn to scents? Maybe you are attracted to the trappings of the person—her dog, her

252

snazzy car. It might be the status that turns you on. Many lesbians are erotically excited by women who are vets (animal doctors or veterans in uniform, take your pick) or nurturing women who like to process (wow, to have your own personal therapist!). Other are more practical and seek out partners with skills that they lack, such as ability to cook, word process, fix the computer, or change the oil in the car. Those among us with fetishes may have to explore a potential partner's shoe closet or the power tools in the garage before knowing if we are attracted to her.

Lesbian Personality/Behavior Scale

Now that you have located yourself and your partner attraction patterns on the gender expression scale, things can get even more interesting. Gender expression is how others see you as well as how you see yourself physically. But you can get tripped up if you rely only on gender expression and do not consider your unique personality and behavior traits, which are only loosely related to the gender expression and biological body. There are many factors to consider in personality traits and styles, and these personality factors may influence how you behave in the world and in relationships. The following questions offer just a few things to consider that may create personality clashes in relationships. Be honest; if you lie, you are only hurting yourself!

1. *Are you*
   a. Aggressive—demand what you want
   b. Assertive—politely, but strongly request what you want
   c. Passive-Aggressive—manipulate and play games to get what you want
   d. Wishy-washy—don't know what you want so can't make decisions

2. *Do you*
   a. Never cry, no matter what
   b. Cry only at sad movies, like Bambi
   c. Cry at sappy commercials or when your girlfriend rags on you
   d. Cry at every occasion, happy or sad

3. *What is your opinion about drama in relationships?*
   a. Hate it, avoid it
   b. Like to watch it, but only as a spectator out of harm's way

   c.   Will engage in it if enticed into the drama

   d.   Are easily sucked into drama

   e.   Instigate the drama—the more the better!

4. When you are having problems in a relationship, what do you want to do about it?

   a.   Just have sex, that will fix everything

   b.   Don't talk about it, because that makes it worse

   c.   Look for logical solutions as soon as possible

   d.   Have a rational discussion about it, then look for solutions

   e.   Process, process, process and never get around to solutions

5. Where are you on the political spectrum?

   a.   A-political or non-political

   b.   I watch Rachel Maddow just because she's cute but don't really listen

   c.   I get involved in elections and special issues

   d.   I am totally involved—politics are my life

6. Are you a pet person?   Yes   No**

If yes, are you

   a. A cat person exclusively

   b. A dog or cat or any kind of pet person (ambipexterious)

   c. A dog person exclusively

7. What is your idea of the perfect party?

   a.   You and your girlfriend having sex

   b.   2-3 close friends over for dinner

   c.   4-6 people to play cards

   d.   7-10 people to play charades

   e.   More than 10 people jammed into your house with dancing, loud music and perhaps an orgy

8. How do you dance?

   a.   I don't

   b.   I gyrate my hips without moving my feet

   c.   I have a few moves and stick to what I know

   d.   I have a repertoire of dances and love to try new things

   e.   Dancing with the Stars, here I come

9. When I go out
    a. Go out? What's that?
    b. I want my partner to dance every dance with me
    c. I want my partner to dance the slow dances with me
    d. I want my partner to watch me dance with other women

Some of these factors have a "gendered" component to them, of course, but as lesbians we all have at least some socialization into the cultural ideas of "femme-nine" ways, so sometimes even the most butch of lesbians will sometimes behave like the most stereotypical of women. Some people think that opposites attract, but consider the potential conflicts that can arise in partners who are at opposite ends of any of these characteristics. Once you have determined your own location on these personality characteristics, you can use the quiz to assess potential girlfriends.

Changing your BF?

Most theorists believe that the BF is an inborn, genetdyk trait that is relatively stable throughout the lifetime and not easily altered. In particular, the body type component is quite resistant to change. For example, Janet Reno, a 3.1 on the BF scale, attempted to femme up her BF number by wearing power suits and high-heels, but only changed the public perception to a 3.3. The other three aspects of the BF equation are somewhat more modifiable, but at what cost? Butch lesbians often give up trying to be more feminine after the first bikini wax, and femme lesbians flee in horror of giving up the eyebrow tweezers. Some who are especially motivated are able to effect shifts of 2 points. Ellen Degeneres, as a covergirl model, scores a 6.1, but at home in the evening, is a 3.9. Pressures to alter one's BF are different, depending on whether the source of the pressure, is from heterosexuals or other lesbians. Heterosexual people, whether bosses, parents, or others, almost exclusively advocate for a change to a higher BF number, that is, more femi-nine. Lesbian communities, especially Lesbian Mother Superiors, often pressure dykes to lower their scores, or become more androgynous, or even butch. For most dykes, however, the best course of action is to find your natural BF and embrace it. Butch/femme satisfaction is a major predictor of high dyke quality of life.

Conclusion

Locate yourself on the butch-femme scale. Everyone should know her BF number, just like you should know your credit rating or sleep bed number. Then find your ideal partner choice, and give those potential partners the personality characteristics quiz as a screening tool. If their answers are too far from yours, do not date her, no matter how hot she is. If you don't find this assessment particularly relevant, well then, develop your own lesbian gender scale. For most of us, however, gender is a rich part of our lesbian identity and erotic attractions, so further understanding our patterns can improve the texture of our lives!

DO-IT-YOURSELF LESBIANALYSIS

Unfortunately, very few therapists have yet been trained in the identification and treatment of dyke diagnoses, nor are they skilled in reducing dyke drama at the individual or community levels, because of the heterosexist nature of their formal psychology training. Until more therapists are trained on the DDM classification system, we will need stop-gap self-help measures to reduce dyke drama. The form of therapy that is best attuned to the unique issues of dykes is called lesbianalysis. This section will provide you with the basics of lesbianalysis so that you can cure your own DDM issues. Exert extreme caution in applying these techniques to girlfriends and ex-lovers, however, as dykes are notoriously independent and stubborn, and resist efforts to change them from the external world. Lesbianalysis works best when used as self-help, or in the hands of a highly trained DDM-certified therapist. The following section outlines the 12 Steps of Self-Lesbianalysis. I recommend that you keep this list of 12 steps on your person at all times.

The Dyke 12 Steps

Step 1. Purchase a copy of the DDM, if you do not already have one. If you do have one, purchase copies for your girlfriend, ex-lovers, best friends, and anyone in your life who needs a deeper understanding of dyke drama and lesbian dynamics, and give one copy to every lesbian in your life who is creating dyke drama for you. The author has a shoe fetish to support (she is allergic to cats and dogs and thus must have an alternative fetish) and needs the additional income. Besides, there are few rule books for lesbian conduct, and this obviously is the best one. If you heed all the advice in this book, you will not require any further intervention and will become a healthy and functional lesbi-buddha. Donate a copy to your old high school library as well. The more people who read this book in your community, the lower the dyke drama quotient will be, and the healthier the overall community.

Step 2. Read the DDM cover to cover at least three times to commit the categories to memory, and then proceed to step 3.

Step 3. Make sure you have access to a personal journal for the remaining steps. We estimate that a dozen 200-page journals should be sufficient. Review signs and symptoms of each DDM category in this book to determine if you have any dykignoses, compare your symptoms to the descriptions in the DDM, and record your current dykignoses here:

1.
2.
3.
4.
5.
[add as many as needed]

The average dyke has 2.3 DDM categories active at any given time (range of 0 to 6), and a lifetime history of 7.1 diagnoses (range of 1 to 15). Co-occurring dyke dykignoses are extraordinarily common, so do not be alarmed by the sheer number of conditions that you may have now or in your lifetime. This book will guide you through reducing or eliminating many of the signs and symptoms, or alternately, to consciously embracing your dyke condition. It is perfectly acceptable to embrace being the crazy dyke cat lady of your neighborhood or having an obsessive relationship with MSNBC, as long as you are aware of the potential hazards of your condition. However, if there are dyke conditions that are causing you distress and that you wish to change, proceed to step 4.

Step 4. Choose the disorder that is causing the greatest degree of poor dental health for you at this point in time. If you cannot determine which one to work on first, try a bite test. Put a piece of cardboard between your teeth and think of the stressors in your current life. The one that makes you bite down the hardest is the one to start with—what dykignosis might be related to your stress? List it in your journal, along with the most painful symptoms that you are currently experiencing:

Dykignosis:

Symptoms:

Step 5. Read the DDM section on treatment for that condition, and rate your response to the treatment guidelines that are outlined for the condition. Which statement best describes your feelings about the treatment?

- o That is bulls*#t, I'm not doing that!
- o I can see the wisdom, but I have to ease my way into this.
- o Ok, if that's what it takes, I will do it!

If you answered "a" you are obviously not ready to acknowledge and deal with this problem yet. Go back to step 4 and start over with a new dykignosis until you find one that you can address comfortably. If you answered "b" you still lack motivation. Go on to Step 6. If you answered "c" you can skip Step 6 and go directly to Step 7.

Step 6. Write a thousand-word essay or a poem about the development of the condition. If writing makes you uncomfortable, make a collage that symbolizes your issues, using old copies of Curve magazine. When did you first notice the impact of this dykignosis on your life? What have your girlfriends, ex-lovers, or best friends said to you about this disorder? Be brutally honest now! It is for your own good. Put the essay aside for two days and then re-read. Gauge whether your motivation to rid yourself of this affliction has increased, and if so, you may move on to step 7. If not, repeat step 6 until you are ready. Unfortunately, some lesbians stay at step 6 for months or even years, ruminating about a past break-up or rationalizing her behavior. If you have a trusted ex-lover in your life who is not in a fused relationship with you, she may be able to help you face your conditions and own your behavior.

Step 7. Consider other factors that might need to be taken into account before you outline your treatment plan. The first of these is your BF number. Record it in your journal. If you scored a 3 or above, find someone to talk to about your treatment plan and who can listen to you, provide support and help you to gently process your way to recovery. If you scored below a 3, do this plan in secret, telling no one about your diagnoses or treatment plan. If you reveal the plan, you may be forced into painful processing sessions.

The second consideration is the number of years that you have had this condition. Record that number in your journal as well. If you have been afflicted for less than year, you can develop a 30-day treatment plan. If you have had this condition for 1-3 years, go for a 60-day plan. If 4-6 years, a 90-day plan is necessary. If you have suffered from this for more than six years, this could be your remaining life's work. Ask your bartender, chiropractor, or hairdresser for support, and get a dog instead of a girlfriend until you have made significant progress. A cat may be too hard on your ego until you are farther along in your lesbianalysis.

Step 8. Using the DDM treatment guidelines for your condition, outline a plan of action for changing your behavior. Share your plan with another person, or your cat, for moral support. Write out your plan in your journal and consider any barriers to implementing your plan.

Step 9. Implement the plan. Try out your new behaviors at the next lesbian event, on your next date, or when you have an argument with your partner, depending on the type of plan you have developed. Start a dyke treatment plan journal to record your efforts, and the responses you get from others.

Step 10. Evaluate the plan. What response did you get from implementing new behaviors? Have you improved your dental health? Reduced the dentists' bills and number of visits? Have moments of lesbi-buddha bliss? Celebrate the successes and evaluate the reasons for lapses into dyk-functional behaviors.

Step 11. Modify the plan as needed, or continue to implement the plan for a minimum of 90 days. That's how long it takes to change a dyke behavior pattern. Ninety days with the DDM leads to a better life or your money back!

Step 12. Congratulate yourself briefly, and then start over on the next disorder. You may need to purchase another copy of the DDM by this time to replace the dog-eared, well-thumbed, or cat-pee stained copy with which you began. Repeat the 12 steps as many times as needed to rid yourself of all dyke drama generators, but do pay close attention to the signs and symptoms of the Dyke two-stepping 12 step condition. It can be easy to lapse from productive therapy into an unhealthy reliance on the 12 steps.

CONCLUSIONS

This manual has highlighted the need for further research on the prevalence and symptoms of dyke disorders and their prevention and treatment. There are thousands of resources for heterosexual couples and families about improving the quality of their individual and collective lives, and countless types of therapies for the mental health problems that they may experience. On the other hand, there is very little research on what makes a good lesbian relationship or family, and far fewer psychological and social resources designed to better their lives. Heterosexually oriented educational materials widely available in book stores and on the internet hardly ever mention dyke-specific issues, such as how to negotiate ex-lover relationships, but those ex-relationships are the cornerstone of many dyke communities. A separate user's manual with guidelines for creating and maintaining dyke ex-lover relationships is sorely needed. In addition, resources for successfully navigating dyke dating challenges are critical, including guidelines for setting up online dating profiles that cover all the nuances of lesbian sexual and gender identifications, preferences, and quirks. Dictionaries of lesbian terminology would also be helpful for school-based lesbian educational classes, as well as for newly out dykes. This manual offers a preliminary glossary of terms, but only scratches the surface of lesbian terminology.

Clearly, national resources are also needed to develop the lesbian dating and sex education classes called for in this manual, as well as for training and preparation of lesbian therapists, softball coaches, collective counselors, lesbian step-pet therapists and mediators, and life dyke coaches. The newly formed Dycology Academy Collective, if it stays healthy and avoids lesbian collectivitis (see DDM 17), will create the training mechanisms, curriculum, and research capacity needed to expand this manual and to develop effective dyke disorder treatment programs across the country. The collective is exploring using lesbian land communes run by Barn OWLS for residential treatment centers. It will also undertake the effort to expand the diagnostic system to consider international and interspecies dysfunctions. The Dycology Academy is now accepting applications for membership (see DDM 17 for guidance on whether or not you are qualified to apply).

Realistically, however, one academic institution is not sufficient to address the pressing problems faced by dyke individuals, dyads, triads, families, and laggles. Therefore, this manual ends with an impassioned plea for additional resources to be devoted to prevention, screening, and treatment of DDM conditions. Fully functioning and emotionally healthy dykes could dramatically change the world, reverse climate change, eliminate world hunger, resolve the U.S. budget deficit, and end war on a global level if their creative impulses could be channeled for the greater good rather than for dyke drama. The DDM Academy needs a patroness. MP lesbians, it is time to step up and support your sisterhood.

GLOSSARY OF TERMS

Academic butch: this term refers to a basically butch lesbian, one who falls somewhere on the masculine side of the gender continuum, but has to conform to some of the conventions of the academy. So rather than blue jeans and sweatshirts, she wears men's pants and sweater vests, or all black polyester pants suits, depending on the brand of feminism to which she subscribes.

Ambisexual: like ambidextrous, the ambisexual is versatile in her sexuality and may have attractions to men (bisexual), objects or pets (lesbian fetishes), or be equally skilled in masturbation with her right or left hand. In one more obscure meaning, the term is related to the sleeping pill Ambien, so ambisexual means boring sex that puts one to sleep.

Baby dyke: a newly out lesbian, typically representing her first year since coming out, regardless of her chronological age. It is important to note, however, that a 16-year-old baby dyke has very different issues and characteristics than a 63-year-old baby dyke. At whatever age a woman becomes a baby dyke, however, she experiences some of the developmental transitions of the adolescent, such as overactive sex drive, intense crushes, and mood swings.

Bi-dyke: this term has three meanings. In the first, this is a lesbian who can easily navigate both the butch and femme sides of the gender continuum. Secondly, this may be a lesbian-identified bisexual, or a woman with sexual feelings for men and women, but who adopts a dyke consciousness or politics. Thirdly, the term refers to bicycle-riding lesbians.

Bisexual: a woman who has sexual attractions to women and men, whether she acts on them or not. Alternatively, a bisexual is a person who is attracted to people on the basis of something other than their gender. Oddly, bisexual women are sometimes treated with suspicion in lesbian communities.

Boidyke: a lesbian more to the butch side of the continuum, or one who carries her tomboy ways into adulthood. A boidyke has elements of both butch and femininity.

Bulldagger: A lesbian who is far to the masculine side of the gender continuum.

Bulldyke: see bulldagger

Chapstick lesbian: this typically refers to a woman on the middle to butch side of the gender continuum. Her "make-up" kit consists of the tube of chapstick that is typically carried in the right hand pocket (left for left-handers) for ready access. It has not been scientifically established whether dry lips or frequent use of lip balm are causative factors in a dyke identity.

Dykecycle: A modification of lifecycle research adapted to the unique patterns of lesbians. The dyke-cycle consists of four stages based on age of coming out rather than chronological age. The first stage is pre-dyke, before the woman recognizes or acknowledges her attractions to women. Baby dyke is the first phase after coming out, and shares many characteristics with the chronological adolescence phase of life, with considerable self-centeredness, sexual and romantic explorations, and raging her-mones. The third phase is the adult lesbian relationship phase, whereby the baby dyke settles into (hopefully) more mature adult lesbian communities and relationships. The final stage, called variously elder dyke, crone, OWL (Older Wiser Lesbian), or other geographic community specific terms, represents the wisdom years.

Dyke-sickle: Derived from popsicle, a tasty treat that one licks, sucks, or bites, a dyke-sickle refers to a common lesbian sexual practice.

Dykignosis: The labeling of a unique lesbian condition that may cause dyke drama or relationship failure among lesbians. Not to be confused with a diagnosis, a medical term.

Ellen: Degeneres, of course. Arguably, the most well known lesbian in popular culture.

Femme: A term to refer to a woman who is on the feminine side of the gender scale, although in common usage it typically refers to a woman who is at least a 7 on the 0-10 gender scale.

Friend of Dorothy: A code word used in the 1960s to refer to lesbian or gay people. Refers to the affinity of some queer folk to Judy Garland, particularly her role in The Wizard of Oz, hence the "Dorothy." Other historians suggest that gay men were drawn to Dorothy, but that dykes were more attracted to the witches; the butch Wicked Witch of the West or the femme Good Witch Glinda, depending on their overall attraction patterns and BF number. Others are not attracted to witches per se, but admire them as role models or become witches themselves.

Gay: A term that sometimes means gay and lesbian, and sometimes means men who have sex and relationships with other men. This term can also mean "happy." Fundamentalist Christians are furious with the gay liberation movement for removing this simple word from their vocabulary. They are only allowed to use the term "homo-SEX-sual "to refer to people with same-sex inclinations, and can never use "gay" to refer to a carefree attitude.

Genetdik: hereditary factors that create uniquely lesbian or gay conditions or traits, such as the gene for gaydar or the U-Haul pathways in the brain.

Glamour butch: The woman who is definitely on the masculine side of the scale, but is an impeccable dresser and always very well groomed.

Goldstar lesbian: A lesbian who has only had sex/relationships with other women. These are exceedingly rare and precious, much like gold itself. Only 12% of lesbians are goldstars.

Granola dyke: A lesbian who appears to be a healthy eater in public; in private she may munch on Krispy Kreme donuts and Fritos.

Her-mones: chemical substances made in the corpus lesbosis that regulate the menstrual cycle and emotional closeness.

High Femme: A woman who is at the extreme end of the feminine gender scale. Along with high feminine appearance often comes a rather dramatic and theatrical personality. Some may refer to high femmes as high priestesses, divas, or high maintenance.

Hor-mones: chemical substances made in the corpus lesbosis that affect sex drive and lesbian lust reactions.

Kiki: A lesbian who is not easily classified as butch or femme; or one who slips between these categories. For example, depending on hairstyle and dress may appear as a 4, 5, or 6 on the gender scale on different days.

Ladyslipper catalog: Named for an endangered form of wild lily, Ladyslipper is a non-profit organization dedicated to cataloging women's music. It began distributing its catalog/music resource guide in print form in 1976, and most politically conscious lesbians bought most of their music from this source. Lesbian mother superiors of the past often coerced their minions into only buying music from this source.

Ladder, The: A lesbian newsletter published 1956 to 1972; originally mimeographed and mailed out in a brown paper wrapper to thousands of lesbians across North America. It was associated with the Daughters of Bilitis, the first lesbian political organization, and was edited by Phyllis Lyon and Del Martin. Lesbians who subscribed to this publication are necessarily Elder Dykes by now. Younger dykes are puzzled by the references in lesbian literature to The Ladder and have no idea what "mimeographed" means.

Land-dyke: a lesbian who lives in a communal setting with other dykes or pets, usually in remote or rural settings. Lesbians who are part of a "back to the land" movement and are often separatists.

Laverne and Shirley Syndrome: refers to a 1970s television program about two supposedly heterosexual female roommates with an enmeshed relationship. Dykes read the story line as Laverne, the athletic butch with an L (for lesbian) monogrammed on all of her shirts, being in love with Shirley, the femme with her "boo-boo kitten" stuffed cat as her prized possession.

Lesbic: epic, in a lesbian manner.

Lesbianage: has at least three possible meanings, including turning straight girls into dykes; being a secret lesbian (closeted); and being a lesbian spy. There are probably more cases of the second type than the other two combined.

Lesbianary: being legendary in a lesbian community; or better than legendary, like this book.

Lesbianarianism: a form of religion practiced by some dykes that includes the worship of Sappho and/or other historical dyke figures, and involves the consuming of dyke-approved food (such as hummus).

Lesbibob: a short haircut; a specialty of some dyke hairdressers.

Lesbidextrous: a dyke who is equally skillful in sexual practice with both hands.

Lesbicide: when a lesbian makes a conscious decision to become heterosexual. This is usually done in a desperate attempt to escape dyke drama.

Lesbidude: a man who poses as a lesbian in a chat room or online dating site.

Lesbigious: a woman who is conflicted or uncertain about her sexuality.

Lesbiology: the study of lesbian physiology, anatomy, and neurobiology.

Lesbian Compatibility. There are several forms of incompatibility among lesbian couples. The most common are
- Income-patibility, referring to couples with disparate income levels;
- incom-cat-ability, where one dyke is a cat lover and the other is allergic to or dislikes cats;
- incom-bark-ability refers to a mismatch related to dog affinities;
- In-cum-patibility refers to differences in opinions about how often a couple should engage in sex;
- Ink-compatibility is the disparity between two women related to technology. If one is a Luddite and the other a techie, the relationship is unlikely to work;

- incom-bustibility refers to a dyke who wants to reduce drama in her life, thus is mis-matched with drama queens.

LC (lesbian correctness): Akin to the term "politically correct," lesbian correctness refers to the unwritten rules of a particular lesbian community, political group, or theoretical perspective. For example, 1970s lesbian separatist literature espoused the superiority of lesbians to heterosexual women, therefore, to suggest that dykes might be just as screwed up as straight women is not LC. This manual stands to be labeled as not LC by some segments of the dyke community.

LGBTQQAID2SSGL: Refers to lesbian, gay, bisexual, transgender, queer, questioning, allies, intersex, down E, two spirit, and same gender loving. There are many variations on this theme, depending on how inclusive the speaker wishes to be. Some refer to this as "alphabet soup." Dykes are one unique subset of the alphabet soup, probably represented by the kale component of the soup.

Lone star lesbian: a lesbian who has had only one female partner in her lifetime. This includes 73% of Baby Dykes, 32% of Adult Dykes, and 18% of Elder Dykes.

Log cabin lesbian: This term has two meanings. In the first, it refers to a dyke who belongs to the Log Cabin Republicans, an inexplicable contradiction. Some believe that the term "conservative lesbian" is an oxymoron. In the second meaning, the term refers to a land-dyke who builds her own home by hand, often with rustic hand-hewn logs.

LP (lesbian potential): a common game played by lesbians in groups in public places, whereby the they assign a number or a descriptor indicating the likelihood that a passing woman could be a dyke, such as "She has high LP."

LUG: lesbian until graduation. A woman who explores her sexuality in college, but resumes a heterosexual life after graduation.

LUT: similar to LUG, but refers to lesbian until thirty, based on current educational patterns that delay graduation until later in the lifecycle. Some LUTS may delay graduation because of a relationship with a woman, but after the breakup, reverts to heterosexuality. For some women, LUT may refer to experimenting with sexuality with a college classmate who becomes a roommate for a few years after graduation (see Laverne and Shirley Syndrome), delaying the return to heterosexuality for a few more years.

Menopause: a phase of life experienced by the elder dyke when irrational behaviors, memory loss, and power surges are common.

Men O'Pause: an episode in the life of a heterosexual woman when she wearies of men's antics and considers trying to be a dyke. In the vast majority of cases, she reverts to heterosexuality when she encounters dykes with DDM dykignoses.

Metrosexual butch: a butch woman with a sense of fashion and style.

Pictionary: a game similar to Charades whereby teams must guess common words or phrases, names of movies, etc, from clues drawn on paper by their teammate. For some unknown reason, this was the game of choice for lesbian game nights in the 1980s.

Plumber femme: a basically feminine woman who is not afraid to get her hands dirty, and thus, will help with gardening, home remodeling or other necessary but messy household activities. She may, however, be paranoid about being seen in her work clothes.

Queer: a term used by some dykes who affiliate with a larger community of men, women, and gender benders who defy societal categories of sex and gender.

Same gender loving: A term often used by African American lesbians (and gay men) to refer to having same-sex partners/attractions. Sometimes represents a rejection of western terms like lesbian.

Sapphite/Sapphic: referring to someone who is like the poet Sappho, that is, loving women.

Saturday Night Butch: the woman who appears androgynous or even feminine during the week, perhaps for her job, but assumes a butch appearance and behavior when out with dyke friends on the weekends.

Scattergories: another game popular at lesbian game nights. There are purported addictions to Scattergories among dykes in northern climates with long winters. There is no plausible explanation as of yet for the dyke affinity for Scattergories and Pictionary, but neuroimaging studies may eventually locate the brain pathways that create these preferences.

Soft Butch: a woman who is on the butch side of the continuum, but closer to center than to hard-core butch. The term may also refer to a butch lesbian who is out of shape.

Stem: a term used to refer to women in the middle of the gender continuum (halfway between STud and fEMme) or a woman who switches positions on the gender continuum. This can also refer to a part of a flower, often missing in the Georgia O'Keefe flower prints favored by some lesbians.

Stone butch: A lesbian far on the masculine side of the continuum who wants to please her partner sexually, but does not want to be touched in return. Selfish femmes often think they want a stone butch, but are disappointed to find that there are fairly rare.

Stud: refers to a lesbian on the butch side of the continuum; one who is also known for her sexual prowess (often more mythical than actual). For a DIY lesbian, stud may have a different meaning entirely, so listeners must consider the context.

Toaster Oven: The prize given for recruiting a woman into a dyke lifestyle. Popularized in the sitcom *Ellen* (not to be confused with *Ellen*, the talk show).

Two spirit: a term used in Native American culture to refer to having both male and female spirits, and often having same-sex attractions as well.

Vagitarian: like the vegetarian who has given up meat; the vagitarian has given up man meat in preference for vaginas.

Wimmin/womyn/wymyn: attempts to take the "man" or "men" out of references to female-bodied individuals. Often used by separatist lesbians such as Barn OWLS. Sadly, one can take the "man" out of the

270

word, but can never eliminate the influence of men on lesbians' lives. Interestingly, many separatist lesbians are studying to be, or claim to be "shamans" but do not seem to mind the "man" in shaman.